My
iPad®
for Seniors

FOURTH EDITION

Michael Miller

800 East 96th Street,
Indianapolis, Indiana 46240 USA

Real Possibilities

My iPad® for Seniors, Fourth Edition

Copyright © 2017 by Pearson Education, Inc.

AARP is a registered trademark.

No part of this publication may be reproduced, stored in a retrieval system, or transmitted in any form or by any means, electronic, mechanical, photocopying, recording, scanning, or otherwise, except as permitted under Section 107 or 108 of the 1976 United States Copyright Act, without the prior written permission of the Publisher. No patent liability is assumed with respect to the use of the information contained herein.

Limit of Liability/Disclaimer of Warranty: While the publisher, AARP, and the author have used their best efforts in preparing this book, they make no representations or warranties with respect to the accuracy or completeness of the contents of this book and specifically disclaim any implied warranties of merchantability or fitness for a particular purpose. No warranty may be created or extended by sales representatives or written sales materials. The advice and strategies contained herein may not be suitable for your situation. You should consult with a professional where appropriate. The publisher, AARP, and the author shall not be liable for any loss of profit or any other commercial damages, including but not limited to special, incidental, consequential, or other damages. The fact that an organization or website is referred to in this work as a citation and/or a potential source of further information does not mean that the publisher, AARP, and the author endorse the information the organization or website may provide or recommendations it may make. Further, readers should be aware that Internet websites listed in this work may have changed or disappeared between when this work was written and when it is read.

ISBN-13: 978-0-7897-5793-7

ISBN-10: 0-7897-5793-1

Library of Congress Control Number: 2016954608

Printed in the United States of America

1 16

Trademarks

Unless otherwise indicated herein, any third-party trademarks that may appear in this work are the property of their respective owners, and any references to third-party trademarks, logos, or other trade dress are for demonstrative or descriptive purposes only. Such references are not intended to imply any sponsorship, endorsement, authorization, or promotion of Que Publishing products by the owners of such marks, or any relationship between the owner and Que Puglishing or its affiliates, authors, licensees, or distributors.

Screen shots reprinted with permission from Apple, Inc.

Warning and Disclaimer

Every effort has been made to make this book as complete and as accurate as possible, but no warranty or fitness is implied. The information provided is on an "as is" basis. The author, AARP, and the publisher shall have neither liability nor responsibility to any person or entity with respect to any loss or damages arising from the information contained in this book.

Special Sales

For information about buying this title in bulk quantities, or for special sales opportunities (which may include electronic versions; custom cover designs; and content particular to your business, training goals, marketing focus, or branding interests), please contact our corporate sales department at corpsales@pearsoned.com or (800) 382-3419.

For government sales inquiries, please contact governmentsales@pearsoned.com.

For questions about sales outside the U.S., please contact intlcs@pearsoned.com.

Editor-in-Chief
Greg Wiegand

Senior Acquisitions Editor
Laura Norman

Marketing
Stephane Nakib

Director, AARP Books
Jodi Lipson

Development/ Copy Editor
Charlotte Kughen,
The Wordsmithery LLC

Managing Editor
Sandra Schroeder

Senior Project Editor
Lori Lyons

Indexer
Larry Sweazy

Proofreader
Cheri Clark

Technical Editor
Vince Averello

Editorial Assistant
Cindy Teeters

Cover Designer
Chuti Prasertsith

Compositor
Kim Scott,
Bumpy Design

Contents at a Glance

Table of Contents

6   Keeping Your iPad Safe and Secure

12 Getting Social with Facebook, Pinterest, and Other Social Networks   221

About the Author

Michael Miller is a popular and prolific writer of close to 200 non-fiction books, known for his ability to explain complex topics to everyday readers. He writes about a variety of topics, including technology, business, and music. His best-selling books for Que include *My Facebook for Seniors, My Social Media for Seniors, My Internet for Seniors, My Samsung Galaxy S7 for Seniors, My Windows 10 Computer for Seniors, Easy Computer Basics,* and *Computer Basics: Absolute Beginner's Guide.* Worldwide, his books have sold more than 1.5 million copies.

Find out more at the author's website: www.millerwriter.com

Follow the author on Twitter: molehillgroup

Dedication

To my musician friends and family here in Minnesota, who make it fun to play.

Acknowledgments

Thanks to all the folks at Que who helped turned this manuscript into a book, including Laura Norman, Greg Wiegand, Charlotte Kughen, Lori Lyons, Kim Scott, and technical editor Jeri Usbay. Thanks also to the kind folks at AARP for adding even more to the project.

About AARP and AARP TEK

AARP is a nonprofit, nonpartisan organization, with a membership of nearly 38 million, that helps people turn their goals and dreams into *real possibilities*™, strengthens communities, and fights for the issues that matter most to families such as healthcare, employment and income security, retirement planning, affordable utilities, and protection from financial abuse. Learn more at aarp.org.

The AARP TEK (Technology Education & Knowledge) program aims to accelerate AARP's mission of turning dreams into *real possibilities*™ by providing step-by-step lessons in a variety of formats to accommodate different learning styles, levels of experience, and interests. Expertly guided hands-on workshops delivered in communities nationwide help instill confidence and enrich lives of the 50+ by equipping them with skills for staying connected to the people and passions in their lives. Lessons are taught on touchscreen tablets and smartphones—common tools for connection, education, entertainment, and productivity. For self-paced lessons, videos, articles, and other resources, visit aarptek.org.

Note

Most of the individuals pictured throughout this book are of the author himself, as well as friends and relatives (used with permission), and sometimes pets. Some names and personal information are fictitious.

We Want to Hear from You!

As the reader of this book, you are our most important critic and commentator. We value your opinion and want to know what we're doing right, what we could do better, what areas you'd like to see us publish in, and any other words of wisdom you're willing to pass our way.

We welcome your comments. You can email or write to let us know what you did or didn't like about this book—as well as what we can do to make our books better.

Please note that we cannot help you with technical problems related to the topic of this book.

When you write, please be sure to include this book's title and author as well as your name and email address. We will carefully review your comments and share them with the author and editors who worked on the book.

Email: feedback@quepublishing.com

Mail: Que Publishing
ATTN: Reader Feedback
800 East 96th Street
Indianapolis, IN 46240 USA

Reader Services

Register your copy of *My iPad for Seniors* at quepublishing.com for convenient access to downloads, updates, and corrections as they become available. To start the registration process, go to quepublishing.com/register and log in or create an account*. Enter the product ISBN, 9780789757937, and click Submit. Once the process is complete, you will find any available bonus content under Registered Products.

*Be sure to check the box that you would like to hear from us in order to receive exclusive discounts on future editions of this product.

In this chapter, you learn about the various iPad models and how to unbox and set up your new iPad.

→ What Is an iPad?
→ Choosing the Right iPad for You
→ Unboxing Your New iPad

Buying and Unboxing Your iPad

Apple's iPad is the most popular tablet today. In fact, Apple pretty much defined the tablet market when it released the very first iPad in 2010. Today you can use the latest iPads to browse and search the Web, keep in touch with people through Facebook and other social media, send and receive email and instant messages, participate in video chats, watch movies and TV shows, listen to music, take and view photographs and video, play games, and even do word processing, create spreadsheets, and manage other productive activities. There are lots of reasons why iPads are popular among users of all ages.

This chapter examines the various models of iPads available and what they offer, and then it explains the "out of box experience"—what to expect when you unbox and first turn on your new iPad. (If you've had a previous version of an iPad, you can probably skip over parts of this chapter.)

What Is an iPad?

Before we start talking about different models of iPads, we need to discuss the iPad itself. What, exactly, is an iPad—and what can you do with it?

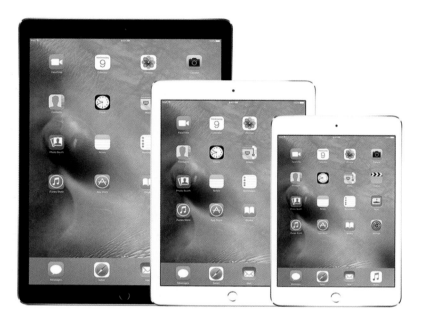

Put simply, the iPad is a *tablet computer*—that is, a small computer in the shape of a handheld tablet. Instead of a keyboard and separate display screen, you have a touch-sensitive display. Not only do you view whatever is on the screen, you can also touch or tap or otherwise poke and prod the screen with your fingertips to make things happen. Instead of tapping the keys on a physical keyboard, you tap the virtual keys and buttons on the display, and the tablet reacts.

The tablet itself is relatively small and thin. Most tablet computers weigh less than two pounds, with newer ones being markedly lighter and thinner than older models. The displays come in all sizes for your viewing pleasure, from around 8 inches diagonal (for so-called mini models) to around 10 inches (for the standard model) to almost 13 inches (for the larger "pro" units). A typical tablet computer, iPad included, looks pretty much like those tablet things the crew used in the *Star Trek: The Next Generation* TV shows and movies.

The iPad was not the first tablet computer, but it was the one that defined the market. When Apple released the original iPad in 2010, it established a new product category. That original iPad sold like proverbial hotcakes, and millions of people discovered that they needed something that really hadn't existed before. People thronged to Apple Stores everywhere to get this newfangled device that promised to redefine their everyday lives.

Like I said, the iPad wasn't the first tablet out there and it wasn't the last, either. Before long, Apple had plenty of competition, primarily from tablets running the rival Android operating system. (Apple's operating system is called iOS, and we'll discuss it a little later in this chapter.) Even though many of these competing tablets were significantly lower priced, the iPad remained the gold standard and the singular best seller.

What can an iPad (or any tablet computer, for that matter) do? Like a computer, it can run productivity programs that let you write letters, crunch numbers, and give presentations. You can use a tablet to communicate with others, via email, text messaging, and video chats. You can use a tablet to access the Internet and do whatever it is you want to do online, from surfing and shopping to keeping in touch via Facebook and Twitter. You can even use a tablet for fun stuff, like watching movies and playing games. Like I said, it's like a computer but crammed into a very small package.

Most of what you do on a tablet is done via *apps*. An app (short for "application") is nothing more than a software program running on the tablet. You tap to open an app, then use that app to do some specific task. There are apps for just about every task imaginable, from editing photos to writing music to tracking your weight and heart rate.

Now, you may read all of this and note that everything a tablet can do, you can also do on your smartphone. This is true. In many ways, a tablet is just a larger smartphone without the phone functionality. Or maybe a smartphone is just a smaller tablet with calling capability. However you approach it, the two types of devices are very similar in what they can do.

The big difference between smartphones and tablets is the size of the screen. Even the largest smartphones have relatively small screens. The larger tablet displays—even on the mini models—simply make it easier to view and do certain things. Watching a movie or reading an ebook or online newspaper is more enjoyable on a larger tablet than on a smaller phone, and it's a lot easier to edit photos, create newsletters, and even play virtual musical instruments on a tablet than on a smartphone.

For many people, a tablet is a viable replacement for a notebook or desktop computer, especially if you don't do a lot of heavy-duty technical stuff. Or you may view a tablet as a useful supplement to your smartphone, one that's just easier and more comfortable to use for many tasks.

In any instance, tablet computers have proven quite popular over the past few years, and the most popular of them are all Apple's various iPads.

Choosing the Right iPad for You

Apple has offered various models of iPads since its introductory model, with new types and sizes being released on an annual basis.

All of Apple's iPads share a number of common features. They all have touchscreens, so you can control what you see with a tap or drag of your finger. They all have built-in speakers for listening, as well as a headphone jack to which you can connect your own earphones or headphones. They all have two cameras, one on the rear for shooting normal photos and one on the front for shooting selfies or doing video chats. They all have built-in storage, to store those photos you take, as well as other data and apps. All will last about 10 hours on a battery charge, depending on your usage. And they all have built-in Wi-Fi so you can wirelessly connect to the Internet.

Beyond that, the models differ mostly in terms of screen size and resolution, storage capacity, processing speed, and a few extra features, such as cellular connectivity (so you can connect your iPad to your mobile phone network). Naturally, the bigger models with more speed, storage, and features cost more than the smaller, less fully featured ones.

So which model you choose depends on a number of factors—how big a screen you want, how much storage capacity you need, what you want to do with the iPad, and how much money you want to spend. Let's look at what's available.

iPad mini

The smallest and most affordable iPad in Apple's line up is the iPad mini. The mini is smaller than the original iPad, with a 7.9-inch screen (compared to the traditional iPad's 9.7-inch screen). This makes the mini both smaller and lighter overall, which a lot of people prefer; you don't need to use both hands to hold it.

Of course, the smaller display also makes it a little more difficult to read what's on the screen. The text on some web pages gets a tad small for some readers, who might be more comfortable with the larger screen on the traditional iPad. That said, the screens on the latest minis have the same resolution as the larger models (measured in terms of pixels, or individual screen elements), which actually provides a sharper picture on the smaller models.

Retina Display

All of Apple's latest iPad models feature what it calls the Retina display. The Retina display has more pixels per square inch, which makes text and images appear extremely crisp onscreen. For example, the screens on the latest iPad minis offer 2048×1536 pixels, which translates to 326 pixels per inch (ppi). (That same Retina display on the larger iPad Air translates to 264 ppi.) In general, the higher the resolution (the more pixels per inch), the sharper the display.

Beyond the smaller size and weight, the big advantage to the iPad mini is the price. The older iPad mini 2 is quite affordable, starting at just $269 for 32GB of storage. The newer iPad mini 4, which offers a faster processor and two storage options (32MB and 128GB), is priced at $399 and $499, respectively.

Cellular Connectivity

All iPads come with Wi-Fi built-in, so you can connect to the Internet from your home Wi-Fi network or any public Wi-Fi hotspot. Select models are also available that add cellular connectivity, so you can connect the iPad to your mobile phone's data network when Wi-Fi is not available. Cellular connectivity adds about $130 to the price of a comparable Wi-Fi-only model; because of this price differential, the non-cellular iPads are Apple's best sellers.

iPad Air

Apple's flagship tablet is the iPad Air. This is the mainline iPad, with the larger 9.7-inch screen and all manner of storage options. The current iPad Air 2 is pretty much a larger version of the iPad mini 4, offering the same Retina display and processor. The iPad Air 2 is available in 16GB and 128GB versions, priced at $399 and $499.

iPad Pro

Apple's latest iPad is the iPad Pro. This is a fully featured model, available in two screen sizes, that is optimized for business productivity. Apple sells a special stylus (dubbed the Apple Pencil) and Smart Keyboard that turn the Pro into a viable replacement for a traditional desktop or laptop PC.

The 9.7-inch iPad Pro starts at $599 for 32GB of storage, and goes up to $799 for a 256GB model. The larger 12.9-inch model, which is better suited for office use, starts at $799 and goes up to $999. Both Pro models utilize a faster processor than you'll find in the iPad Air, and the 12.9-inch model even has a higher-resolution display (2732 × 2048 pixels).

>>>*Go Further*

iOS—THE iPAD OPERATING SYSTEM

All iPad models are powered by a special operating system designed just for mobile devices, dubbed iOS. The same operating system is on Apple's iPhones.

The current version of the operating system is iOS 10. This latest version has many major and minor improvements to the older iOS 9, including redesigned screens and notifications, as well as changes to some of Apple's most popular apps, such as Photos, Maps, Music, News, Phone, and Messages.

All current iPads come with iOS 10 preinstalled; if you have an older model, you can easily upgrade to iOS 10 by tapping Settings on your iPad, then tapping General, then Software Update. You can also upgrade through the iTunes software when you connect your iPad to your computer.

This book covers iPads running iOS 10. If your iPad is running an older version of iOS, you can either upgrade your device or purchase a previous version of this book.

Which iPad Should You Buy?

As noted previously, which iPad is best for you depends on how you intend to use it, along with what size screen you want and how much you want to spend.

In general, most home and casual users go with either the iPad mini or the iPad Air. The iPad Pro is targeted at business users, and is priced a little high for casual personal use.

Between the mini and the Air, many users prefer the smaller size of the iPad mini. It's certainly the most affordable option, and it is Apple's best-selling model; the mini line accounts for almost half of Apple's iPad sales.

If the mini's screen is a little too mini for you, then the larger iPad Air is a better option. The bigger screen of the Air is also better suited for many apps that just need a little more display space.

Whichever iPad you choose, they all run the iOS 10 operating system, and all run pretty much the same apps you can find in Apple's App Store. It really is a matter of size and storage capacity; choose the one that best fits your needs.

More Storage Is Better

If you have extra money to spend, buy a model with more internal storage. The extra storage not only lets you store more photos and videos but it also gives you room to install more apps!

Unboxing Your New iPad

Whichever model iPad you choose, it comes in a stylish white box with minimal text and graphics. (Apple is all about the style!) What's inside that box? Let's take a peek!

What's Inside the Box

All iPad models come in similar packaging. Open the box and you see the iPad itself. Take out the iPad and remove the plastic screen protector.

Underneath the iPad are a white cable and power adapter, which you use to both charge your iPad and connect it to a computer. One end of the cable has a small Lightning connector that plugs into the bottom of the iPad; the other end of the cable has a USB connector that you can connect to a computer's USB port or to the USB port on the power adapter. The power adapter, of course, plugs right into any wall outlet.

Charging Your iPad

Your new iPad's battery probably has a slight charge out of the box, so you can use it right away. However, you'll soon want to recharge the battery to get maximum use out of your new device. Learn how in Chapter 2, "Getting Started with Your iPad."

Turn It On—For the First Time

Now is the moment of truth—time to power up your iPad for the very first time! It will take about five to ten minutes to get everything set up, but it's as simple as following the instructions you see onscreen.

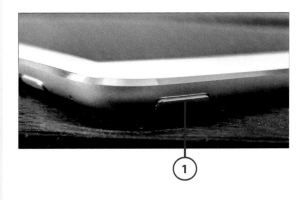

(1) Turn on your iPad by pressing and holding the On/Off button (at the top right of the case) until you see the Apple symbol.

Start Over

When you're setting up your iPad, you can start over at any point by pressing the Home button.

(**2**) You see the word "Hello" in many languages. Swipe or slide your finger from left to right anywhere on this screen to continue.

(**3**) Tap to select your language. (This determines which language is used for onscreen prompts and notifications.)

(4) Tap to select your country or region. (This determines how specific information, such as date and time, appears on your device.)

(5) Tap the name of your home wireless network or nearby Wi-Fi hotspot to connect to it. If prompted to sign into the network, enter your password or other required information. Tap Next (not shown) to activate your iPad.

Cellular Connection

If you're setting up an iPad that offers cellular connectivity, tap Use Cellular Connection to connect to your phone's data network.

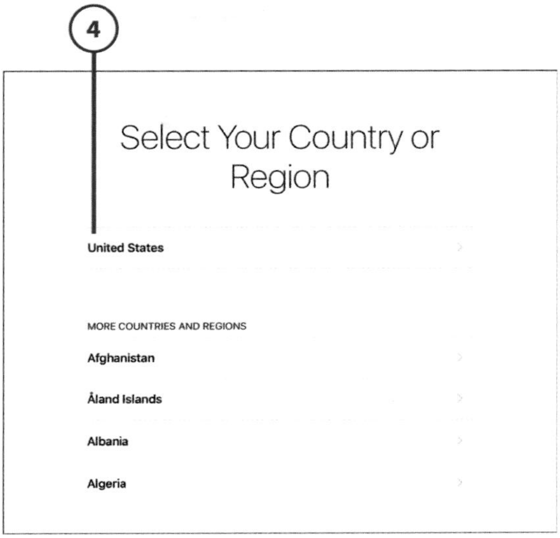

(4)

Select Your Country or Region

United States

MORE COUNTRIES AND REGIONS

Afghanistan

Åland Islands

Albania

Algeria

Choose a Wi-Fi Network

attwifi

Dr. Miller   **(5)**

Google Starbucks

(6) Tap Enable Location Services. (This enables you to fully use Maps and other apps that need to know your current location.)

(7) Place your finger or thumb on the home button until your fingerprint is registered. This lets you unlock your iPad by tapping the home button—no other password or PIN required. You will have to place and lift your finger or thumb multiple times to register your fingerprint.

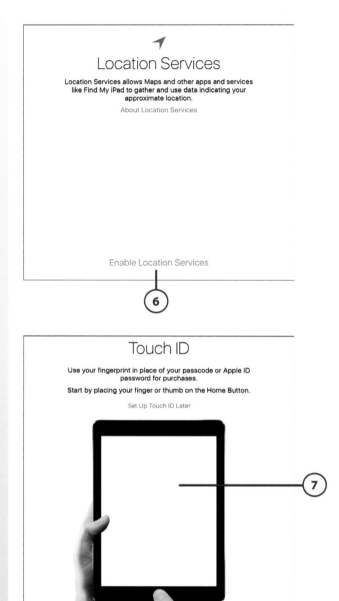

(8) Tap Continue after your fingerprint is registered.

Passwords and PINs

Learn more about protecting your
iPad with passwords, PINs, and Touch
ID in Chapter 6, "Keeping Your iPad
Safe and Secure."

(9) When prompted, create a six-
digit numeric passcode you can
use in case the fingerprint login
doesn't work. (You also use the
passcode for certain device features, such as Apple Pay.) When
prompted to re-enter your passcode, do so.

Complete

Touch ID is ready. Your print can be used
for unlocking your iPad.

Continue

(8)

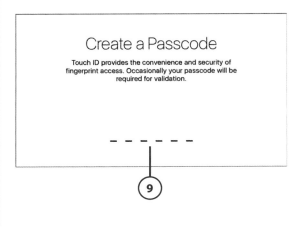

Create a Passcode

Touch ID provides the convenience and security of
fingerprint access. Occasionally your passcode will be
required for validation.

(9)

(10) If you're transferring apps and data from a previous iPad, you use the Apps & Data screen. If this is your first iPad, tap the Set Up as New iPad option.

(11) You are prompted to sign in with your Apple ID. If you already have an Apple ID and password (which you probably do if you also use an iPhone or a Mac computer), enter them now, *or…*

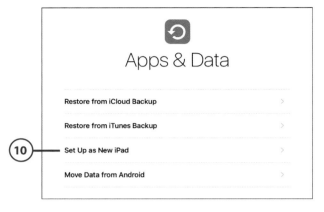

Apple ID

You don't need an Apple ID to use your iPad, although it's necessary to take advantage of many popular features and services, including iCloud online storage and the iTunes Store. You can create a new Apple ID at any time by using your web browser to go to https://appleid.apple.com.

(12) If this is your first Apple product, you need to create an Apple ID. Tap Don't Have an Apple ID or Forgot It? and then follow the onscreen instructions.

Apple Services

After you've created and/or signed in with your Apple ID, you might be asked to set up various services, such as iCloud Drive and Apple Pay. Do so now if you want, or skip each option and set them up later.

13 You are prompted to turn on Siri, the iPad's virtual personal assistant. You use Siri to control your iPad with voice commands. Tap Turn On Siri.

14 You are asked if you want to send diagnostic information to Apple. You don't need to do this, so tap Don't Send. (Or, if you want to, tap Send to Apple.)

15 Tap Get Started to begin using your new iPad—and turn to Chapter 2 to learn what happens next!

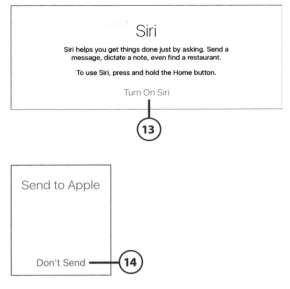

In this chapter, you learn the basic operation of your new iPad.

→ Getting to Know Your iPad
→ Turning Your iPad On and Off
→ Using Your iPad
→ Performing Basic Operations
→ Managing Your iPad's Battery

Getting Started with Your iPad

Now that you've taken your new iPad out of the box, charged it up, and performed the initial setup, it's time to start using the thing. To do so, you need to know what's what and what's where on the iPad itself—and what you need to do to operate the darned thing!

Getting to Know Your iPad

Your iPad is a large, flat tablet with a screen on one side and a fairly plain back on the other. You can hold it either vertically (with the Home button on the bottom) or horizontally (with the Home button to the left or right side); the screen flips to accommodate how you're holding it.

There are physical buttons along the top and sides of the iPad, and on the bottom front. Let's look at these buttons now.

Front

Looking at the iPad from the front, the first thing you see is the screen itself. This is the touchscreen (technically, Apple calls it a Multi-Touch Display), which is how you perform most of the device's operations—by literally touching the screen with your fingers. We'll go over all the touch gestures (tapping, swiping, pinching, and more) later in this chapter, but let's move to everything else you see on the front of the device.

FaceTime HD camera

Multi-Touch Display

Home button/
Touch ID sensor

The round button just beneath the screen is the Home button. You press this button to return at any time to the iPad's Home screen. The Home button also doubles as the Touch ID sensor; if you've configured your iPad to unlock with your fingerprint, this is where you press your finger to unlock the device.

Touch ID

Learn more about fingerprint unlocking in Chapter 6, "Keeping Your iPad Safe and Secure."

Directly above the screen is a small hole. This is the lens for the iPad's front-facing camera—the one you use to take selfies or conduct video chats. Apple calls this the FaceTime HD camera, and you probably don't want to cover it up.

Top

There are two important items along the top edge of your iPad. On the left top you find a standard 3.5mm headset jack, for connecting earphones or head-phones. On the right top is a small button for turning your iPad on or off, appro-priately called the Sleep/Wake button. Press this button to wake your iPad when it's asleep, or put it to sleep if you're using it.

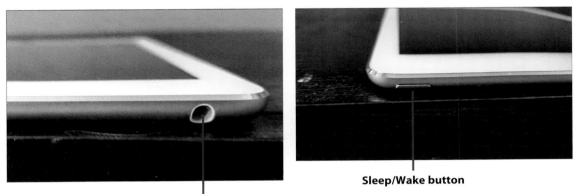

Sleep/Wake button

Headset jack

Sides

If you have an iPad Air or iPad mini, there's nothing on the left side of the unit. If you have an iPad Pro, however, you'll see the Smart Connector in the very middle of the left side. The Smart Connector is used to magnetically connect so-called "smart" accessories, such as the iPad Pro Smart Keyboard. (Learn more about these accessories in Chapter 23, "Accessorizing Your iPad.")

On all iPad models, you find the up and down volume buttons on the right side of the unit. Use these controls to raise and lower the iPad's volume.

There's also a small hole located just above the top volume button. This is a microphone, for when you're using your iPhone for video calls or recording videos.

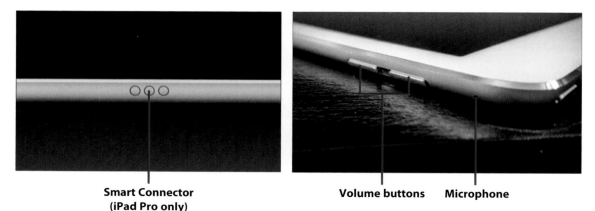

Smart Connector
(iPad Pro only)   Volume buttons   Microphone

Cellular Models

If your iPad offers cellular connectivity (in addition to the normal Wi-Fi wireless), you'll find a removable tray on the right side of the unit. This tray contains the iPad's Nano-SIM card; insert the included removal tool (or a plain old paperclip) into the small hole to eject the tray.

Bottom

There are two (actually, three) important items along the bottom edge of your iPad.

In the very middle bottom is a small connector, dubbed the Lightning connector. You use this connector to plug in the cable that came with your iPad; the other end of the cable can connect to either your computer (via USB) or the power adapter that you plug into the wall.

There are also two speakers on the bottom of the iPad, on either side of the Lightning connector. Don't cover up these speakers or you'll adversely affect the sounds you hear.

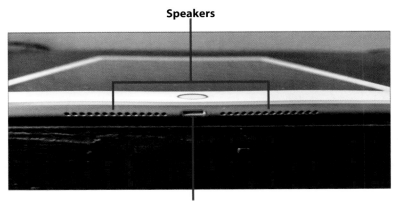

Speakers

Lightning connector

Back

Finally, turn your iPad over and examine the back of the unit. The most obvious thing on the back is the big Apple logo, but that really doesn't do anything.

Instead, direct your attention to the top-left corner. The big round thing you see there is the main camera. Apple calls this the iSight camera, and you use it to take pictures and videos of others.

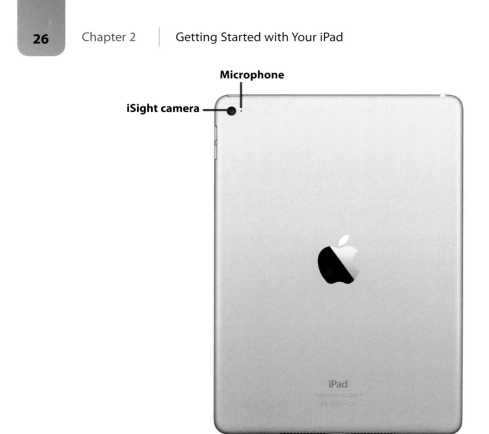

Just to the right of the iSight camera is a small hole that contains another micro-phone. Don't cover up either the camera or the microphone, or they won't work.

Turning Your iPad On and Off

Turning your iPad on and off is a little more complex than you might think. That's because you can completely power off your unit or just put it to sleep. When the unit is completely powered off, it takes a minute or so to power back on. When it's in sleep mode (or "locked," as Apple puts it) it can immediately come back to life, with the same apps running as when you put it to sleep.

Power On Your iPad

When your iPad is completely powered off (as it is when you first remove it from its box), you need to power it back on.

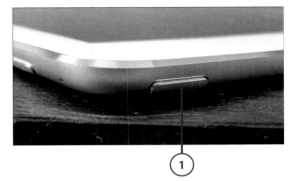

(1) Press and hold the Sleep/Wake button until the Apple logo appears onscreen.

(2) After the Apple logo disappears, you're prompted to enter your passcode. Do so now to display your device's Home screen. (If you haven't set up a password, you won't see this prompt and instead are directly shown the Home screen.)

Lock Your iPad

You put your iPad to sleep (but not turn it completely off) by locking the device. This is how you most often "turn off" your iPad.

(1) Press the Sleep/Wake button.

(2) The screen goes blank and the iPad is now locked.

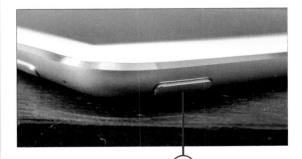

Inactivity Lock

By default, your iPad locks automatically if you haven't touched the screen for two minutes. You can change this auto-lock time on the Settings screen, as discussed in Chapter 3, "Personalizing the Way Your iPad Looks and Works."

Unlock Your iPad

To reawaken a sleeping iPad all you have to do is unlock it.

(1) Press either the Home or the Sleep/Wake button.

(2) If you've configured your iPad for fingerprint operation, press the Home button (Touch ID sensor) with your finger or thumb.

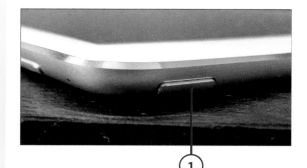

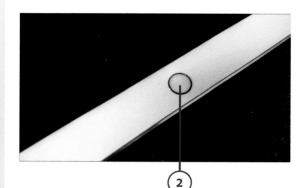

3 If you've configured your iPad for passcode operation, press the Home button again and then enter your passcode.

4 If you have not configured your iPad with either a passcode or fingerprint, press the Home button again to unlock the device.

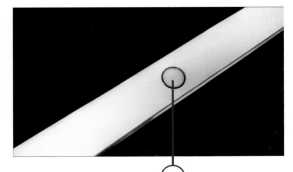

Power Off Your iPad

Turning off the iPad shuts down all open apps and removes all power. You have to power it back up again the next time you want to use it.

(**1**) Press and hold the Sleep/Wake button for a few seconds, until the slider appears onscreen.

(**2**) Drag the Slide to Power Off slider to the right. The iPad now powers down.

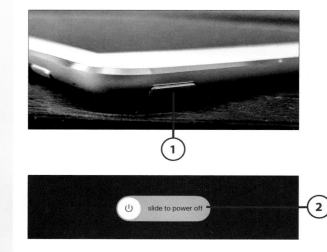

Force a Restart

On rare occasions an iPad may become frozen—tapping the screen does nothing. In this instance, you need to force a restart of your device.

(**1**) Press and hold both the Sleep/Wake and Home buttons at the same time for at least ten seconds.

(**2**) When the Apple logo appears onscreen, your iPad is restarting.

>>>Go Further

SMART COVERS

Many companies (Apple included) sell so-called "smart" covers and cases for the various models of iPads. A smart cover or case not only protects your device, but interacts with your iPad to wake it up when opened and put it to sleep when closed. Learn more about smart covers and cases in Chapter 23.

Using Your iPad

Okay, now you can turn your iPad on and off (and lock it and unlock it, too). But what do you do with it once you turn it on?

Learn Essential Multi-Touch Gestures

You operate your iPad with your finger(s). You can perform different operations with different gestures.

Most everything you can do onscreen is based on a half dozen basic gestures. These are detailed in the following table.

Basic Touch Gestures

Gesture	Looks Like	Description
Tap		Touch and quickly release a point on the screen with your finger.
Press		Touch your finger to the screen and hold it there.
Drag		Touch and hold your finger on an item on the screen, then slowly move your finger to drag the item to a new position. Release your finger to "drop" the item to the new position.

Gesture	Looks Like	Description
Swipe		This is like dragging, except faster. Place the tip of your finger on the screen, then quickly move it in the appropriate direction. You use swiping to scroll up or down a screen, or move the screen left or right.
Pinch		Position your thumb and forefinger apart on the screen, then pinch them together. This is typically used to zoom out of a page or image.
Expand		This is the opposite of pinching. Position your thumb and forefinger together on the screen and then slide them apart. This is typically used to zoom into a page or an image.

>>>Go Further

HIDDEN GESTURES

You can expand on the basic gestures to perform other common operations. These are kind of "hidden" gestures, so now the secret's out!

Try these hidden gestures to get more out of your iPad:

- Within an app, return to the top of a long page by tapping the top menu bar.

- Display the iPad's Spotlight Search page by swiping down on any Home screen. (This screen displays alerts, notices, and a Search box.)

- Display notifications by swiping down from the very top edge of any screen.

- Display the Control Center by swiping up from the bottom edge of the screen. (You use the Control center to adjust basic device settings.)

- Display two apps side-by-side onscreen (what Apple calls "multi-tasking") by displaying the first app and then swiping in from the middle of the right edge of the screen. This displays a list of apps in a narrow column; tap the second app you want to display.

- Return to the Home screen by pinching four or five fingers together.

- View all your open apps by swiping up with four fingers and your thumb.

- Switch to the next or previous open app by swiping left or right with four or five fingers.

- Split the onscreen keyboard into two halves by expanding the keyboard with your thumb and forefinger. (Some people find this makes typing a little easier.) Pinch your fingers back together to rejoin the two halves into a whole keyboard.

- In a document or web page, select a word by double-tapping it. Alternatively, press and hold a word to select it.

Navigate the Home Screen

On your iPad, the Home screen is where everything starts. When you press the Home button, you see the Home screen—or, more accurately, the first of several Home screens. All Home screens display a grid of icons that represent the apps installed on your device. You have as many Home screens as you need to display all your apps.

(1) Press the Home button to display the first Home screen.

(2) At the bottom of the screen is the Dock, where up to six app icons can be "docked" so that they appear on every Home page.

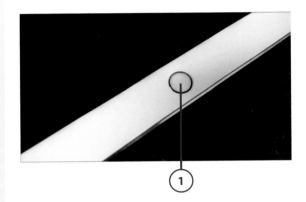

3 The number of Home screens on your iPad is indicated by a grouping of dots above the Dock; you see as many dots as you have Home screens. The screen you're currently viewing is the solid white dot in the group.

4 Swipe left or right to view the next or previous Home screen.

5 Tap an icon to open the corresponding app.

View the Search Screen

The very first screen on your iPad actually isn't a Home screen. This screen, to the left of the main Home screen (the one you see when you press the Home button), is called the Search screen and displays a search box along with a variety of "widgets." These are small panels that display specific information, such as news, weather, appointments, and the like.

Widgets on Lock Screen

You can also display widgets on the Lock screen, before you unlock your iPad. Just swipe to the right from the Lock screen and you'll see all your notifications and widgets.

1 Press the Home button to display the first Home screen.

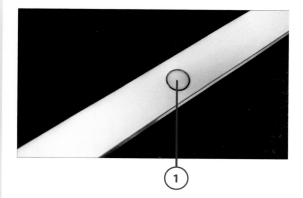

2 Swipe to the right to display the Search screen.

3 When held horizontally, you see two columns of widgets, as shown here. When held vertically, you see a single column of widgets. Tap any widget or notification to view more details or to open the corresponding app.

Customizing the Search Screen

To add new widgets to the widgets screen, tap the Edit button. Learn more in Chapter 3.

View and Close Open Apps

You open apps on your iPad by tapping the app's icon on one of the Home screens. You can have multiple apps open at the same time, and easily switch between them.

1 To view all open apps, press the Home button twice.

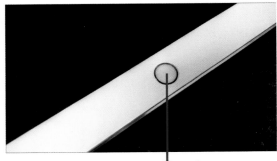

(2) You now see all your open apps, in a type of carousel. (Apple calls this the App Switcher.) Swipe left or right to focus on other apps.

(3) Tap an app to go to that app.

(4) Drag an app up and off the screen to close it.

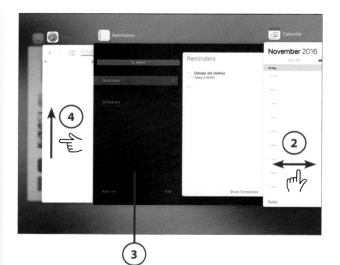

Understand the Status Bar

Running across the top of every iPad screen is a transparent status bar. This status bar displays icons for various system operations and provides information that shows you how your iPad is working.

Status bar

The following table details the more common icons you'll find on the status bar, and what they mean.

Status Bar Icons

Icon	Name	Description
🔒	Lock	The device is locked.
🔋	Battery	Shows the battery level or charging status.
⏰	Alarm	An alarm is set.

Icon	Name	Description
	Activity	There is currently app or network activity.
	Orientation Lock	Screen orientation is locked.
	Wi-Fi	The iPad is connected to a Wi-Fi network; the more bars, the stronger the connection.
	Airplane Mode	Airplane Mode is engaged (Wi-Fi and Bluetooth are both turned off).
	Do Not Disturb	Do Not Disturb mode is turned on.
	Personal Hotspot	The iPad is providing a personal hotspot for other devices.
	Syncing	The iPad is connected to your computer and syncing with iTunes.
VPN	VPN	The iPad is connected to a virtual private network (VPN).
	Location Services	An app is using Location Services to establish the current location.
	Bluetooth	If the icon is blue or white, Bluetooth is turned on and the iPad is paired with a device, such as a Bluetooth headset. If the icon is gray, Bluetooth is turned on and the iPad is paired with a device, but the device is turned off or out of range.
	Bluetooth Battery	Shows the battery level of the connected Bluetooth device.

Cell Icons

If you have an iPad with cellular connectivity (Wi-Fi+Cellular), there are also icons for your cell signal and 3G/4G/LTE/EDGE/GPRS networks.

Performing Basic Operations

Now that you know where (almost) everything is on your iPad, let's learn some of the most common operations necessary to get things done.

View and Respond to Alerts

When your iPad or a specific app has something to tell you, you see an alert pop up onscreen. Depending on your settings and the importance of the alert, it may appear briefly at the top of the screen and then fade away, or remain in the center of the screen until you take some necessary action. Some alerts also appear on your iPad's Home or Search screens.

(1) Pull down on the alert to respond to it without leaving your current app.

(2) Swipe the alert from right to left to respond to an alert when your iPad is locked.

Configure Alerts
To determine which alerts you see (and how you see them), turn to Chapter 3.

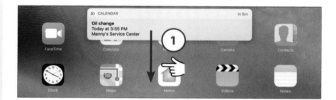

Display the Control Center

When you want instant access to key system settings, such as screen brightness and volume, open your iPad's Control Center.

1. Swipe up from the bottom of the screen to display the Control Center.

2. Tap any icon to turn on or off that control.

3. Drag any slider to adjust that control.

4. Swipe from right to left to display the second screen of the Control Center.

5. Close the Control Center by swiping down until it moves off the bottom of the screen.

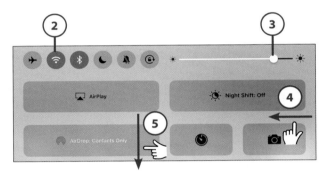

Adjust the Brightness

As noted, most of the more immediate iPad settings are accessed via the Control Center. This includes the device's screen brightness control.

1. Swipe up from the bottom edge of any screen to display the Control Center.

(2) Drag the brightness slider to the right to increase screen brightness and to the left to decrease screen brightness.

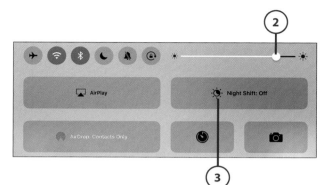

Conserve Battery Usage

Lower the screen brightness to conserve the battery.

(3) Tap the Night Shift button to turn on the feature, which makes the screen colors warmer and easier to see at night. Tap the button again to return to normal screen colors. (The first time you enable this feature, you are prompted to set the Night Shift schedule.)

Change the Volume Level

Use the volume controls on the right side of your iPad to raise and lower the sounds you hear from the iPad's speakers.

(1) Press the volume up button to increase the device's volume level.

(2) Press the volume down button to decrease the device's volume level.

(3) Press and hold the volume down button to temporarily mute the sound. Press the volume up button to increase the sound again.

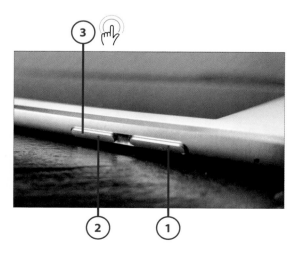

Control Center Muting

You can also mute the sound from the Control Center. Just open the Control Center and tap the Mute button. (It turns red when the sound is muted.) Tap the Mute button again to return to the previous volume level.

Rotate the iPad

As previously noted, you can use your iPad in either vertical (portrait) or horizontal (landscape) modes. The Home screen and most apps automatically rotate and adjust their displays to optimize how they work in either mode.

1. To switch from horizontal to vertical mode, simply rotate the iPad 90 degrees left or right. (Rotating left—counterclockwise—puts the volume controls on top of the iPad, and the Home button on the right.)

2. The Home screen automatically adapts to the new orientation.

Activate Do Not Disturb Mode

There may be times when you don't want to be disturbed by alerts and notifications or by requests to video chat via FaceTime. When you don't want to be bothered by these and similar requests, activate your iPad's Do Not Disturb mode. When Do Not Disturb is activated, you won't see or hear notifications, alerts, and system sound effects. (Audio from music, movies, and TV shows is *not* muted.)

(1) Swipe up from the bottom edge of any screen to display the Control Center.

(2) Tap the Do Not Disturb button to mute all system alerts and notifications. Tap the button again to return to normal operation.

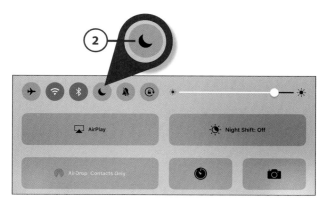

Enter Text with the Onscreen Keyboard

Many applications let you (or even require you!) to enter text onscreen. You may be writing a note or memo, or browsing a web page that asks you to enter information into an onscreen form.

When you need to enter text onscreen, use your iPad's onscreen keyboard. In most instances, the keyboard appears automatically, on the bottom half of the screen, when you tap within a form field or document.

1. Tap within a document or form field to display the onscreen keyboard.

2. Tap a key on the keyboard to enter that character onscreen.

3. Tap the Shift key to enter a capital letter. Double-tap the Shift key to engage caps lock.

4. Tap the Number key to display numbers and special characters.

5. Tap to enter a number or special character.

6. Tap the ABC key to return to the normal alphanumeric keyboard.

7. Tap the Emoji key to display and enter a range of emoji.

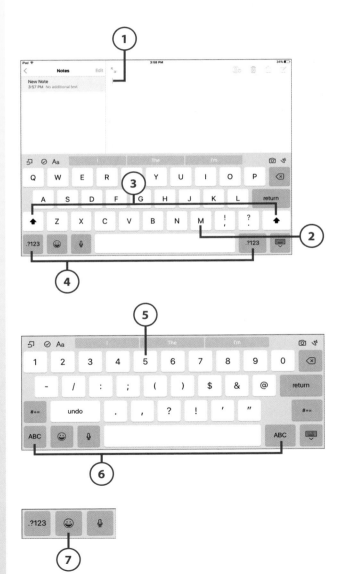

(8) Tap a tab to display different types of emoji.

(9) Tap to enter an emoji.

(10) Tap the ABC key to return to the normal alphanumeric keyboard.

(11) Tap the Keyboard key to hide the onscreen keyboard.

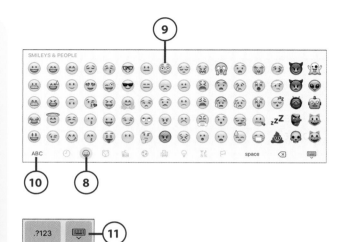

>>>Go Further

PREDICTIVE KEYBOARD

Your iPad uses what is called a *predictive keyboard*, in that it tries to figure out what you're typing and enter the word for you. You see the recommended words at the top of the keyboard; tap a word to insert it into the form or document.

The predictive keyboard lets you type without having to completely enter long words, and it can help you type faster. It also helps you avoid common spelling mistakes.

If you don't like the suggestions made by the predictive keyboard, you can turn off the predictive part of it. From the Settings screen, select General; then select Keyboard. On the Keyboards screen, tap "off" the Predictive switch.

Predictive keyboard suggestions

Copy and Paste Text

Whether you're using your iPad to write long letters or short Facebook posts, it's handy to be able to copy and paste text from one location to another.

(1) Press the screen to make the magnifying glass appear.

(2) Move your finger left or right to position the insertion point.

(3) Lift your finger to display the pop-up menu. Tap Select to select the current word.

(4) Tap and drag the starting and end points to select more or less text.

(5) Tap Cut to cut this selection (move it to another location).

(6) Tap Copy to copy this selection (duplicate it in another location).

(7) Press or double-tap the screen where you want to paste the cut or copied text. This displays a different menu of options. (The options available differ from app to app.)

(8) Tap Paste.

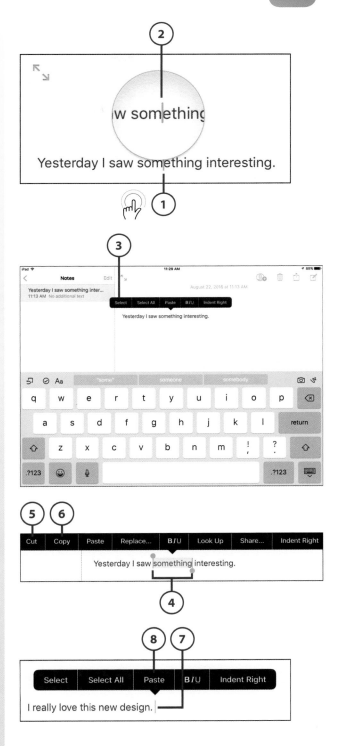

Set an Alarm

Your iPad includes a Clock app that lets you set a timer or an alarm. It also functions as a stopwatch.

If you want to use your iPad as a (very expensive!) alarm clock, use the Clock app to set an alarm.

(1) Tap the Clock icon to open the Clock app.

(2) Tap the Alarm icon at the bottom of the screen.

(3) Tap the + icon to create a new alarm.

(4) Use the clock control to set the alarm time.

(5) To have the alarm repeat on later days, tap Repeat and select which day(s) you want to use it.

(6) Tap Label to create a name for this alarm.

(7) Tap Sound to select the sound you want to hear when the alarm goes off.

(8) Tap "off" the Snooze control if you don't want to be able to snooze through the alarm.

(9) Tap Save. The alarm is created and activated.

Turn Off an Alarm

When an alarm sounds, turn it off by pressing the iPad's Home button.

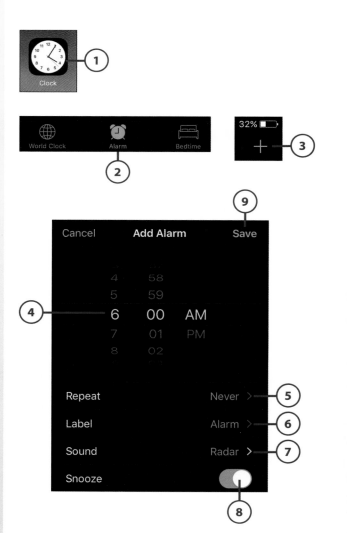

Onscreen Switches

iOS utilizes a variety of onscreen switches to activate and deactivate various settings and functions. Just tap the switch to change its condition from "off" to "on," or vice versa. An "on" switch is to the right with a green background; an "off" switch is to the left with a white background.

Set a Timer

There are times when you need to set a timer—when you're cooking in the kitchen, for example, or putting the grandkids in a timeout. You can use the Clock app for all your timer needs.

(1) Tap the Clock icon to open the Clock app.

(2) Tap the Timer icon.

(3) Use the timer controls to set the length of the timer.

(4) Tap the sound icon to set the sound you hear when the timer goes off.

(5) Tap Start to start the timer.

Turn Off the Timer

When the Timer ends, press the Home button to turn it off.

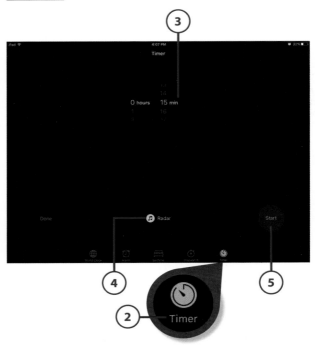

Use the Stopwatch

Finally, the Clock app also lets you use it as a stopwatch, so that you can time any ongoing event.

(1) Tap the Clock icon to open the Clock app.

(2) Tap the Stopwatch icon.

(3) Tap Start to start the stopwatch.

(4) Tap Stop to stop the stopwatch. The elapsed time is displayed onscreen.

Managing Your iPad's Battery

Your iPad is powered by an internal battery that recharges when you connect it to the included power charger. How long the internal battery lasts before needing to be recharged depends on a lot of different factors—how you're using the device, which apps you're running, how bright you've set the screen, and so forth.

Recharge the Battery

Use the included power adapter to charge your iPad when you're not using it—although you can continue to use the device when charging.

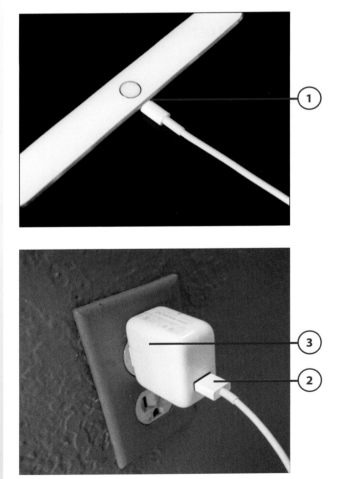

 Connect the Lightning connector on the cable to the Lightning port on the bottom of the iPad.

Lightning Connector
One nice thing about Apple's Lightning connector is that it's symmetrical; you can plug the cable in right side up or upside down, it's all the same. No more twisting and turning to fit cables into connectors!

2 Connect the USB connector on the cable to the USB port on the power adapter.

3 Connect the power adapter to any power outlet. Your iPad should fully charge in about 5 to 7 hours—longer if you're using it while charging (which you can).

It's Not All Good

USB Charging

You can also charge your iPad's battery by connecting the Lightning cable to a USB port on your computer instead of to the power adapter. Recharging via computer, however, is much slower than recharging via a traditional power outlet. In addition, if you connect your iPad to a computer that is turned off or in sleep or standby modes, it may drain the iPad battery instead of charging it!

Monitor Battery Usage

The battery icon on the right side of the status bar indicates how much charge you have left. When the charge gets too low, the status bar displays the image of a nearly empty battery, and you'll need to plug in and charge up your iPad before you can continue to use it.

If you want to know which apps are using the most battery power, you can do that.

1. From the Home screen, tap the Settings icon to open the Settings screen.

2. Tap Battery in the left column.

Settings

(**3**) You see a list of those apps
and system functions that have
used the most battery power,
in descending order. Tap to display usage for the last 24 hours
or the last 7 days.

(**4**) Tap any item to view how many
minutes this and other items
have been used.

(**3**)

BATTERY USAGE	
Last 24 Hours	Last 7 Days

Home & Lock Screen	29%
Photos	27%
Music	23%
Calendar	10%
Settings	7%
Reminders	4%

Shows proportion of battery used by each app in the last 24 hours.

(**4**)

In this chapter, you learn how to personalize various aspects of your iPad experience.

→ Personalizing Your Home Screens
→ Configuring Device Settings
→ Managing System Settings

3

Personalizing the Way Your iPad Looks and Works

Every iPad looks and acts the same right out of the box. But that doesn't mean that you can't configure your iPad to your own personal tastes.

Want a different background picture? You can do that. Want a brighter or dimmer screen? You can do that, too. Don't like the way you receive notifications onscreen, and from which apps? Then change the notification settings.

Truth is, there's a lot you can do to personalize your very own iPad. This chapter walks you through managing your screens, backgrounds, and more detailed settings. Change is coming!

Personalizing Your Home Screens

One of the most visible things that people like to change is the look of the iPad screens. You can change the background wallpaper of the Lock and Home screens, as well as the way app icons are arranged onscreen.

Change the Wallpaper

The default wallpaper you see on your iPad's Home and Lock screens is pretty enough, but you can probably find something more to your liking. You can choose different wallpaper for the Lock and Home screens, or use the same wallpaper for both.

① From the Home page, tap the Settings icon to display the Settings screen.

② Tap Wallpaper in the left column. Your current wallpaper is displayed on thumbnails of your Lock (left) and Home (right) screens.

③ Tap Choose a New Wallpaper.

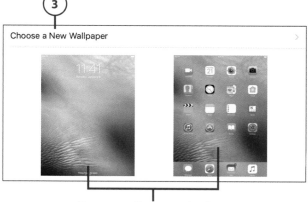

Current wallpaper selections

4) Tap Dynamic to select one of Apple's dynamic (moving) wallpapers. *Or…*

5) Tap Stills to select one of Apple's supplied still photos.

6) Tap to select one of the available choices, then skip to Step 9. *Or…*

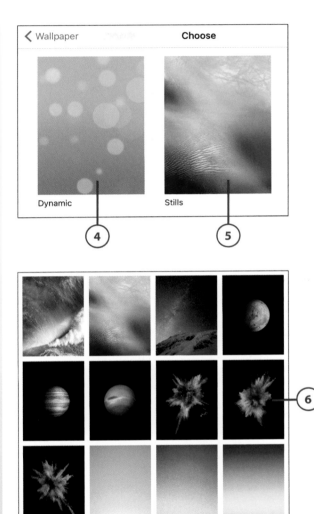

(7) Tap one of the photo folders to use one of your own pictures as wallpaper.

(8) Tap to select a specific photo. That picture is applied as your Lock screen wallpaper.

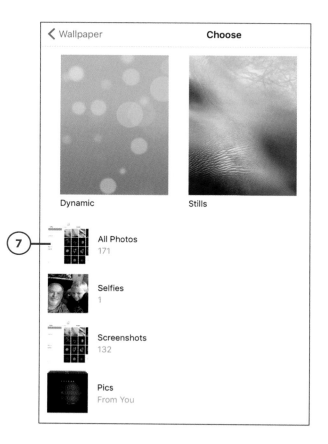

⑨ Tap and drag the background photo to position it as you like on the screen.

⑩ To create a slight motion effect for the background, tap to turn on Perspective Zoom.

Perspective Zooming

When you select Perspective Zoom you enable what experts call a *parallax effect*. It essentially creates a slight motion effect on the Home or Lock screens when you tilt your iPad; the background seems to follow you as you move your device. Some people like it, some people don't. It's not really a big thing.

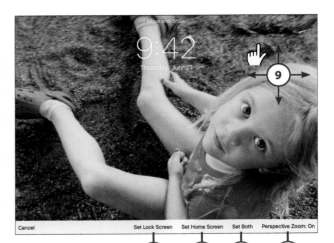

⑪ Tap Set Lock Screen to set this picture for only your Lock screen.

⑫ Tap Set Home Screen to set this picture for only your Home screen.

⑬ Tap Set Both to use this picture as the background for both your Lock and Home screens.

Arrange App Icons

Whatever size iPad you have, app icons are displayed on the Home screen in the same 4 × 5 grid. (That's 4 columns by 5 rows if held vertically, or 4 rows by 5 columns if held horizontally.) There's also the Dock at the bottom of the screen, where you can permanently "dock" icons for your most-used apps.

iOS Apps

Learn more about apps on your iPad in Chapter 8, "Installing and Using Apps."

Which icons appear where on your Home screens is totally up to you. You can easily move icons from one position to another, and even from one screen to another. You can also move icons to and from the dock.

(1) Press and hold the icon you want to move until all the icons onscreen start to jiggle. (You also see a little X next to each icon, which means you're in editing mode.) You can tap the X to delete an app, if you want.

(2) Drag the icon to a new position. The other icons rearrange themselves to make room.

(3) Lift your finger when the icon is in place.

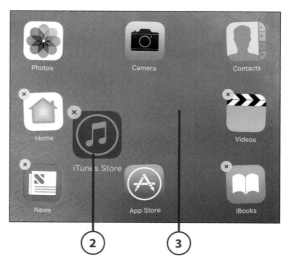

4 Press the Home button to return to normal screen mode.

Screen to Screen

To move an icon to a different Home screen, drag the icon to the side of the screen until the adjacent screen appears. You can then "drop" the icon to a new position on this screen. If you try to drag an icon to a screen that's already full, it pushes the last icon (on the bottom right) to the next screen.

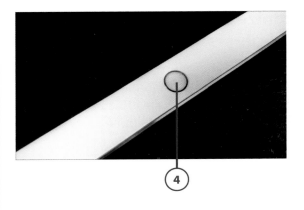

Move an Icon to the Dock

The Dock is that area at the bottom of every screen that "permanently" holds icons for your most-used apps. I say "permanently" in quotes because you can easily change which icons appear in the Dock, whenever you want.

1 Add an icon to the Dock by dragging it from any screen down to the Dock.

2 Rearrange icons on the Dock by dragging any icon to a new position.

3 Remove an icon from the Dock by dragging it from the Dock to any Home screen.

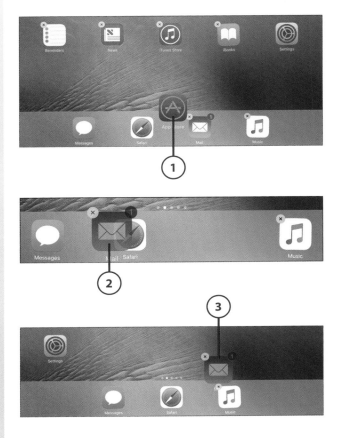

Organize Apps with Folders

If you have too many apps crowding too many screens, you can organize those apps into folders. Each folder can contain multiple apps; to open a folder, tap it and then tap the appropriate app inside.

(1) Create a new folder by dragging one icon on top of another. This creates the folder and displays it full screen.

(2) Tap anywhere outside the folder to close the folder and return to the desktop. The folder is displayed in position there. (You can drag the folder to move it to another position, if you like.)

(3) Add another app to this folder by dragging the app icon on top of the folder icon.

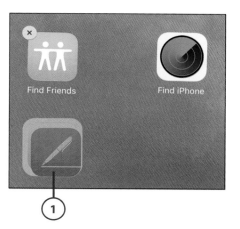

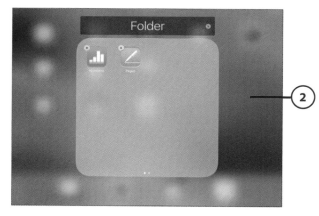

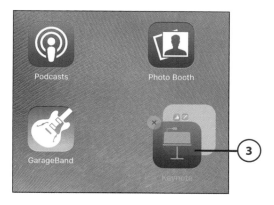

4 Remove an app from a folder by opening the folder and then dragging the icon outside of the folder.

5 Rename a folder by opening the folder, tapping the default name, and then using the onscreen keyboard to edit or enter a new name.

>>>Go Further
ORGANIZE BY TYPE

I find it useful to organize my lesser-used apps into folders. Those apps I use all the time I want to tap immediately from the Home screen; those I use less regularly I put into folders so they're not cluttering my screens.

When I use folders, I try to put similar apps together. For example, if I have a half dozen or so games, I might create a folder labeled Games to hold them all. Similarly, I might group my music, video, and photos apps into a folder labeled Lifestyle, or the Numbers, Pages, and Keynote apps into a Productivity folder.

The point is to group similar apps together in folders where I can quickly and easily find them. I've found that creating a folder labeled Misc is the best way to "lose" apps on my device!

Configure the Search Screen

When you swipe from left to right on the main Home screen, you display your iPad's Search screen. There's a search box at the top of this screen, as you might expect, but also a variety of *widgets*. These are small panels that display specific types of information—weather, news, and the like.

You can personalize which widgets you display on the Search screen. This makes this screen more useful for you.

(**1**) Swipe to the right from the main Home screen to display the Search screen.

(**2**) Your current widgets are displayed. If you have many widgets installed, you can scroll up and down through the left and right columns to view all of them. Tap a widget to display more information or open a given app.

(**3**) Tap Edit to display the Add Widgets screen.

(**4**) Your current widgets are listed by their position, in either the Left Column or Right Column list. To move a widget to another column or to another position within the same column, press and drag it to its new position.

(**5**) Tap the red – button to remove a widget from the Search screen, and then tap the Remove button.

(**6**) Add a new widget by scrolling to the More Widgets section and tapping the green + for the widget you want to add. (You can then reposition the new widget in the Left Column and Right Column lists.)

(**7**) Tap Done to return to the Search screen.

Add Widgets

Get timely information from your favorite apps, at a glance.
Add and organize your widgets below.

LEFT COLUMN

- Reminders
- Calendar

RIGHT COLUMN

- News
- Siri App Suggestions
- Music

(**5**)   (**4**)

(**6**)   (**7**)

Cancel   Done

- Siri App Suggestions
- Music

MORE WIDGETS

- Find Friends
- Mail
- Maps Destinations
- Maps Nearby
- Maps Transit
- Notes
- Photos

Configuring Device Settings

There are many other settings you can configure to better personalize your iPad. You configure all these settings from the iPad's Settings page.

Display the Settings Page

The Settings page is organized into a series of tabs, which are accessible from the left column. Tap a tab to view the individual settings of a given type.

(1) From the Home screen, tap the Settings icon to open the Settings screen.

(2) Tap the tab on the left to display related settings.

Configure Notifications

Many apps display notifications for various types of events. The Mail app, for example, can display notifications when you receive new emails; the News app can display notifications with recent news headlines.

You can determine what types of notifications you receive on an app-by-app basis. For that matter, you can opt to turn off all notifications for specific apps, thus reducing the number of annoying notifications you have to deal with.

Different Notifications

Different apps will have different notification options. This how-to discusses some of the more common notification options.

(1) From the Settings page, tap to display the Notifications tab.

(2) Tap the app you want to configure.

(3) Disable all notifications from this app by tapping off the Allow Notifications switch.

(4) Show notifications from this app in the Notification Center by tapping on the Show in Notification Center switch.

(5) Tap Sounds to change the notification sound for this app. Make a selection from the list.

(6) Some apps display a number on top of the icon to indicate the number of notifications or actions pending. (For example, the icon for the Mail app displays a red "2" if there are two unread emails in the inbox.) Turn on this numbering by tapping on the Badge App Icon switch.

(7) Show notifications from this app on the Lock screen by tapping on the Show on Lock Screen switch. Tap off this switch to not display notifications from this app on the Lock screen.

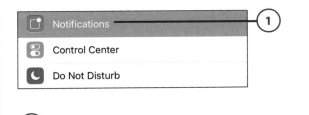

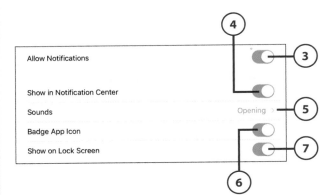

(8) In the Alert Style When Unlocked section, tap None to not display alerts on the Lock or Home screen.

(9) To display alerts as banners that automatically fade way, tap to select Banners.

(10) To display alerts in the middle of the screen that don't go away until some action is taken, tap to select Alerts.

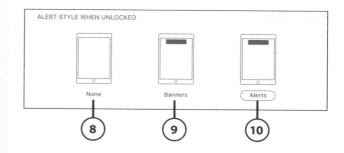

Hide the Control Center

The Control Center—which enables quick access to volume, brightness, wireless, and other settings— appears when you swipe up from the bottom of any screen. If you'd rather not display the Control Center within apps or from the Lock screen, you have that option. (It always displays from the Home screens.)

(1) From the Settings page, tap to display the Control Center tab.

(2) Tap off the Access on Lock Screen switch to not display the Control Center from the Lock screen.

(3) Tap off the Access Within Apps switch to not display the Control center from within apps.

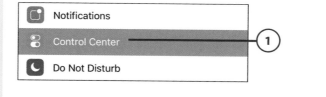

Configure the Display and Brightness

You can adjust how bright your iPad's display appears, along with several other display-related settings.

(1) From the Settings page, tap to display the Display & Brightness tab.

(2) Drag the Brightness slider to the left to make the screen less bright, or to the right to make it brighter. (Remember, the brighter the screen, the faster it drains your battery.)

(3) To let your iPad automatically adjust the screen brightness when lighting conditions change (darker in darker rooms, brighter in brighter conditions), tap on the Auto-Brightness switch.

(4) To let your iPad automatically shift the display colors warmer (more reddish) after dark, tap on the Night Shift switch. You see the Night Shift panel.

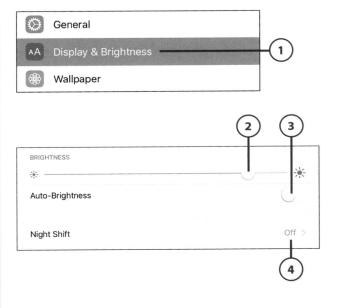

5 Schedule when Night Shift is enabled by tapping on the Scheduled switch and making a selection.

6 Manually enable Night Shift from now to daylight tomorrow by tapping on the Manually Enable Until Tomorrow switch.

7 Adjust just how warm the Night Shift colors appear by dragging the Color Temperature slider to the left (less warm) or right (warmer).

8 Tap the left arrow to return to the Display & Brightness screen.

9 Change the amount of idle time that must elapse before your iPad automatically locks by tapping Auto-Lock and making a new selection (2 minutes, 5 minutes, 10 minutes, 15 minutes, or never).

10 If you have a Smart Cover on your iPad, you can disable it so that your device doesn't automatically unlock when the cover is opened—just tap off the Lock/Unlock switch.

11 Tap Text Size to change the size of the text you see onscreen.

8   **5**

< Display & Brightness   **Night Shift**

Night Shift automatically shifts the colors of your display to the warmer end of the color spectrum after dark. This may help you get a better night's sleep.

Scheduled

From   10:00 PM
To   7:00 AM

Manually Enable Until Tomorrow

COLOR TEMPERATURE

Less Warm   More Warm

7   **6**

10   **9**

Auto-Lock   5 Minutes >

Lock / Unlock

Automatically lock and unlock your iPad when you close and open the iPad cover.

Text Size

Bold Text

11

(12) Drag the slider to the left to make the text smaller, or to the right to make the text larger. Tap the left arrow to return to the previous screen.

(13) To make the text for icons and other system elements bold (and thus, perhaps, easier to read), tap on the Bold Text switch. Your iPad restarts.

Change System Sounds

You can select different sounds for different system actions, such as sending an email or making a Facebook post. You can also opt to hear sounds when your iPad locks or when you tap the keys of the onscreen keyboard.

(1) From the Settings page, tap to display the Sounds tab.

(2) Drag the Ringer and Alerts slider to the left to decrease the volume; drag to the right to make them louder.

(3) To control these system sounds with your iPad's physical volume buttons, tap on the Change with Buttons switch. (Otherwise, the volume buttons only control the volume of music and videos you're listening to or watching.)

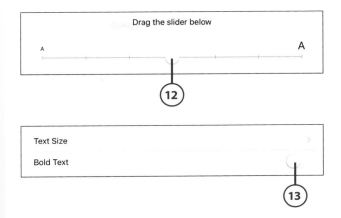

Drag the slider below

A   A

12

Text Size   >

Bold Text

13

General

Display & Brightness

Wallpaper

Sounds   1

Siri

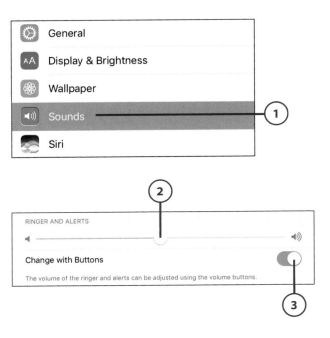

2

RINGER AND ALERTS

Change with Buttons

The volume of the ringer and alerts can be adjusted using the volume buttons.

3

(4) Change the sound for any specific system function by going to the Sounds section, tapping that function, and selecting a new sound.

(5) Tap off the Lock Sounds switch to turn off sounds when you lock or unlock your iPad.

(6) Tap off the Keyboard Clicks switch to turn off sounds when you tap your iPad's onscreen keyboard.

(4)

SOUNDS	
Ringtone	Opening >
Text Tone	Note >
New Mail	Ding >
Sent Mail	Swoosh >
Tweet	Tweet >
Facebook Post	Swish >
Calendar Alerts	Chord >
Reminder Alerts	Chord >
AirDrop	Pulse >

Lock Sounds	
Keyboard Clicks	

(5) **(6)**

Configure Individual Apps

Most of the apps installed on your iPad have their own individual settings you can configure. Use the Settings screen to adjust settings for any app.

(1) From the Settings page, scroll down to the list of individual apps in the left column.

(2) Tap an app to display and configure its settings.

- Mail **(1)**
- Contacts
- Calendar
- Notes
- Reminders **(2)**
- Messages
- FaceTime
- Maps
- Safari
- News
- Home

Managing System Settings

We've covered some of the most used settings you may want to configure on your iPad. But there are more settings available, on the General tab, that let you fine-tune various system options—and show you information about your device.

Display and Manage General Settings

The General tab on the Settings page is home to a variety of settings that affect all the apps on your iPad—as well as the iPad itself.

1. From the Settings page, tap to select the General tab.

2. Tap About to see information about your device—how many items of various types you have stored, total capacity, available storage space, model and serial number, and more.

3. Tap Software Update to manually force any available software update.

Automatic Updates
Most available software updates will automatically install; manual updates are not typically needed.

4. Tap Spotlight Search to deactivate Apple's Spotlight Search for any specific application (including use by Siri).

⚙	General
ᴀA	Display & Brightness
✱	Wallpaper

About	>
Software Update	>
Spotlight Search	>
Handoff	>
Multitasking	>

(5) Tap Handoff to deactivate the ability to start work on one device and resume that work on another device.

(6) Tap Multitasking to deactivate the abilities to use multiple apps, display a persistent overlay when playing videos, or use four- and five-finger touch gestures.

(7) Tap Accessibility to configure your device for enhanced accessibility.

Accessibility Options

To learn more about your iPad's accessibility options, see Chapter 4, "Making Your iPad More Accessible."

(8) Tap Storage & iCloud Usage to view how much storage space you've used and have left, both on your device and online in iCloud.

(9) Some apps automatically refresh themselves in the background. To turn this off, tap Background App Refresh.

(10) Tap Restrictions to enable restrictions for specific apps (useful if small children are using your iPad).

(5)

About	>
Software Update	>
Spotlight Search	>
Handoff	>
Multitasking	>

(6)

(7)   **(8)**

Accessibility	>
Storage & iCloud Usage	>
Background App Refresh	>
Restrictions	Off >

(10)   **(9)**

11 Tap Date & Time to set your iPad's date and time.

12 Tap Keyboard to configure various options for the onscreen keyboard.

13 Tap Language & Region to reset the language and region for your iPad.

14 Tap Dictionary to select which dictionary your iPad uses when checking text you enter.

15 Tap iTunes Wi-Fi Sync to manually sync data on your iPad with your computer via Wi-Fi.

16 Tap VPN to configure your iPad to use a virtual public network.

17 Tap Profile to view your configuration profile.

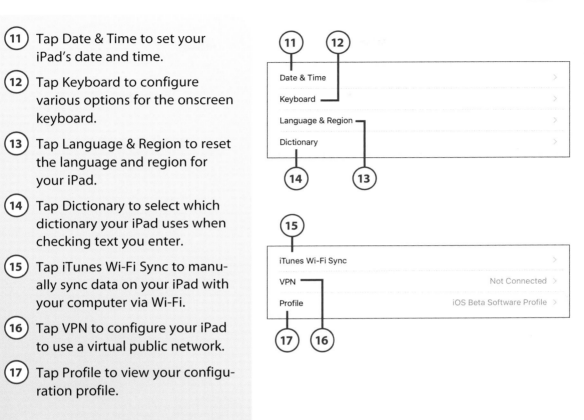

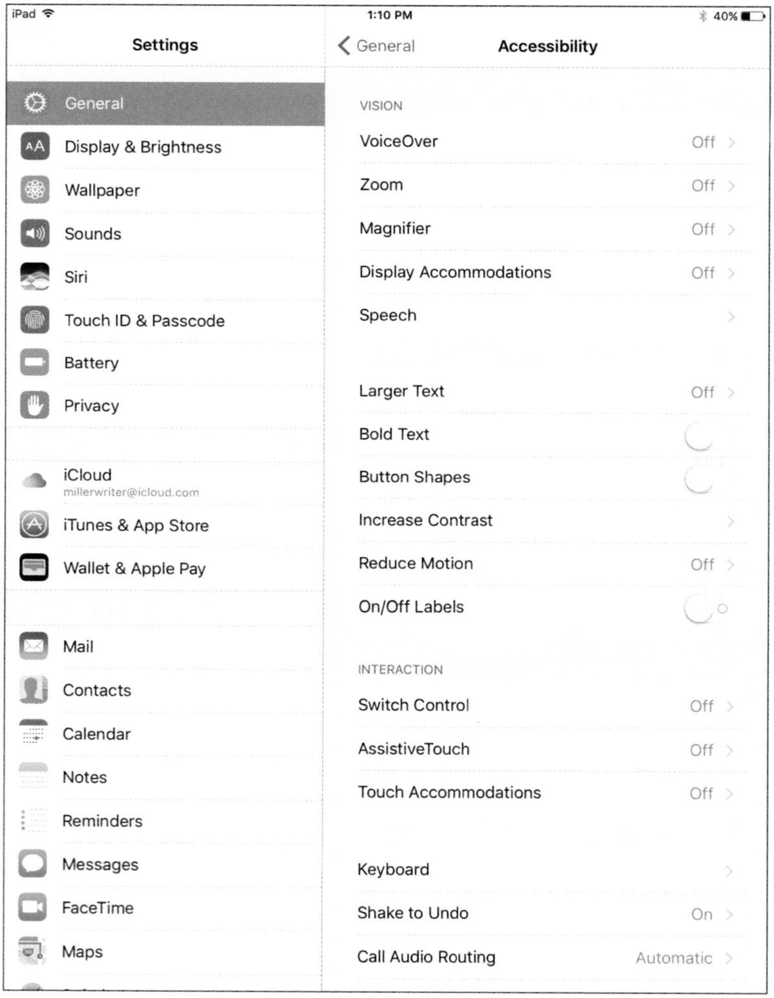

Settings	‹ General	Accessibility

⚙ General

AA Display & Brightness

⊛ Wallpaper

🔊 Sounds

Siri

Touch ID & Passcode

Battery

✋ Privacy

☁ iCloud
millerwriter@icloud.com

Ⓐ iTunes & App Store

Wallet & Apple Pay

✉ Mail

👤 Contacts

Calendar

Notes

Reminders

💬 Messages

🎥 FaceTime

Maps

VISION

VoiceOver	Off ›
Zoom	Off ›
Magnifier	Off ›
Display Accommodations	Off ›
Speech	›

Larger Text	Off ›
Bold Text	⬭
Button Shapes	⬭
Increase Contrast	›
Reduce Motion	Off ›
On/Off Labels	⬭ ○

INTERACTION

Switch Control	Off ›
AssistiveTouch	Off ›
Touch Accommodations	Off ›

Keyboard	›
Shake to Undo	On ›
Call Audio Routing	Automatic ›

In this chapter, you explore how to configure your iPad's accessibility options—and make it easier to use.

→ Making the iPad Easier to Use for the Vision Impaired
→ Making the iPad Easier to Use for the Hearing Impaired
→ Making the iPad Easier to Operate

4

Making Your iPad More Accessible

Let's face it. As we get older, it often becomes more difficult to read fine print and sometimes to perform fine motor functions. And because even the largest iPad has a relatively small screen, some of us may have trouble seeing what's onscreen, or tapping where we need to tap.

Fortunately, there are several settings on your iPad that can make it easier to use. We'll discuss them in this chapter.

Making the iPad Easier to Use for the Vision Impaired

Let's start with those features that can make things displayed onscreen easier to see. Many of us have some degree of vision loss, even if it's just the need for reading glasses to see fine print. Given the relatively small size of text on the iPad screen (especially on many web pages), you may want to avail yourself of these features that make onscreen text easier to read.

Read the Screen with VoiceOver

Probably the most useful accessibility feature for those with vision difficulties is Apple's VoiceOver. VoiceOver describes out loud any screen element or text. Just touch an item or text selection and VoiceOver either reads it or tells you about it. In some instances, VoiceOver even tells you how to use a given item—"double-tap to open," for example.

When VoiceOver is activated, all you have to do is touch the screen or drag your finger over an area to hear information about what's onscreen. When you go to a new screen, VoiceOver plays a sound and then selects and reads the first item on the new screen.

Note that because VoiceOver requires you to tap the screen to "read" an item, most traditional touch gestures change when you've activated VoiceOver. Where you would normally use a single-tap, for example, you now use a double-tap.

Other Screen-Reading Options

Although VoiceOver is the best and most full-featured screen-reading option on your iPad, other options are available. Go to the Accessibility screen and tap Speech and you can enable the Speak Selection (for reading text), Speak Screen (for reading screen elements), and Typing Feedback (for reading words while you type) options. Give them a try; they're less functional but also less intrusive than VoiceOver.

---

1. To activate VoiceOver, go to the Settings screen, select the General tab, tap Accessibility, and then tap VoiceOver.

2. From the VoiceOver page, tap on the VoiceOver switch. (Alternatively, press and hold the Home button and tell Siri, "Turn VoiceOver on.")

3. To "read" any onscreen item, touch it. (The item is now surrounded by a black border—the VoiceOver cursor.)

4. To activate any operation normally done by single-tapping, instead select the item and then double-tap the screen.

5. To activate any operation normally done by double-tapping, instead triple-tap that item.

Turn It Off

To deactivate VoiceOver, press and hold the Home button and tell Siri, "Turn VoiceOver off."

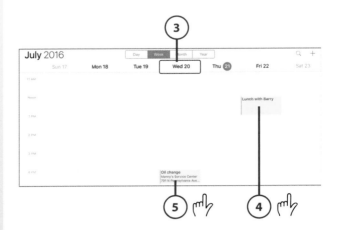

>>>Go Further

VOICEOVER GESTURES

When you're using VoiceOver, how you use your iPad changes in subtle ways. Because basic tapping or touching now "reads" that onscreen item, you need to use different touch gestures to do just about anything onscreen.

The following table shows you some of the more common operations and their new VoiceOver-enabled touch gestures.

Operation	VoiceOver Gesture
Select and read an item	Single-tap
Select the next or previous item	Swipe right or left
Read all elements from the top of the screen	Two-finger swipe up
Read all elements from the current position	Two-finger swipe down
Stop or resume speaking	Two-finger tap
Dismiss an alert or go back to a previous screen	Move two fingers back and forth quickly in a Z pattern
Scroll one page at a time	Three-finger swipe up or down
Go to the next or previous page (including on the Home page)	Three-finger swipe right or left
Speak additional information about the selected item	Three-finger tap
Select the first item on the page	Four-finger tap at the top of the screen
Select the last item on the page	Four-finger tap at the bottom of the screen
Activate the selected item	Double-tap
Double-tap an item	Triple-tap

Operation	VoiceOver Gesture
Use a standard gesture	Double-tap and hold one second, and then perform the standard gesture
Initiate an action or pause an in-progress action	Two-finger double-tap
Change an item's label	Two-finger double-tap and then hold
Open the Item Chooser	Two-finger triple-tap
Mute or unmute VoiceOver	Three-finger double-tap

There are also a number of settings you can configure to personalize the way VoiceOver works for you. Just go to the Settings page, select the General tab, tap Accessibility, and then tap VoiceOver.

Braille Displays

Your iPad is fully compatible with most third-party braille displays. Use the braille display to control your iPad when VoiceOver is activated. Connect a braille display to your iPad via Bluetooth, and then go the Settings page, select the General tab, tap Accessibility, tap VoiceOver, and then tap Braille.

Magnify the Screen with Zoom

Having VoiceOver take over your iPad's screen may be too much for those of us with only mild vision difficulties. In this instance, you might need only to zoom into an area of the screen to make it larger and more legible.

Many apps let you zoom in by either double-tapping the screen or expanding your fingers apart. (You zoom out by pinching your fingers together.) Apple also offers a dedicated Zoom feature that lets you magnify any screen.

1 To activate Zoom, go to the Settings screen, select the General tab, tap Accessibility, and then tap Zoom.

2 Tap on the Zoom switch to display the zoom box onscreen.

3 Drag the bottom of the zoom box to move it around the screen. (Not shown.)

4 Hide the zoom box by double-tapping the screen with three fingers. Doubletap with three fingers again to re-display the zoom box. (Not shown.)

1

< General   **Accessibility**

VISION

VoiceOver   Off >

Zoom   Off >

Magnifier   Off >

Display Accommodations   Off >

Speech   >

2

Zoom

Zoom magnifies the entire screen:
• Double-tap three fingers to zoom
• Drag three fingers to move around the screen
• Double-tap three fingers and drag to change zoom

Invert Screen Colors

If you're having trouble distinguishing elements onscreen, it may be an issue of contrast. I've found that increasing the contrast between light and dark elements can help me read even very small type onscreen.

With this in mind, Apple enables you to invert your colors onscreen. With inverted colors, black text on a white background becomes white text on a black background, and other color highlights appear against that same black background.

1 Go to the Settings screen, select the General tab, tap Accessibility, and then tap Display Accommodations.

< General   **Accessibility**

VISION

VoiceOver   Off >

Zoom   Off >

Magnifier   Off >

1 Display Accommodations   Off >

Speech   >

2 Tap on the Invert Colors switch. The screen colors automatically change.

Invert Colors	
Enabling Invert Colors will automatically disable Night Shift.	

2

3 Return to your iPad's normal color scheme by returning to the Display Accommodations screen and tapping off the Invert Colors switch. (Not shown.)

Colorblind Users

If you're fully or partially colorblind, you simply can't see some color combinations. Fortunately, you can configure your iPad with color filters, to make those otherwise hard-to-see colors pop. Just go to the Display Accommodations screen, tap Color Filters, and then choose a color and tap on the Color Filters switch.

Make Onscreen Text Larger and Bolder

Another way to make an iPad screen more readable is to increase the size of the onscreen text, or perhaps even bold that text.

General		
Accessibility		>

1

1 Go to the Settings screen, select the General tab, and tap Accessibility.

2 Make onscreen text bold by tapping on the Bold Text switch. (Selecting Bold Text will restart your iPad.)

3 Increase the size of onscreen text by tapping Larger Text.

3   **2**

Larger Text	Off >
Bold Text	
Button Shapes	
Increase Contrast	>
Reduce Motion	Off >
On/Off Labels	

(4) Tap on the Larger Accessibility Sizes switch.

(5) Drag the slider to the right to make text larger. Drag the slider back to the left to make larger text smaller.

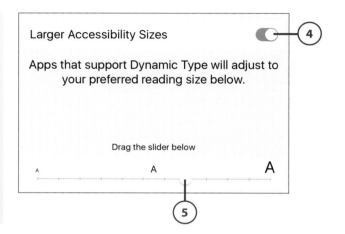

Making the iPad Easier to Use for the Hearing Impaired

Whether you're a little hard of hearing or completely deaf, you'll be pleased to know that your iPad can accommodate various types of hearing devices, as well as compensate for hearing damage in one ear or another.

Use a Hearing Aid with Your iPad

Many companies make "Made for iPad" hearing aids that are officially compatible with most iPad models. When you pair these hearing aids via Bluetooth, you can use the iPad to adjust their settings, stream audio direct to the hearing aids, and more. All you have to do is configure your iPad for the type of hearing aid you have.

(1) Make sure Bluetooth is enabled on your iPad (tap Bluetooth from the Settings screen), then go to the Settings screen, select the General tab, and tap Accessibility.

(2) Scroll to the Hearing section and tap Hearing Devices.

(3) Close the battery doors on your hearing aids and wait for them to appear in the Devices list. When the hearing aid appears, tap its name and respond to the pairing request. You can then adjust settings specific to your hearing aids from the Hearing Devices page.

HEARING	
Hearing Devices	>

(2)

< Accessibility	**Hearing Devices**
DEVICES	
Searching...	
Pair Made for iPad Hearing Aids. Other hearing aids are paired in Bluetooth settings.	

(3)

Mix Stereo Audio to Mono

If your hearing is weaker in one ear than another, you might have trouble hearing sounds coming from either the left or right speaker in your iPad. To compensate, you can mix all stereo sound to mono and have your iPad play back only mono sounds.

(1) Go to the Settings screen, select the General tab, and tap Accessibility.

(2) Tap on the Mono Audio switch.

(3) Drag the slider to the left or right until you can best hear all sounds coming from the iPad speakers.

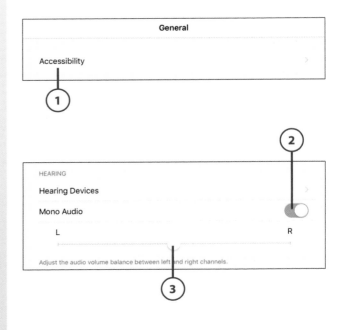

General

Accessibility

(1)

Turn On Closed Captioning When Watching Videos

Many streaming video services and video player apps, such as Apple's own Videos app, offer closed captioning for the hearing impaired. You can typically enable closed captioning within the individual app, or universally via your iPad's general settings.

1. Go to the Settings screen, select the General tab, tap Accessibility, and then tap Subtitles & Captioning.

2. Tap on the Closed Captions + SDH switch.

3. Tap Style to select a closed-captioned style.

MEDIA

Subtitles & Captioning   >

Audio Descriptions   Off >

Closed Captions + SDH

When available, prefer closed captioning or subtitles for the deaf and hard of hearing.

Style   Default >

Making the iPad Easier to Operate

If you have trouble performing the necessary touch gestures to operate your iPad, there are some options available to you. You can fine-tune how various gestures work, enable an assistive technology called AssistiveTouch, or just use the Siri personal assistant to operate your iPad via voice commands.

Adjust the Touchscreen Display

Sometimes I find my iPad's touchscreen display to be a little too touchy. If you find yourself tapping or swiping things without meaning to, you can adjust the sensitivity of the display itself.

1. Go to the Settings screen, select the General tab, tap Accessibility, and then tap Touch Accommodations.

2. Tap on the Touch Accommodations switch.

3. Adjust how long you must touch the screen before that touch is recognized by tapping on the Hold Duration switch and then setting a new time. (The default is 0.10 seconds.)

4. If your single touches sometimes register as double touches, tap on the Ignore Repeat switch and increase the time limit.

5. If you have trouble precisely tapping onscreen elements, enable Tap Assistance by tapping either Use Initial Touch Location or Use Final Touch Location. Tap Off to disable this feature.

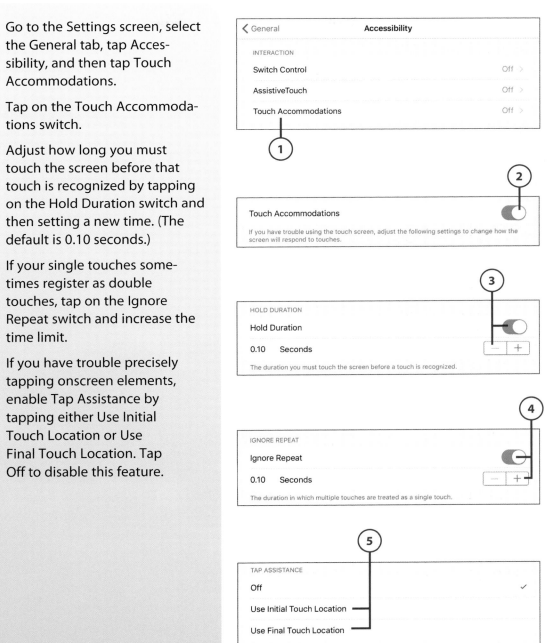

‹ General   **Accessibility**

INTERACTION

Switch Control   Off ›

AssistiveTouch   Off ›

Touch Accommodations   Off ›

Touch Accommodations

If you have trouble using the touch screen, adjust the following settings to change how the screen will respond to touches.

HOLD DURATION

Hold Duration

0.10   Seconds   − +

The duration you must touch the screen before a touch is recognized.

IGNORE REPEAT

Ignore Repeat

0.10   Seconds   − +

The duration in which multiple touches are treated as a single touch.

TAP ASSISTANCE

Off   ✓

Use Initial Touch Location

Use Final Touch Location

Enable Tap Assistance to allow any single finger gesture to perform a tap.

Enable AssistiveTouch

Your iPad includes an accessibility feature dubbed AssistiveTouch that overlays a group of large icons onscreen for common functions. With AssistiveTouch enabled, just tap the AssistiveTouch icon and then tap an icon for Notification Center, Device, Control Center, Home, Siri, or Custom (any operation of your choice).

1. Go to the Settings screen, select the General tab, tap Accessibility, and then tap AssistiveTouch.

2. Tap on the AssistiveTouch switch.

3. The AssistiveTouch icon now appears at the bottom-right corner of the iPad screen. Tap this icon to display the Assistive-Touch menu, and then tap the action you want to initiate. (Tap anywhere outside the Assistive-Touch menu to close the panel.)

Use Siri

If you have trouble managing the fine gestures you need to operate your iPad, just skip the screen entirely and use voice commands, instead. This is accomplished via Apple's personal digital assistant, dubbed Siri.

We discuss Siri in more detail in Chapter 7, "Controlling Your iPad—and More—with Siri." Turn there to learn more.

Activating Accessibility Features with Siri

You can activate many accessibility features by talking to your iPad via Siri. Just say "Siri, turn on VoiceOver," for example, and that feature will be turned on.

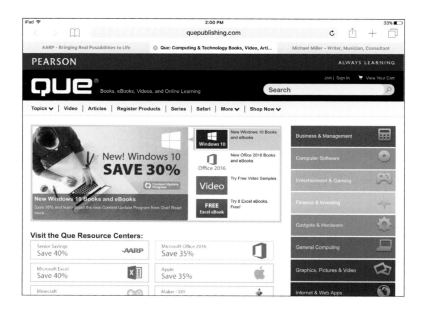

In this chapter, you learn how to connect your iPad to Wi-Fi networks and hotspots to access sites and information on the Internet. You also learn how to use the Safari web browser to surf the Web.

→ Connecting to a Wi-Fi Network
→ Using the Safari Web Browser
→ Making the Web More Readable
→ Searching the Web

Connecting to the Internet and Browsing the Web

A lot of what you do with your iPad requires a connection to the Internet. Sending and receiving email, searching for information, video chatting with FaceTime, watching streaming videos or listening to streaming music—all of these activities require an Internet connection.

You connect your iPad to the Internet via a Wi-Fi wireless connection. Your iPad has built-in Wi-Fi, so it's just a matter of connecting to a private Wi-Fi network (like you probably have at home) or a public Wi-Fi hotspot. After you're connected, you can do all that fun Internet-related stuff—as well as use those apps that also require an Internet connection.

Connecting to a Wi-Fi Network

To get the most out of your iPad, you need to connect it to the Internet, via a wireless network. You can connect to your home Wi-Fi network, or to any public Wi-Fi network or hotspot.

Wi-Fi

Wi-Fi (short for *Wireless Fidelity*) is the consumer-friendly name for the IEEE 802.11 wireless networking standard. Most of today's wireless networks are Wi-Fi networks and use Wi-Fi-certified products.

Connect to Your Home Wireless Network

Obviously, if you have a wireless network in your home you'll want to connect your iPad to that. Once you've initially connected, you won't need to manually reconnect in the future; your iPad remembers the network settings and reconnects automatically.

To connect to your home network, you need to know the name of the network (sometimes called an SSID, for *service set identifier*) and the network password (sometimes called a *security key*).

(1) Tap the Settings icon to open the Settings page.

(2) In the left column, tap Wi-Fi. (If you're not yet connected, it should say "Not Connected.")

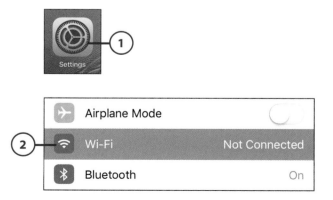

(3) Make sure the Wi-Fi switch is in the on position. If it isn't, tap to turn it on.

(4) You see a list of the wireless networks within range. Tap to select your home network. This displays the password panel.

Public Versus Private Networks

Private wireless networks require a password to connect, and are indicated with a lock icon in the network list. Public networks (sometimes called *open networks*) let you connect without a password, and are not accompanied by the lock icon.

(5) Use the onscreen keyboard to enter the password for your network.

(6) Tap Join. You are now connected to the network and can access the Internet.

Current Connection

If you're currently connected to a wireless network, you see that network's name in the Wi-Fi field in the left column of the Wi-Fi page. You can connect to a different network if you like; see the "Change Networks" task later in this section.

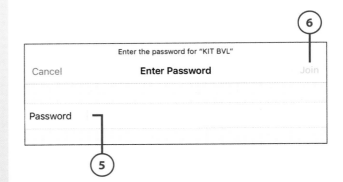

Public network (3)

Wi-Fi

CHOOSE A NETWORK...

Caribou Coffee

DIRECT-fd-HP M426 LaserJet

Gharvest

KIT BVL

KIT GUEST

WaxCenterBurnsville

Other...

(4) **Private network**

(6)

Enter the password for "KIT BVL"

Cancel **Enter Password** Join

Password

(5)

Connect to a Public Wireless Hotspot

Most wireless networks and hotspots you find out in the real world are public networks—that is, you don't need a special password to connect. All you have to do is identify the network from the list and click to connect. (You'll know you're connected when you see the Wi-Fi icon in the status bar at the top of the screen.)

Some public networks, however, do require you to read through and agree to their terms of service after you connect but before you can use the network.

If this is the case, the site typically launches a connection page in your web browser. (In some instances, you may need to launch the Safari browser manually and try to access a web page; this will then launch the wireless connection page.) When you see the connection page from the wireless network or hotspot, you might need to check an "I read that" option or click a "connect" button.

For example, if you connect to the wireless networks at your local Starbucks or McDonald's, you need to manually log in from their respective log-in pages. In some instances, there may be a fee to use the wireless network, in which case you'll need to enter your credit card number to proceed.

Hotel Wi-Fi

If you're connecting to the wireless network in a hotel without free Wi-Fi, you typically enter your room number to add the charges to your bill. Given that some hotels charge $10 or more per night, it's always a smart idea to shop around for hotels that offer free Wi-Fi.

---

(1) From the Settings page, tap Wi-Fi in the left column.

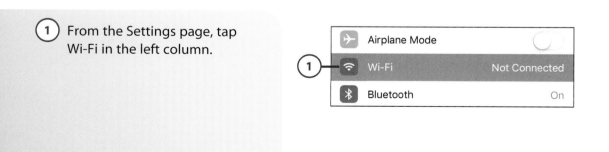

(**2**) Make sure the Wi-Fi switch is in the on position. If it isn't, tap to turn it on.

(**3**) You see a list of the wireless networks and hotspots within range. Tap to select the desired network.

(**4**) If the hotspot requires you to sign in, it should launch the Safari web browser and display a sign-in page. (If this doesn't happen automatically, you might need to launch Safari manually and then enter any web page address to open the sign-in page.) Check Agree to any terms and conditions and then click the "accept" or "sign in" button.

Change Networks

Sometimes, especially out in public, you may have several different Wi-Fi networks available to you—and your iPad might automatically connect to one other than the one you wanted to connect to. If this is the case, it's easy enough to switch networks.

Airplane Mode		
Wi-Fi	Caribou Coffee	— 1
Bluetooth	On	

(1) From the Settings page, observe the Wi-Fi field in the left column. The currently connected network is displayed. If you don't want to connect to this network, tap the Wi-Fi field to display a list of other available networks.

CHOOSE A NETWORK...

Gharvest

KIT BVL

KIT GUEST

WaxCenterBurnsville

Other...

(2) Tap the network you want to connect to. Your iPad disconnects from the previous network and connects instead to the newly selected one.

Connect to a Network You've Previously Connected To

This one's easier. When you're in range of a wireless network or hotspot you've previously connected to, your iPad automatically connects to it again. You don't have to choose it from the list; the iPad automatically discovers the network and makes the connection.

If it's a private network, like your home network, your iPad remembers the previously entered password and enters it for you. If it's a public network or hotspot that requires logging in via your web browser, you might be asked to agree to terms and click the "sign in" button again. (Or you might not; some sites allow reconnection without having to sign back in.)

It's Not All Good

Connection Problems

Not all Internet connections are good. Sometimes the Wi-Fi network or hotspot you connect to has problems, which can keep your iPad from connecting to the Internet.

For example, the Wi-Fi hotspot I use at one of my local coffeehouses has a tendency to go missing every few hours. That is, I'll be connected one minute and the next minute find that I'm not connected—and that the hotspot itself is no longer visible on my iPad. Normally I wait a minute or two, the hotspot reappears, and my iPad reconnects. The best I can figure is that the coffeehouse's Wi-Fi router has rebooted, for some reason, which kicks everyone using it off until it powers back on.

You can also run into similar connection problems with your home Wi-Fi network. In many cases, the problem corrects itself automatically within a few minutes. If the problem persists, try turning off your iPad's Wi-Fi and then turning it back on. This forces your iPad to establish a new connection to the wireless network or hotspot, which often fixes the problem.

Using the Safari Web Browser

After your iPad is connected to a Wi-Fi network or hotspot, you should have access (via that network) to the Internet. That's where all the fun stuff happens—including surfing the Web.

To surf the Web you need an app called a *web browser*. You're probably familiar with using a web browser on your computer or phone, and it works similarly on your iPad.

The browser that Apple includes with your iPad is called Safari. It works like most other web browsers, and it's ready for use whenever you are.

Other Web Browsers

Safari is preinstalled on your iPad, but you can use other web browsers, if you like. The most popular non-Apple browser is Google Chrome, which is available for free from the iTunes App Store. Many people prefer Chrome to Safari, especially if they use Chrome on their computer or other devices.

Launch the Safari Browser

The icon for the Safari browser is located by default in the Dock at the bottom of all Home screens.

(1) From the Dock on any Home screen, tap the Safari icon to open the Safari browser.

(2) The first time you launch Safari, it opens to a blank page. If you've previously used the browser, it opens your last open page.

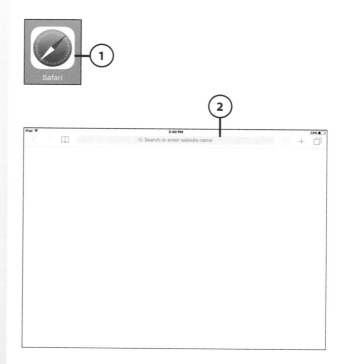

Enter a Web Address

To go directly to a given website or web page, you must enter the web address of that page into the Address box at the top of the browser screen.

(1) Tap within the Address box to display the onscreen keyboard.

2 Enter the address of the web page you want to visit.

3 As you type, Safari might suggest matching web pages. Tap any page to go to it *or*…

4 Finish entering the full address and then tap Go on the keyboard to go to that page.

5 The web page appears onscreen. Swipe up to scroll down the page.

6 If a page has trouble loading, or if you want to refresh the content, you can reload the page by tapping the Reload button.

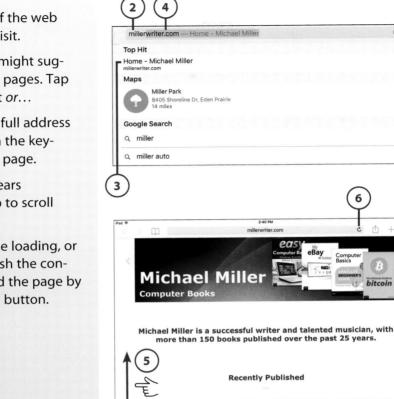

>>>*Go Further*
WEB ADDRESSES

A web address is called a Uniform Resource Locator, or URL. Technically, all URLs start with either http:// or (for secure sites) https://. You don't need to type this part of the URL, however; Safari assumes it and enters it automatically.

The main part of most web addresses starts with www followed by a dot, then the name of the website, then another dot and the domain identifier, such as com or org. As an example, my personal website is www.millerwriter.com. (You don't have to enter the "www."; Safari does this for you.)

Use Web Links

Pages on the Web are often connected via clickable (on your iPad,
tappable) links, called *web links*.
A web link can be within a page's text
(typically underlined or in a different
color) or embedded in an image. Tap
a link to go the linked-to page.

1. On the current web page, tap
   the web link.

2. The linked-to page displays.

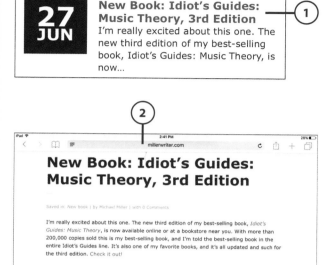

View Multiple Pages in Tabs

Safari, like most modern web
browsers, lets you open more than
one page at a time, using *tabs*. You
can open different web pages in
different tabs, and easily switch
between them.

1. Tap the + icon to create a
   new tab.

2. Enter the desired web address
   into the new tab's Address box.

3. Tap a different tab to view that
   tab. *Or…*

4. Tap the tabs icon to view
   thumbnails of all open tabs.

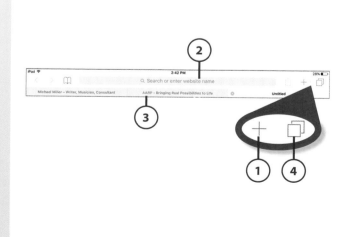

5 Tap to switch to a different tab.

6 Swipe a tab to the left to close it. *Or…*

7 Tap the X on any tab to close it.

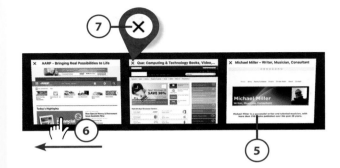

Bookmark Pages

You can save any page you visit by *bookmarking* that page. It's easy, then, to revisit those pages you've bookmarked.

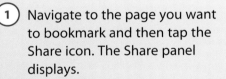

1 Navigate to the page you want to bookmark and then tap the Share icon. The Share panel displays.

2 Tap Add Bookmark.

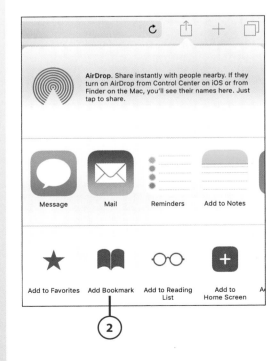

(3) Edit the web page name in the Add Bookmark panel, if you like.

(4) Tap Save. The page is now saved in your bookmarks.

Favorites

Safari offers a special category of bookmarks, called Favorites. You save a page to your Favorites list by tapping Add to Favorites in the Share panel. All Favorites can be accessed by selecting Favorites in the Bookmark panel; Favorites are also displayed when you tap + to open a new empty tab.

(5) Tap the Bookmark icon to open the Bookmark panel so you can view and revisit bookmarked pages.

(6) Make sure the Bookmarks tab is selected.

(7) Some bookmarks are organized into folders. Tap a folder name to view all bookmarks in that folder.

(8) Tap the name of a bookmark to open the corresponding web page.

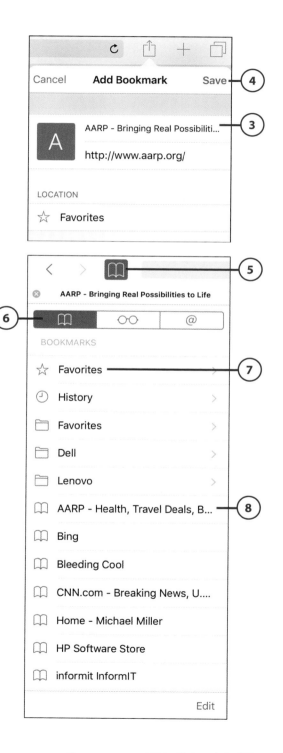

>>>*Go Further*
ADD TO HOME SCREEN

If you find yourself visiting a given web page with regularity, you might want to create a shortcut to it on your iPad's Home screen. When you add an icon for a page to the Home screen, tapping that icon launches Safari and opens that page.

To add an icon for a given web page, navigate to that page, tap the Share icon, and then tap Add to Home Screen. When the Add to Home panel appears, tap Add.

Revisit Past Pages

How easy is it to return to a web page you've previously viewed? Safari keeps track of all your web browsing history, and revisiting a page is as easy as tapping it in the Bookmark panel.

1. View the page you just visited by tapping the back (left arrow) icon.

2. Return to the next page by tapping the forward (right arrow) icon.

3. Tap the Bookmark icon to open the Bookmark panel.

4. Tap History to view pages you've visited, newest first.

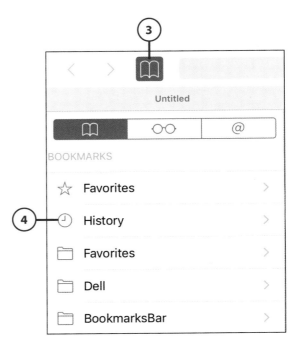

Browse the Web in Private

There are some web pages you might want to browse in private, and not let others know you've seen. When you want to browse anonymously, use Safari's Private mode. Pages you visit while in Private mode are not stored to your history, and are not otherwise tracked on your device or elsewhere.

1. From within Safari, tap the Tabs icon.

2. Tap Private.

3. Tap Done. You are now in private browsing mode.

4. Use Safari as normal. None of your activity will be tracked.

5. Tap the Tabs icon to exit private browsing mode.

6. Tap Private. You now see any tabs you had open before entering private browsing mode.

7. Tap Done.

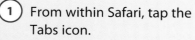

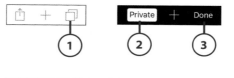

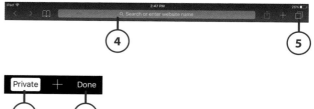

Configure Safari Settings

Safari is configured perfectly for most users by default, but there are a number of settings you can change to better personalize your Safari browsing experience. You access all these settings from your iPad's Settings screen.

(1) From your iPad's Home screen, tap the Settings icon to open the Settings screen.

(2) Scroll down the left column to the apps section and tap Safari.

(3) Tap to edit any setting.

Settings

(1)

Maps	
Safari	(2)
News	

Safari

SEARCH

Search Engine   Google >

Search Engine Suggestions

Safari Suggestions

Quick Website Search   On >

Preload Top Hit

About Search & Privacy...

GENERAL

Passwords   (3)

AutoFill   >

Frequently Visited Sites

Favorites   Favorites >

Open New Tabs in Background

Show Favorites Bar

Show Tab Bar

Block Pop-ups

>>>Go Further

BLOCK ONLINE ADS

If you're like me, you quickly tire of all the online ads displayed on various web pages. (There are even ads on Facebook and many web-based email services!) Fortunately, you can block many if not all of these ads by installing an ad blocker extension in the Safari web browser. With an ad blocker installed, ads simply don't display on a web page—you see a blank space where the ad is supposed to be. Ad blockers don't hurt your browser or your iPad, and make browsing the Web that much more pleasant.

There are a variety of different ad blockers available in the iTunes App Store. Some are free; some aren't. The most popular ones include 1Blocker, Adblock Plus, Crystal Adblock, and Sanitize.

You may have to manually enable any ad blocker you install. From your iPad's Settings page, tap Safari in the left column and then tap Content Blockers. (This option is not available until you install an ad blocker.) You can then enable or disable any ad blocker you've installed.

Making the Web More Readable

Viewing web pages in Safari might not always be easy. Some pages, especially those not optimized for mobile viewing, may contain very small type or columns that wrap too far off the side of a page, making them less than readable.

Fortunately, there are ways to make small type on web pages a little larger—and web pages more readable, in general.

Zoom into a Page

If you find a particular web page difficult to read, the first thing you can do is try to zoom into the text—that is, make the text larger onscreen.

1 Double-tap a block of text to make it fill the screen. (This works on some web pages, but not all.) Double-tap again to return the text to normal size.

2 Place two fingers together on the screen and then expand them. As you move your fingers apart, you zoom into that portion of the page. To zoom back out, pinch your two fingers back together.

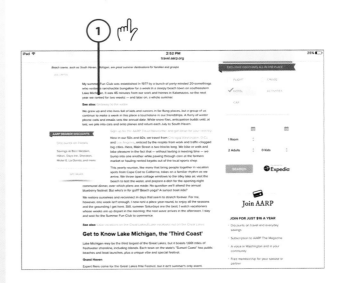

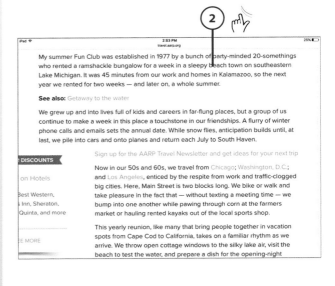

Read Articles with Safari Reader

Safari Reader is a special reading mode that makes some web pages easier to read by removing ads, images, videos, and other extraneous elements. Not all web pages can be viewed with Safari Reader, but those that can are a lot easier to read than normal cluttered web pages. (Safari Reader is especially useful for reading articles on web news sites.)

① If a page can be viewed with Safari Reader, it has a Reader icon in the Address bar. Tap this icon to switch to Reader mode.

② Tap the Reader icon again to return to normal web page view.

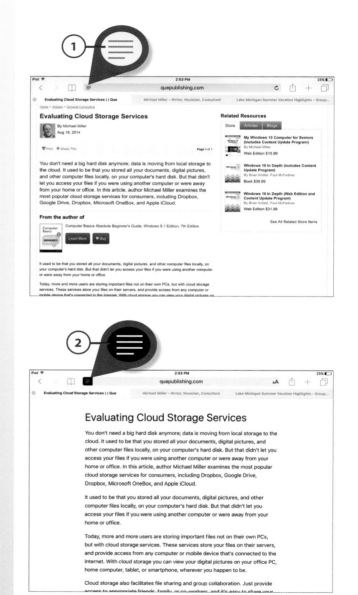

Searching the Web

With so much information available on the Web, how do you find the stuff you want or need to know? It's easy, thanks to Google.

Search the Web with Google

Google is the default search engine for the Safari web browser. You can search Google from within Safari, or from Google's own website.

(**1**) To search within Safari, tap within the Address box and enter your query.

(**2**) As you type, Safari displays several suggested searches. Go to the Google Search section and, if the search you want is listed, tap it.

(**3**) Otherwise, continue entering your query and tap Go on the onscreen keyboard. *Or….*

(**4**) Go directly to the Google web page at www.google.com, enter your query into the Search box, and tap the Search button.

(5) Google displays a page of search results. Tap to open a given web page. *Or…*

(6) Display different types of results by selecting a results type along the top of the page— All, Images, Shopping, Videos, News, Maps, and so forth.

(7) Further refine your results by tapping Search. This displays a new search bar; tap to filter results by time and other options.

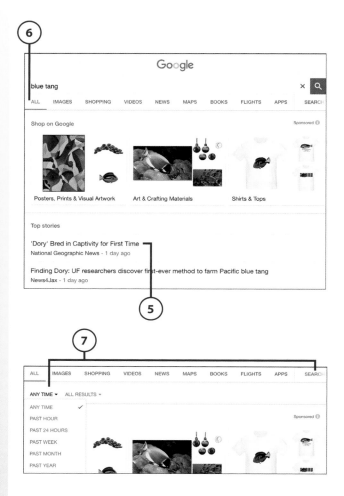

Change Your Search Engine

If you'd rather use a different search engine with Safari, such as Microsoft's Bing or Yahoo!, you can do that.

(1) From your iPad's Settings page, tap Safari in the left column.

2 In the Search section, tap Search Engine.

3 Tap to select your desired search engine.

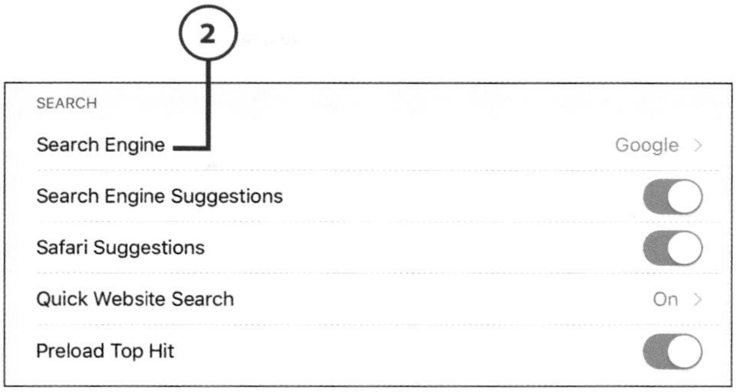

2

SEARCH	
Search Engine	Google >
Search Engine Suggestions	
Safari Suggestions	
Quick Website Search	On >
Preload Top Hit	

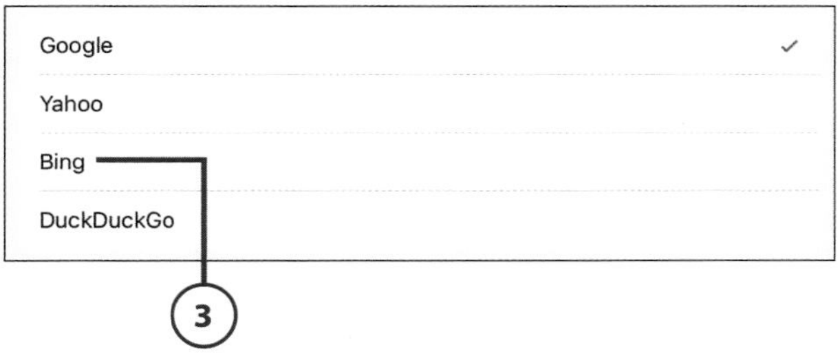

Google	✓
Yahoo	
Bing	
DuckDuckGo	

3

Keeping Your iPad Safe and Secure

Your iPad is a small portable device. That means that it could be relatively easy for someone to walk away with it while you're not looking. If someone takes your iPad—accidentally or on purpose—do you really want them digging around in everything you have stored inside?

Fortunately, there are ways to keep the information on your iPad safe from prying eyes. And there are lots of things you can do to minimize the risk of data theft if your iPad is lost or stolen.

In addition, there are things you can do to keep your information and identity safe when using your iPad to go online. The Internet can be a dangerous place, so it makes sense to be as safe as possible when you're connecting with your iPad.

Creating a Safer Lock Screen

When it comes to keeping unwanted users away from the information stored on your iPad, your first and best line of defense is the device's Lock screen. If you play your cards right, strangers simply won't be able to get past the Lock screen to see anything else on your iPad.

Set a Simple Passcode

By default, you unlock your iPad by simply pressing the Home button. That's convenient but far from secure; anybody picking up your device can unlock and see what you've stored inside.

A better approach is to establish a passcode (like a personal identification number, or PIN) to use to unlock your phone. Your passcode should consist of six numbers and be fairly random—or as random as you remember, in any case.

When you've enabled passcode operation, you're prompted to enter your passcode after you've restarted your iPad or woken it from sleep.

(**1**) Tap the Settings icon to open the Settings screen.

(**2**) Tap Touch ID & Passcode in the left column.

⚙	General
AA	Display & Brightness
✿	Wallpaper
◀))	Sounds
〰	Siri
⊙	Touch ID & Passcode
▭	Battery
✋	Privacy

(3) Tap Turn Passcode On to display the Set Passcode panel.

(4) Enter your desired six-digit passcode.

Creating a Passcode

Your passcode should be a series of digits you can remember but not something easily guessed. For example, you shouldn't use your birthdate as your passcode, nor should you set a common series of digits, such as 123456.

(5) When prompted, re-enter your six-digit passcode. Your passcode is now enabled, and you'll need to use it to unlock your device in the future—so write it down somewhere only you can find it!

Data Encryption

Creating a passcode also turns on your iPad's data encryption. This uses your passcode as a key to encrypt Mail messages and all attachments stored on your device.

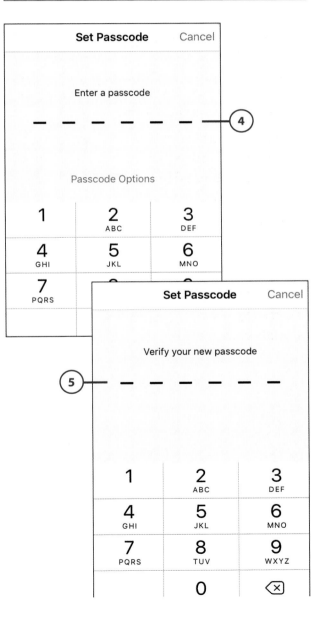

Use Fingerprint Recognition with TouchID

On most newer iPads (iPad mini 3 and later, iPad Air 2 and later, and all iPad Pros), you can employ even stronger security by using your fingerprint to unlock your device. This is called TouchID, and you can also use it to make purchases in the iTunes Store and App Store, provide debit and credit card payment information, enter billing and shipping addresses, and provide contact info when making in-app purchases on apps that offer Apple Pay as a payment method.

To unlock your phone using Touch ID, all you have to do is press your thumb or finger (whichever fingerprint you registered) on the Home button, which doubles as the Touch ID sensor. When the iPad recognizes your fingerprint, it unlocks.

(1) Tap the Settings icon to open the Settings screen.

(2) Tap Touch ID & Passcode in the left column.

(3) Tap Add a Fingerprint.

Settings
1

🔊	Sounds
〰️	Siri
🖐️	Touch ID & Passcode
🔋	Battery
✋	Privacy

2

FINGERPRINTS

Add a Fingerprint...

3

(4) Place your finger or thumb on the Home button.

(5) Follow the onscreen instructions to lift and place your finger as many times as necessary to register your fingerprint.

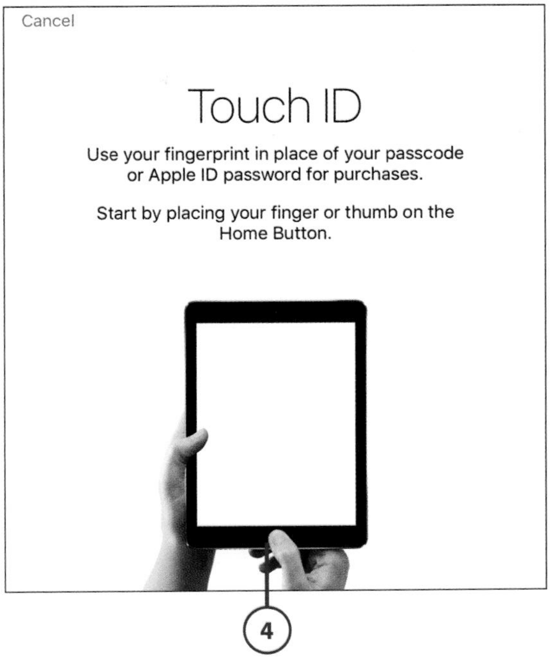

Cancel

Touch ID

Use your fingerprint in place of your passcode or Apple ID password for purchases.

Start by placing your finger or thumb on the Home Button.

(4)

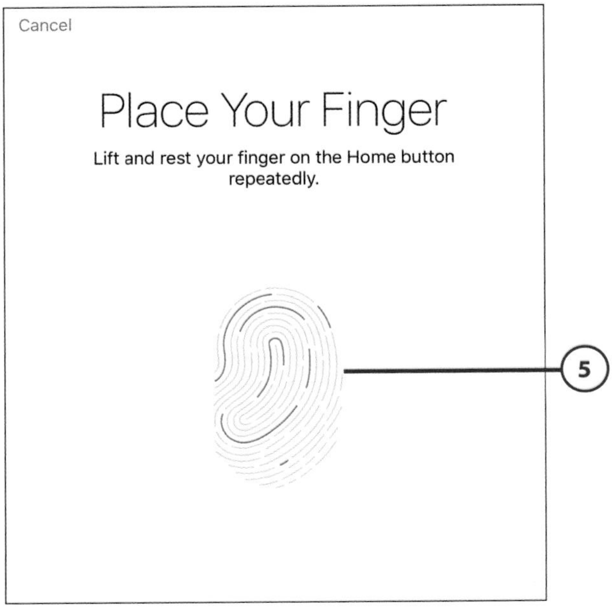

Cancel

Place Your Finger

Lift and rest your finger on the Home button repeatedly.

(5)

(6) When the process is complete, tap Continue. Your device is ready to use with Touch ID enabled.

Erase Data After Too Many Passcode Attempts

As the ultimate "fail-safe" procedure, you can configure your iPhone to erase all its stored data after ten failed passcode attempts. This ensures that none of your data will fall into the wrong hands, especially if your iPad is stolen.

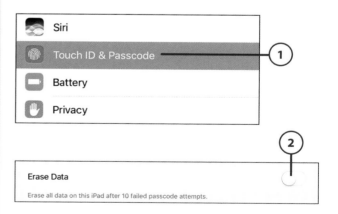

(1) From the Settings screen, tap Touch ID & Passcode in the left column.

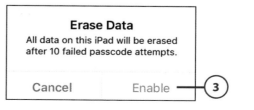

(2) Tap on the Erase Data switch.

(3) Tap Enable in the confirmation box.

It's Not All Good

Don't Forget Your Passcode

If you forget your passcode and enter more than ten passcode attempts, you'll need to restore your iPad to use it again. Restoring your iPad to factory condition also deletes all the apps and data stored on the device. So don't forget your passcode—or you're in for a lot of unnecessary trouble!

Reducing the Risk of Theft

As noted, your iPad (any size, from mini to Pro) is a relatively small device that's usually not plugged into anything, which means it can be easily heisted by those with impure hearts. (It's also easy to lose or leave behind, but that's another issue.) Given the attractiveness of the iPad to would-be thieves, how do you keep it away from sticky-fingered strangers?

Keep Your iPad Safe

Your iPad is a particularly attractive target for thieves. Not only is it small and easy to steal, it's also a high-value item. All Apple products are considered luxury items, and thieves like items that can command a high price when sold or pawned.

Knowing this, you need to take extra care when you take your iPad out in public. If most crime consists of the criminally bent taking advantage of an opportunity, you want to reduce that opportunity as much as possible.

- Don't show it off. You may be very proud of your shiny new iPad, but don't make a big deal out of it. Don't show it off, don't make others aware of what you have. Treat it as low key as you can.

- Keep it hidden—especially when you're not around. An expensive iPad is not the sort of thing you want to leave sitting on the table at Starbucks when you go off to use the restroom. It's also not a good thing to leave visible on the front seat or dashboard of your car when you park. When you're not using it, put it away—in your purse or backpack or briefcase. Or just carry it around with you.

- Be aware of your surroundings. A near-empty coffeehouse with a table near the counter is safer than a crowded McDonald's filled with suspicious-looking characters. If the surroundings look unsafe, keep a firmer grasp on your iPad—or don't bring it out at all.

- Be cautious around strangers. Yes, there will be earnest individuals who see you using your new iPad and want to ask you all sorts of questions about it. There are also smooth-talking heisters who get you to show them your iPad purely as a ruse to grab it out of your hands. Beware the latter.

- Keep it safe even at home. You might think it would be okay to leave your iPad sitting out on the coffee table at your own house or apartment, but that's just tempting fate. If you house is broken into, small expensive items sitting in plain sight are the first things that thieves grab. And if your house has a lot of foot traffic (think friends of your kids or grandkids), a loose iPad on the table is pretty attractive for anyone with money or addiction problems. Even at home, keep your iPad in a safe and private place.

In other words, be smart about how you use and store your iPad, and you can remove a lot of the risk involved.

Enable iPad Tracking

What do you do if your iPad is stolen or even just lost? Fortunately, your iPad includes an app, called Find My iPhone, that you can use to track a lost or stolen device.

iPhone or iPad

The Find My iPhone app gets its name from its original target audience: iPhone users. (Statistically, there are more iPhones lost and stolen than iPads—probably because of the smaller size.) Don't get too hung up on the name, however; you can use the Find My iPhone app to find your lost or stolen iPad.

Before you can track a lost or stolen device, you first have to turn on Find My iPad.

(1) From the Settings screen, tap iCloud in the left column.

(2) Tap Find My iPad.

(3) Tap on the Find My iPad switch. (This may be enabled by default.)

(4) If you want the location of your iPad to be automatically sent to Apple before the battery dies, tap on the Send Last Location switch.

☁ iCloud	**(1)**
millerwriter@icloud.com	
Ⓐ iTunes & App Store	
▭ Wallet & Apple Pay	

🔑 Keychain	On >
🔄 Backup	On >
◉ Find My iPad	Off >

(2)

(3)

‹ iCloud   **Find My iPad**

Find My iPad   ⬤

Find My iPad allows you to locate, lock, or erase your iPad and prevents it from being erased or reactivated without your password. About Find My iPad and Privacy...

Send Last Location   ⬤

Automatically send the location of this iPad to Apple when the battery is critically low.

(4)

Track a Lost or Stolen iPad

If your lost or stolen iPad is connected to a Wi-Fi network (or, for cellular models, to either a Wi-Fi or cellular network), and if you've enabled the app previously, Find My iPhone can locate your missing device. Naturally, you can open Find My iPhone on your missing iPad, but you can use the app on another person's device or from the Web, at www.icloud.com/find.

Let's look at how you use the Find My iPhone on another iPad or iPhone to find a lost or stolen device.

(1) Tap the Find iPhone icon to launch the Find My iPhone app and sign into your Apple account.

(2) All devices registered to your account are listed in the left column. Tap the device you want to track.

(3) Your device appears centered on the map on the right. Tap your device on the map to display a panel of options beneath the map.

(4) Tap Play Sound to play an alert sound on your iPad for two minutes. (This works even if the device has been muted.)

(5) Tap Lost Mode to immediately lock your iPad with a passcode and display a custom message onscreen, along with your contact number. (Lost Mode automatically enables Location Services, which is used to track your device's location.)

(6) Tap Erase iPad to delete all the data and media on your iPad and restore it to the original factory settings. Employ this option as a last resort to keep anyone from accessing your personal data or using your iPad to make unauthorized payments using Apple Pay.

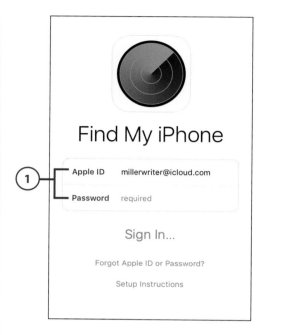

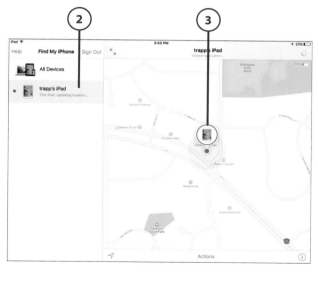

It's Not All Good

Tracking a Lost Device: A True Story

What follows is an iPhone story, but it might as well have involved an iPad. The names have not been changed to protect the innocent.

My granddaughter Alethia received a brand-new iPhone for her birthday. She uses it to text and call her mom when she's at her dad's house, and vice versa. (Her parents are divorced.) She also likes to text with her cousins and play games, of course.

Alethia, her mom, and her siblings were recently on vacation in Michigan, near Traverse City. They had spent a fun day and were relaxing by the docks on Lake Michigan. When they got up to leave, Alethia left her purse on the dock. Inside were all sorts of valuable personal things, along with her iPhone.

When they discovered the purse and the iPhone were missing, Alethia's mom immediately opened the Find My iPhone App on her phone. She put the lost phone into Lost Mode, instructed the phone to play a loud sound, and put a message on the screen with her phone number to contact. Then she settled in to track exactly where the lost phone was.

She tracked the lost phone for the better part of a day. Unfortunately, the location for most of that time was somewhere in the middle of Lake Michigan— apparently, whoever took the phone was on a boat, jetting about from point to point. She called the local police, but they couldn't help as they couldn't identify which boat it was on. Eventually, the phone's battery went dead and so did the signal. At this point, things looked bleak.

There's a happy ending to this story, however. The next week, Alethia's mom got a phone call from a store owner along the lake. He'd found Alethia's purse in one of their trash cans, and inside was the dead iPhone. The owner charged it up (he had an iPhone charger), saw the onscreen message, and called the number listed there. He was nice enough to ship the purse and phone back to my granddaughter, and everybody's happy—thanks in no small part to Apple's Find My iPhone app.

Staying Safe Online

Much of what you do on your iPad is done over the Internet, via either the Safari web browser or apps that use online resources. Unfortunately, the Internet can be a scary place. There are certain predators who target older users online, and for good reasons. Many older computer users are more trusting than younger users, and they're also less tech savvy. In addition, seniors often have large nest eggs that are attractive to online predators, and older computer users are often ashamed to report being taken advantage of.

It all adds up to a potentially dangerous environment for seniors—which means you need to learn how to protect yourself when you're online. You need to be able to identify the most common online threats and scams and know how to avoid becoming a victim.

Protect Against Identity Theft

Online predators want your personal information—your real name, address, online usernames and passwords, bank account numbers, and the like. It's called *identity theft*, and it's a way for a con artist to impersonate you—both online and in the real world. If your personal data falls into the hands of identity thieves, they can use it to hack into your online accounts, make unauthorized charges on your credit card, and maybe even drain your bank account.

There are many ways for criminals to obtain your personal information. Almost all involve tricking you, in some way or another, into providing this information of your own free will. Your challenge is to avoid being tricked.

One of the most common techniques used by identity thieves is called *phishing*. It's called that because the other party is "fishing" for your personal information, typically via fake email messages and websites.

It's Not All Good

Phishing Means Phony

A phishing scam typically starts with a phony email message that appears to be from a legitimate source, such as your bank, the postal service, PayPal, or other official institution. This email purports to contain important information that you can see if you tap the enclosed link. That's where the bad stuff starts.

If you tap the link in the phishing email, you're taken to a fake website masquerading as the real site, complete with logos and official-looking text. You're encouraged to enter your personal information into the forms on this fake web page; when you do so, your information is sent to the scammer, and you're now a victim of identity theft.

How can you avoid falling victim to a phishing scam? There are several things you can do:

- Look at the sender's email address. Most phishing emails come from an address different from the one indicated by the (fake) sender.

- Look for poor grammar and misspellings. Many phishing schemes come from outside the U.S. by scammers who don't speak English as their first language. As such, you're likely to find questionable phrasing and unprofessional text— not what you'd expect from your bank or other professional institution.

- If you receive an unexpected email, no matter the apparent source, do *not* tap any of the links in the email. If you think there's a legitimate issue from a given website, go to that site manually in Safari and access your account from there.

- Some phishing messages include attached files that you are urged to open to display a document or image. Do *not* open any of these attachments; they might contain malware that can steal personal information from your device. (While malware isn't as much of a threat to iPads as it is to personal computers, you still want to avoid opening unexpected email attachments.)

Malware Threats

If you're a long-time computer user, you're probably familiar with the threat posed by computer viruses, spyware, and other malicious software (malware). Computers are easily infected by these harmful programs. Fortunately, your iPad is not as easily infected; due to technological safeguards built into the iOS operating system, the malware risk for iPad users is extremely low. So don't worry too much about malware on your iPad—but still remain vigilant, nonetheless.

Keep Your Private Information Private

Identity theft can happen any time you make private information public. This has become a special issue on social networks, such as Facebook, where users tend to forget that most everything they post is publicly visible—and often share information about birthdays, schools attended, and even phone numbers.

None of this might sound dangerous, until you realize that all of these items are the type of personal information many companies use for the "secret questions" their websites use to reset users' passwords. A fraudster armed with this publicly visible information could log onto your account on a banking website, for example, reset your password (to a new one he provides), and thus gain access to your banking accounts.

The solution to this problem, of course, is to enter as little personal information as possible when you're online. For example, you don't need to—and shouldn't—include your street address or phone number in a comment or reply to an online news article. Don't give the bad guys anything they can use against you!

Protect Against Online Fraud

Identity theft isn't the only kind of online fraud you might encounter. Con artists are especially creative in concocting schemes that can defraud unsuspecting victims of thousands of dollars.

Most of these scams start with an email or social media message that promises something for nothing. Maybe the message tells you that you've won a lottery, or you are asked to help someone in a foreign country deposit funds in a U.S. bank account. You might even receive requests from people purporting to be far-off relatives who need some cash to bail them out of some sort of trouble.

The common factor in these scams is that you're eventually asked to either send money (typically via wire transfer) or provide your bank account information—with which the scammers can drain your money faster than you can imagine. If you're naïve or gullible enough then the damage can be considerable.

Protecting yourself from the huge number of these online scams is both difficult and simple. The difficulty comes from the sheer number of scams and their amazing variety. The simplicity comes from the fact that the best way to deal with any such scam is to use common sense—and ignore it.

Most online fraud is easily detectible by the simple fact that it arrives out of the blue and seems too good to be true. So if you get an unsolicited offer that promises great riches, you know to tap Delete—pronto.

Savvy Internet users train themselves to recognize scam messages at a glance. That's because most scam messages come from complete strangers, and often don't even address you by name. Most of these messages are rife with spelling and grammatical errors, as scammers frequently operate from foreign countries and do not use English as their first language.

A typical scam email promises you large sums of money for little or no effort on your part. Either in the first or subsequent messages (if you respond), you will be asked to provide your bank account number, credit card number, or other personal information—or are asked to provide money upfront for various fees, or to pay the cost of expediting the process.

If you receive a message that you think is a scam, delete it. In fact, it's a good idea to ignore all unsolicited messages, of any type. No stranger will send you a legitimate offer via email or Facebook; it just doesn't happen.

Also, and this should go without saying, but you just shouldn't give in to greed. If an offer sounds too good to be true, it is; there are no true "get rich quick" schemes.

>>>Go Further

WHAT TO DO IF YOU'VE BEEN SCAMMED

What should you do if you think you've been the victim of an online fraud? There are a few steps you can take to minimize the damage:

- If the fraud involved transmittal of your credit card information, contact your credit card company to put a halt to all unauthorized payments—and to limit your liability to the first $50.

- If you think your bank accounts have been compromised, contact your bank to put a freeze on your checking and savings accounts—and to open new accounts, if necessary.

- Contact one of the three major credit reporting bureaus to see if stolen personal information has been used to open new credit accounts—or max out your existing accounts.

- Contact your local law enforcement authorities—fraud is illegal, and it should be reported as a crime.

- Report the fraud to your state attorney general's office.

- File a complaint with the Federal Trade Commission (FTC) via the form located at www.ftccomplaintassistant.gov.

- Contact any or all of the following consumer-oriented websites: Better Business Bureau (www.bbb.org), Internet Crime Complaint Center (www.ic3.gov), and the National Consumers League's Fraud Center (www.fraud.org).

Above all, don't provide any additional information or money to the scammers. As soon as you suspect you've been had, halt all contact and cut off all access to your bank and credit card accounts. Sometimes the best you can hope for is to minimize your losses.

Shop Safely

Many people use their iPads to shop online. It's convenient, and you don't have to bother with driving to the store and dealing with all those crowds.

Despite the huge upsurge in online shopping, many users are still reticent to provide their credit card information over the Internet. It is possible, after all, for shady sellers to take your money and not deliver the goods, or even for high-tech thieves to intercept your credit card information over the Internet—or from a public Wi-Fi hotspot.

All that said, online shopping remains immensely popular, and is generally quite safe. You can make your online shopping even safer by following this advice:

- Don't shop in public. While you can shop over any wireless connection, public connections (like the kind you find at coffeehouses and restaurants) aren't as secure as the private connection you have on your home network. It's possible for individuals with the right equipment to intercept public wireless signals, and thus skim your credit card and other personal information. While this sort of data theft doesn't happen often, it's better to make your online purchases over a safer private connection.

- Shop only at secure websites. Whatever you're shopping for online, make sure you're using a website that offers secure connections. (A secure web address starts with https:, not the normal http:.) A secure website encrypts the data you send to it, so even if it is intercepted by a third party, that party can't read it. Most major online retailers have secure sites.

- Don't leave your credit card number on file with online retailers. As tempting as it is to have your favorite retailer store your credit card info for future purchases, that also means they have a copy of it on their servers—and anyone breaking into their servers can then steal your information. Instead, enter your credit card number fresh with each new purchase; it's just safer.

If you shop at major online retailers, you're probably going to be safe. Same thing if you buy from smaller sellers on eBay or Etsy; those sites have their own robust security mechanisms in place. If it's a retailer you haven't heard of before, check them out by doing a Google search and reading online reviews; if the reviews trend towards the negative, shop elsewhere. And always, always shop from a merchant that offers a toll-free number for customer support, just in case something goes wrong.

Do all of these things and shopping with your iPad will be not only convenient but also safe.

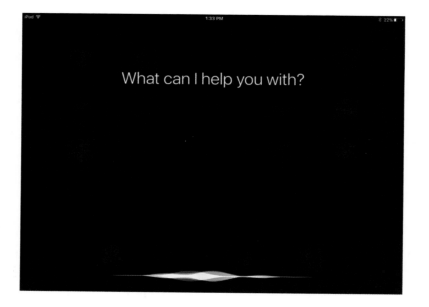

In this chapter, you learn how to use Siri to control iPad operations and query for specific information.

→ Getting to Know Siri, Your iPad's Virtual Personal Assistant
→ Using Siri to Control Your iPad and Apps
→ Using Siri to Find Useful and Interesting Information

7

Controlling Your iPad—and More—with Siri

Siri isn't a person; it's a thing, sort of. To be precise, Siri is a piece of software that functions as a virtual personal assistant on your iPad and other Apple devices. It's a way of both operating your iPad using voice commands and searching the Internet for relevant information.

Siri understands natural speech, so all you have to do is talk to your iPad using plain-English questions and commands and Siri knows what you're asking and responds accordingly. You can use Siri not just to ask questions and find information but also to control the operations of your iPad.

Getting to Know Siri, Your iPad's Virtual Personal Assistant

Siri functions as a high-tech personal assistant on your iPad. In reality, Siri is nothing more than an app on your device, albeit one that's highly functional and very high tech. The Siri app essentially serves as a voice-controlled interface between you and various operations on your iPad, enabling you to perform many operations via voice commands.

You can use Siri to initiate most operations on your iPad. Use Siri to compose and send messages, schedule events, watch videos, and listen to music, as well as launch apps, turn on Do Not Disturb mode, and raise and lower your iPad's volume levels.

Siri can also keep you updated on current sports scores, news events, and weather conditions. You can even ask Siri factual questions, such as "How many miles is it to the moon?" or "How much is five times seven?"

Enable Siri

Before you can use Siri, you have to enable the Siri app on your iPad. You probably did this when you first set up your new device, but you can enable (or disable) Siri manually at any time.

Settings — 1

⚙	General
AA	Display & Brightness
✳	Wallpaper
🔊	Sounds
	Siri — 2
👆	Touch ID & Passcode

(1) Tap the Settings icon to display the Settings screen.

(2) Tap Siri in the list of apps on the left.

(3) Tap on the Siri switch. (It may be on by default.)

3

Siri

Press and hold the home button to start speaking to Siri, then release the button when you are done. About Siri and Privacy...

Configure Siri

There are several things you can change to personalize your own experience with Siri. You can change Siri's voice, the language she speaks, and even whether you can summon Siri merely by saying, "Hey Siri!"

1 From the Settings screen, tap Siri in the list of apps on the left.

2 By default, you can summon Siri from any screen, including the Lock screen (before you unlock it). If you don't want Siri available to your locked device, tap off Access on Lock Screen.

3 To summon Siri without first tapping the Home button, tap on the Allow "Hey Siri!" switch. You are prompted to set up Siri to recognize your voice; follow the onscreen instructions. ("Hey Siri!" only works when your iPad is connected to external power.)

4 Tap Language and then make a selection to change the language that Siri speaks.

5 Have Siri speak in a different voice. Tap Siri Voice and make a new selection. Choose from American (default), Australian, or British accents, in either Male or Female (default) voices.

6 By default, Siri provides voice feedback. To disable this in favor of onscreen feedback, tap Voice Feedback and then tap Hands-Free Only.

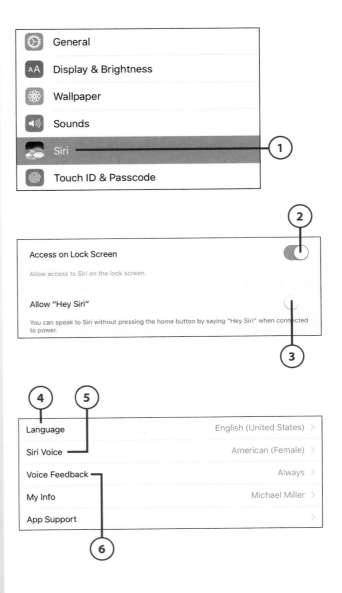

Summon Siri

(1) Press and hold the iPad's Home button. *Or...*

(2) If you've enabled "Hey Siri!" functionality (and your iPad is plugged into external power), simply speak the words "Hey Siri!" into the device.

(3) You'll see the words "What can I help you with?" onscreen. Speak your question or command.

Louder or Softer

To adjust the volume level of Siri's voice, use the volume up and down buttons on the side of your iPad.

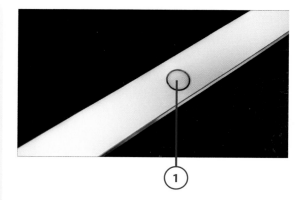

Using Siri to Control Your iPad and Apps

Instead of tapping onscreen icons or controls, you can use Siri's voice commands to perform many operations on your iPad. This makes Siri essential for using the iPad for those with accessibility issues—and just more convenient for the rest of us.

Connect to Query

To use Siri, your iPad must be connected to the Internet.

Launch Apps

The first thing you can do with Siri is launch apps on your iPad. To do so, say something like

Launch app name.

For example, to launch the Facebook app, say

Launch Facebook.

Control System Functions

You can use Siri to enable, disable, and control various system functions on your iPad. Say the following:

Turn Wi-Fi on.

Turn Bluetooth off.

Increase the brightness.

Send and Receive Messages

Siri is useful if you want to send or receive messages via the Messages or Mail apps. To read messages, say the following:

Read my messages.

Read messages from Bob.

Read my last message from Sally.

To reply to a message, say the following, and then say "Send":

Reply I'll see you then.

Reply okay.

To create a new message, say any of the following, and then say "Send":

New email to John Jones.

Send a message to Oliver saying I'm free tomorrow.

Email Clark and say I received the pictures, thanks.

You can also use Siri to initiate FaceTime conversations. Say something like

FaceTime Hayley.

End conversation.

Manage Meetings, Events, and Reminders

If you use your iPad to manage your meetings, events, and reminders, Siri definitely can come in handy.

Here are a few commands to try regarding meetings and appointments:

What's on my calendar tomorrow?

Do I have a meeting at noon?

Where is my ten o'clock meeting?

Set up a meeting with Hal at two.

Cancel my eleven o'clock appointment.

Reschedule my meeting with Dinah to next Friday at ten.

You can even create complex events, complete with other attendees. Just tell Siri as much as possible about the event, like this:

Make an event for nine forty-five tomorrow called Neighborhood Association with Randy Jones, Don Emory, Betsy Griffin, and Samuel Hancock.

Then there are reminders, of which Siri can be quite helpful. Say something like

Remind me to pay the electric bill by the fifteenth.

Remind me to stop at the drug store when I leave here.

Remind me to buy milk.

Remind me to feed the fish when I get home.

You can also use Siri to create notes. Say something like

Create a new note or *Make a note named Parts List*, and then dictate your note.

Find my note about plumbers.

You can even use Siri to set alarms and timers. Say something like

Set an alarm for six am.

Set an alarm for three hours from now.

Turn off all alarms.

Set a timer for fifteen minutes.

Take and View Pictures

If you use the camera in your iPad, you can control it via Siri voice commands. Say something like

Open camera.

Take a picture.

Take a selfie.

To view pictures you've taken, say something like

Show me photos from October.

Show me photos I took last year.

Show me photos of Dave.

Show me photos of Florida.

Show me photos from my Family album.

Listen to Music

If you use your iPad's Music app to listen to music, you can control what you listen to via Siri's voice commands. Try the following:

Play music.

Pause music.

Stop.

Next song.

Previous song.

To play specific music, say something like

Play James Taylor.

Play "Proud Mary."

Play Abbey Road.

Play the playlist My Favorites.

Play the radio station Classic Rock.

You can even shuffle the music you call up:

Play Classic Soul shuffled.

To find out more about the currently playing song, say something like

What's playing?

Who sings this song?

Who is this song by?

>>>*Go Further*

SMART HOME CONTROL

If you use Apple's Home app to control HomeKit-enabled devices in your home, you can use Siri to control those devices via voice commands. For example, you can tell Siri to do the following:

Turn off the lights.

Turn down the dining room lights.

Dim the lights.

Set brightness to 50 percent.

Set the temperature to 72 degrees.

Turn on the coffeemaker.

After you get a device set up, experiment with different commands to see just what Siri can control.

Using Siri to Find Interesting and Useful Information

Siri isn't just about controlling apps and settings on your iPad. You can also use Siri to find information—like searching the Web with voice commands.

Find Information

Probably one of the most used functions for Siri is to find information. It's like using Google, but Siri returns a real answer to any question you ask.

You can ask Siri about the weather:

What's the current temperature?

Is it going to rain today?

What's the weather like this weekend?

Or about sports:

What's the score of the Vikings game?

Who's in first place in the National League West?

Or the stock market:

How is the stock market doing today?

What is Apple's stock price?

Interested in a new movie?

Is the new Avengers *movie any good?*

What time is the Star Trek *movie playing?*

Or just ask Siri about anything in which you're interested. Here are a few queries to try:

How far is it to the moon?

How old is Tom Hanks?

Who is Prime Minister of Canada?

Who wrote War and Peace?

Solve Equations and Make Conversions

Siri is also great for converting various measurements. Here's a sampling of what you can ask:

How many kilometers are there in a mile?

How many dollars in a Euro?

Convert 2.7 ounces to grams.

Convert $47 to pounds.

Conversions are fun, but what about basic math problems? Siri can handle all sorts of equations, such as

What is a 20 percent tip on $83?

What is 238 times 72?

What is 22 divided by 2?

What is the square root of pi?

Find Businesses and Get Directions

Siri can help you find nearby businesses (and information about them). Say something like

Where is the nearest gas station?

Are there any good Chinese restaurants nearby?

How late is Home Depot open?

Is CVS open right now?

You can also use Siri to find and make reservations via the Yelp and OpenTable apps:

Find me a table for two for dinner tomorrow.

Book me a table for four at noon on Thursday at The Fancy Pear.

Then there are directions, of which you can ask Siri:

Show me how to get to the history museum.

Find directions to 10223 Main Street.

You can even ask Siri other travel-related questions, such as

Check flight status of United 231.

When does Southwest 72 arrive?

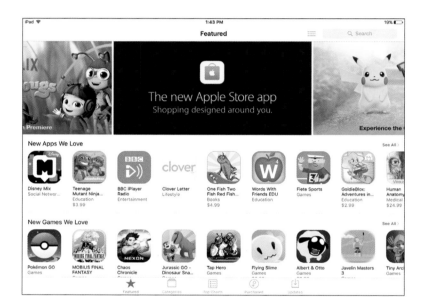

→ Working with Apps
→ Finding New Apps in the App Store
→ Managing Installed Apps
→ Multitasking on Your iPad

Installing and Using Apps

Most of what you do on your iPad you do via *applications*, or *apps*. An app is a self-contained program designed to perform a particular task or serve a specific purpose. There are apps for news and weather, apps for email and text messaging, apps for Facebook and Pinterest, even apps for listening to music and watching videos. Whatever you want to do on your iPad, there's probably an app for it.

Your new iPad came with more than a dozen apps preinstalled, but these aren't the only apps you can use. There are tens of thousands of additional apps available, most for free or low cost, in Apple's online App Store. It's easy to find new apps and install them on your iPad—and then use them every day.

Working with Apps

To do just about anything on your iPad, you have to learn how to work with Apps. All the apps currently installed on your iPad are displayed on the various Home screens. Each icon on the screen represents a different app. When you install a new app, an icon for that app appears on the Home screen.

Launch an App

You open apps from the iPad's Home screen.

1. Press the Home button to return to the main Home screen.

2. Navigate to the Home screen that displays the icon for the app you want to open.

3. Tap the icon to open the app.

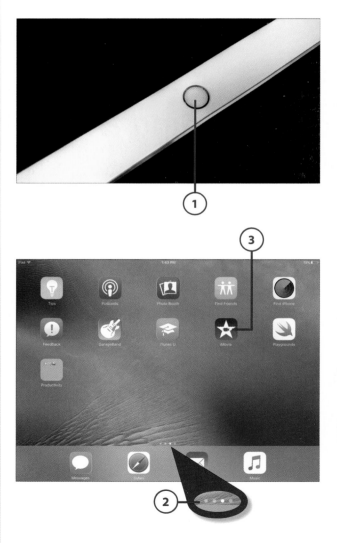

Search for an App

If you have a ton of apps installed on your iPad, it may be challenging to find a specific app you want. (Which Home screen did you put it on?) If this is the case, use your iPad's search function to find that one app you're looking for.

(1) From the main Home screen, drag from left to right to display the Search screen. *Or…*

(2) Drag down from the center of the Home screen to display the Search panel.

(3) Enter the name of the app you want into the Search box.

(4) As you type, your iPad suggests matching apps. Tap the name of an app to open it.

Switch Between Apps

You can have multiple apps open at the same time, and easily switch between them.

 Press the Home button twice to view all open apps.

② You see Apple's App Switcher, which displays all your open apps. Swipe left or right to focus on other apps.

③ Tap an app to go to that app.

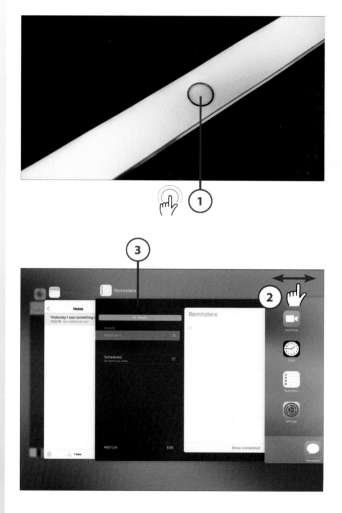

Close an App

Apps remain open until you manually close them. When you're not using an app, it remains paused in the background, but it doesn't consume system resources. Because of this, you don't have to close an app when you're done with it—although you can if you want.

(1) Press the Home key twice to display the App Switcher.

(2) Tap and drag the app up and off the screen until it disappears.

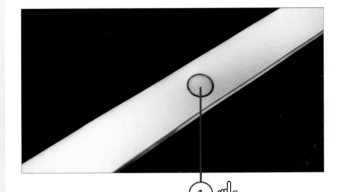

Finding New Apps in the App Store

Where do you find new apps to use on your iPad? There's one central source that offers apps from multiple developers—Apple's App Store.

Browse and Search the App Store

Apple's App Store is an online store that offers apps and games for iPads and iPhones. Most apps in the App Store are free or relatively low cost. It's easy to find new apps by either browsing or searching.

1. Tap the App Store icon to open the App Store.

2. Tap the Featured tab to view apps and games recommended for you.

3. Swipe up to view various lists— New Apps We Love, New Games We Love, and the like.

4. Swipe from right to left to see more apps and games in each list.

5 Tap the Categories tab to browse apps and games in various categories—Games, Kids, Entertainment, Finance, Medical, and the like.

6 Tap a category to view apps in that category.

7 Tap the Top Charts tab to view top-selling paid and free apps and games.

8 Tap an app to view more about that app.

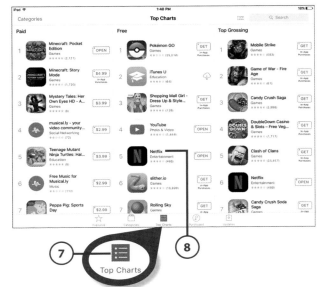

Purchase and Download Apps

Many apps in the App Store are free. Others you have to pay for.

① Download a free app from the app panel by tapping the Get button, which changes to an Install button.

② Tap Install. The app is downloaded to and installed on your iPad.

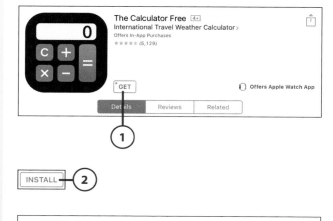

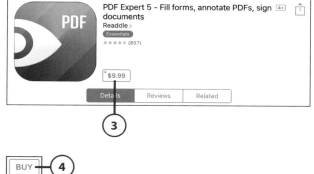

Locating and Moving Apps

When you install a new app, the icon for that app appears in the first empty space on the second or later Home screen. (New apps are not added to your main Home screen.) You can then move that icon to another position or screen if you like. (Learn more about moving and managing app icons in Chapter 3, "Personalizing the Way Your iPad Looks and Works.")

③ The details panel for a paid app displays the app's price. Tap the price button to start the purchase; the button changes to a Buy button.

④ Tap the Buy button.

⑤ The iTunes Store should recognize your Apple ID and then ask you for your password; if not, you need to enter both your Apple ID and password to sign in. The app is purchased and the download begins.

>>>*Go Further*

PAYING FOR APPS

Naturally, you have to pay for those apps that have a price. Payment is automatic when you tap the Buy button, provided you're signed into the iTunes Store and have a credit card on file for your Apple ID.

You may have provided credit card information when you first set up your iPad or created your Apple ID. If not, you can add a credit card to your account at any time by using the Safari app to go to https://appleid.apple.com and signing into your Apple account. On the main page, scroll down to the Payment and Shipping section and tap Edit Payment Information. Enter your credit card number, expiration date, billing address, and the like, and then tap Save. This credit card will then be used for all your App Store purchases.

Managing Installed Apps

Your iPad offers a variety of functions you can employ to better manage the apps you have installed on your device.

View and Manage Purchased Apps

All the apps you've ever purchased are listed in the App Store app. Even if you've deleted an app from your device, you can still see that app and reinstall it on your iPad at any time.

1. From within the App Store, tap to select the Purchased tab.

2. Apps that are currently installed on your phone have an Open button. Tap the Open button to launch a particular app.

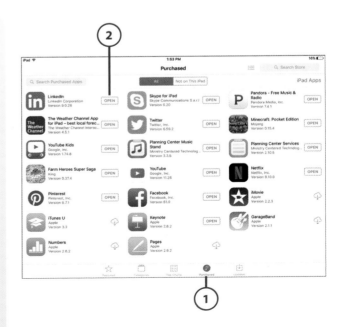

3 Apps you've purchased but have yet to install, or that you've since deleted (so they're not currently installed) have a cloud icon. Tap this Download icon to install an app on your device.

4 The App Store even keeps tracks of apps you've installed on other devices (such as your iPhone) that you can also install on your iPad. Tap Not on This iPad at the top of the page.

5 Tap the Download icon to install an app on your iPad.

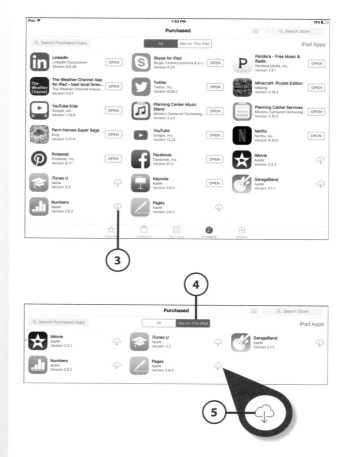

Update Your Apps

From time to time apps get updated. Some apps add new features, some merely include bug fixes. In any case, you need to keep your apps up to date, which you do from the App Store app. All updates are always free.

1 If you have apps that need updating, you see a number on the App Store icon. This number indicates how many apps you need to update. Tap the App Store icon to open the App Store.

2 From within the App Store, tap the Updates tab. All apps awaiting update are listed here.

3 To update an individual app, tap that app's Update button.

4 To update all apps with pending updates, tap Update All.

Delete an App

Over time, you'll probably find that you've installed some apps that you no longer use. You may want to delete these apps to clear up any Home screen clutter, and to free up storage space for new apps.

1 Navigate to the Home screen that contains the app you want to delete.

2 Press and hold the app you want to delete. All the app icons start to wiggle.

3 Tap the X next to the app icon you want to delete.

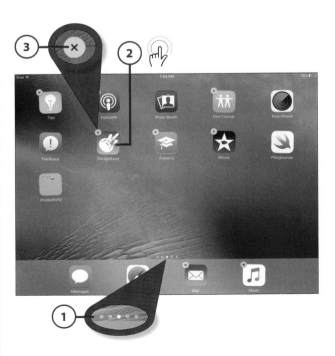

(4) Tap Delete at the prompt.

(5) Press your iPad's Home button to return to the normal, non-wiggly Home screen.

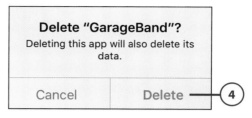

Delete "GarageBand"?
Deleting this app will also delete its data.

| Cancel | Delete —(4) |

No X

If, when you press and hold an app's icon, you don't see a little X in the top-left corner that means you're looking at a system app that can't be deleted. Apps with X's can be deleted; those without can't.

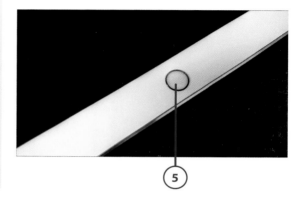

(5)

>>>Go Further

INSTALLED APPS

Your iPad comes with a number of apps preinstalled. You might find that these apps are sufficient for most of your daily needs. Or you may need to install other apps to do other things you want to do.

The apps that Apple preinstalls on your iPad are found on the device's two (by default) Home screens. The following table details what you get—for free!

Icon	App	Description
App Store	App Store	Find and install new apps from the online store
Wednesday 27 Calendar	Calendar	Keep track of appointments and events

Icon	App	Description
	Camera	Shoot digital still photos and videos
	Clock	View current time, set alarms, set timer, use stopwatch
	Contacts	Keep track of friends' contact information for email, video conferencing, and more
	FaceTime	Chat with friends and family in online video chats
	Feedback	Provide feedback to Apple
	Find My Friends	Use location services to locate friends and family
	Find My iPhone	Locate, lock, or erase your iPad if it's lost or stolen
	GarageBand	Create and record music on a variety of virtual instruments
	Home	Manage HomeKit-compatible smart home devices

Icon	App	Description
iBooks	iBooks	Read eBooks on your iPad
iMovie	iMovie	Produce and edit digital movies
iTunes Store	iTunes Store	Purchase music, movies, and TV shows online
iTunes U	iTunes U	Access everything an instructor needs to manage classroom activities, reading, and homework
Keynote	Keynote	Create and give presentations
Mail	Mail	Send and receive email messages
Maps	Maps	Display location maps and turn-by-turn directions
Messages	Messages	Send and receive text messages via iMessage or SMS/MMS
Music	Music	Play digital music

Icon	App	Description
News	News	Read the latest news headlines
Notes	Notes	Take and recall short notes
Numbers	Numbers	Create and manage spreadsheets
Pages	Pages	Create and manage word processing documents
Photo Booth	Photo Booth	Take photos and add various special effects
Photos	Photos	View and edit digital photos on your iPad
Playgrounds	Playgrounds (Swift Playgrounds)	Learn simple coding and programming
Podcasts	Podcasts	Listen to audio podcasts
Reminders	Reminders	Create and recall brief reminders

Icon	App	Description
Safari	Safari	Browse the Web
Tips	Tips	Learn more about how to use your iPad
Videos	Videos	View videos on your iPad

Obviously, if these apps don't do everything you need them to do, you can download and install additional apps from the App Store. The only limit to how many apps you can have is the storage space available on your device!

Multitasking on Your iPad

Your iPad enables you to have multiple apps open simultaneously. Normally, you use one app full screen while the other apps hide in the background; you then use the App Switcher to change from one app to another.

You can also choose to run two apps onscreen at the same time. This type of multitasking is enabled by the Slide Over and Split Screen functions.

Open a Second App with Slide Over

Slide Over enables you to open a second app onscreen without closing the one you're currently in. The second app (called the *side app*) slides in from the right side of the screen in a narrow column. When the side app is visible the focus is there; the main app is dimmed and inactive.

(**1**) With the current app open, swipe left from the right edge of the screen. This displays the most recent app as the side app.

(**2**) Pull down from the top of the side app to display other available apps.

(**3**) Tap to select the side app you want to use.

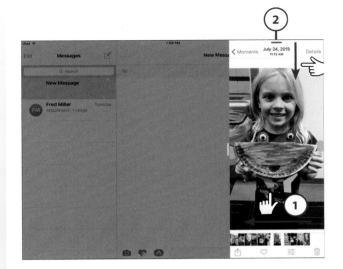

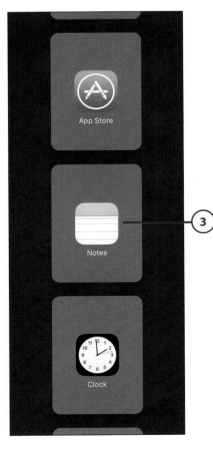

④ Close the side app by tapping the main app on the left or swiping right from the app divider.

④

Display Two Apps at Once with Split View

The Slide Over feature lets you see two apps at once, although only one is active. If you want to display *and* use to apps at the same time, use iPad's Split View.

To use Split View, you start out the same way you do with Slide Over. It's when you take an extra step, however, that you activate both apps on their respective parts of the screen.

① With the current app open, swipe left from the right edge of the screen. This displays the previous app as the side app.

2 Grab the handle in the middle of the app divider and drag it to the center of the screen. This makes both apps active.

3 Select a different app to view on the right by pulling down from the top of the right-hand app.

4 Tap to select the app you want to display.

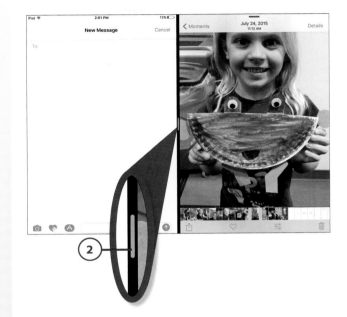

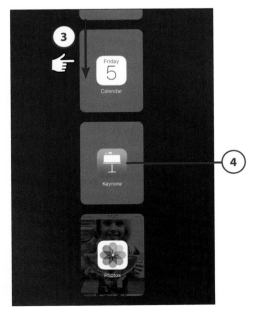

(5) To return to single-app view, drag the app divider handle to the right to close the right-hand app or to the left to close the left-hand app.

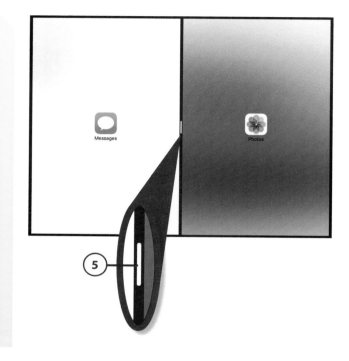

>>>Go Further

PICTURE IN PICTURE

Your iPad also offers a picture in picture mode, for use with certain apps. If you're watching a TV show or movie, or conducting a FaceTime video chat, you can keep that video or chat playing in a separate window while you do other stuff on the iPad screen. The video or chat appears in a small window that floats on top of the active app, so you can keep watching while you work.

To activate picture in picture mode, tap the Picture in Picture icon (in the video app) or press the iPad's Home button (when using FaceTime). The video screen shrinks to a corner of your display. Your Home screen or other apps appear beneath the video window, and you can then use whatever app you want while the video or chat keeps playing.

When you display the picture in picture window, you can make the window bigger by expanding two fingers on the window. Pinch two fingers together to make the video window smaller. And, if you want, you can use your finger to drag the video window to a different corner or position on the screen.

To return the video window to full screen, tap the window to display the control icons and then tap the Picture in Picture icon.

‹ iCloud | **Inbox** | Edit

🔍 Search

● **Michael Miller**   2:18 PM
Monthly meeting
Everybody, just a reminder that the
monthly meeting is coming up next Th...

Fred Miller   2:16 PM
Pics
Mike: Here's a great pic from last
weekend. We had a blast! Fred

Fred Miller   4/14/16
Drums
Here are some pics of you playing
drums last week. Enjoy!

From: Fred Miller   FM
To: Michael Miller ›   Hide

Pics
Today at 2:15 PM

Mike:

Here's a great pic from last weekend. We had a blast!

Fred

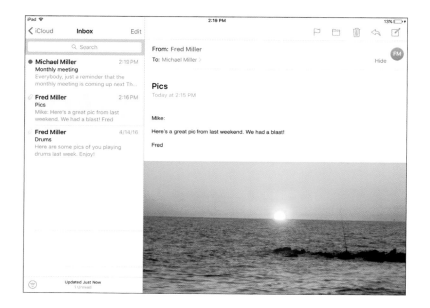

Updated Just Now
1 Unread

In this chapter, you learn how to use your iPad's Mail app to send and receive email messages.

→ Configuring the Mail App
→ Sending and Receiving Messages

9

Sending and Receiving Email

For the past several decades, email has been an important means for people to communicate with each other. Whether you're trading messages with friends and family members, receiving messages from groups to which you belong, or receiving confirmation messages after you've purchased merchandise online, it's important to have an email address and master the workings of a full-featured email program.

The email app included with your iPad is called Mail. You can use Mail to send and receive emails using your Apple email account, or configure the app to work with other email services, such as Yahoo! Mail and Google's Gmail.

Configuring the Mail App

You use your iPad's Mail app to send and receive email messages. It works like most other email apps, and can work with your Apple iCloud email, Microsoft Outlook, Google's Gmail, Yahoo! Mail, and other email services.

Add an Email Account

When you set up your iPad with your Apple ID, that information was automatically added to the Mail app. So if you have an Apple or iCloud email address, that account is already set up in the Mail app—there's nothing more you need to do to get started.

If you have an email address with a different service, however, you can add that account to the Mail app and check that email from the app. The Mail app lets you add multiple accounts and check messages from multiple addresses and inboxes. It's convenient to be able to check all your emails in one place.

While you can still go to the Gmail website for your email, for example, it's just as easy to check your Gmail messages from within the Mail app. All you have to do is configure the Mail app for the new account.

1 Tap the Settings icon to open the Settings screen.

2 Scroll down the left column to the list of apps and tap Mail.

3 Tap Accounts to display the Accounts screen.

4 Tap Add Account to display the Add Account screen.

Settings

1

Mail	**2**
Contacts	
Calendar	

3

Accounts
iCloud

ACCOUNTS

iCloud
iCloud Drive, Mail, Contacts, Calendars, Safari, Reminders, Notes, News and 2 more...

Add Account

4

5 Tap the type of email account you want to add—iCloud, Exchange, Google, Yahoo!, AOL, or Outlook.com. (If you have another type of email, tap Other.)

6 When prompted, sign into the email account you selected with that account's email address and password.

7 If prompted to enable various aspects of your email account (such as calendar or contacts), select those options you want and tap Save. This account is now added to the Mail app.

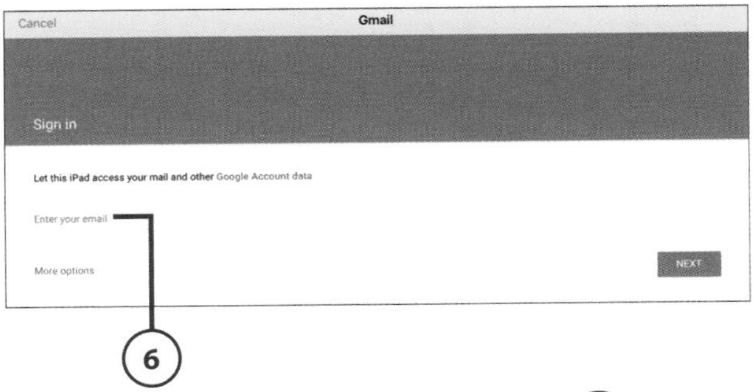

☁ iCloud

E🅱 Exchange

Google — **5**

YAHOO!

Aol.

🅾✉ Outlook.com

Other

Cancel   **Gmail**

Sign in

Let this iPad access your mail and other Google Account data

Enter your email

More options   NEXT

6

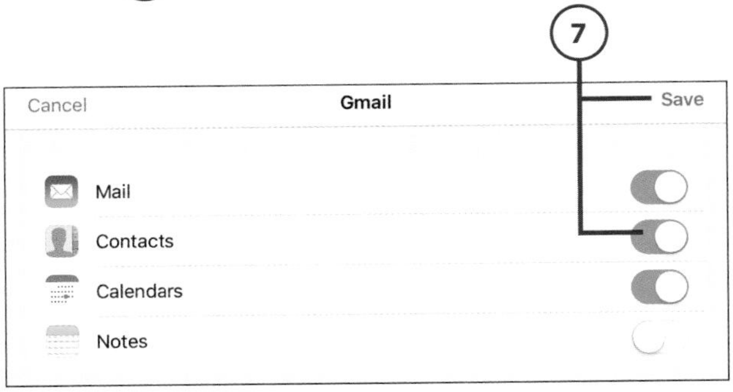

7

Cancel   **Gmail**   Save

✉ Mail

👤 Contacts

📅 Calendars

📝 Notes

>>>*Go Further*
SELECT A DEFAULT ACCOUNT

Although Mail receives messages from all accounts you add, you need to select which account is used when you send messages. This is important if you have, say, both iCloud and Gmail accounts added in the app; you have to decide whether the new emails you send come from your iCloud or Gmail address.

To do this, open the Settings screen, tap Mail, and then scroll down to the Composing section. Tap Default Account and select the account you want to use to send new messages.

You're not stuck with this one account, however. You can select a different sending account when creating a new message. When you create a new message, tap within the From field to display a panel with all your accounts listed, then select a different email account.

Get Notified of New Messages

The Mail app can notify you when you receive new messages.

1. Tap the Settings icon to open the Settings screen.

2. Tap Notifications in the left column.

3. Tap Mail.

Settings ─(1)

☐ Notifications ────────	(2)
☷ Control Center	
☾ Do Not Disturb	

(3)

✉	**Mail** Badges, Sounds, Banners	>
🗺	**Maps** Banners	>
💬	**Messages** Badges, Sounds, Banners	>

4 Tap on the Allow Notifications switch.

5 Tap the account from which you want to receive notifications.

6 Indicate that you want to show notifications from this account in the Notification Center by tapping on the Show in Notification Center switch.

7 Indicate that you want to show notifications from this account on the Lock screen by tapping on the Show on Lock Screen switch.

8 In the Alert Style When Unlocked section, select what type of notifications you want to receive—None, Banners, or Alerts.

9 To display previews of message contents in the alerts, tap on the Show Previews switch.

Allow Notifications

iCloud
Badges, Sounds
Gmail
Badges, Sounds

Show in Notification Center

Sounds   Ding

Badge App Icon

Show on Lock Screen

Show alerts on the lock screen, and in Notification Center when it is accessed from the lock screen.

ALERT STYLE WHEN UNLOCKED

None   Banners   Alerts

Alerts require an action before proceeding.
Banners appear at the top of the screen and go away automatically.

MAIL OPTIONS

Show Previews

Create a Signature

By default, when you send email from the Mail app, it automatically attaches a line of text to the bottom of each message stating "Sent from my iPad." This line is called a *signature*, and you can customize what text you include in yours.

1. Tap the Settings icon to open the Settings screen.

2. Scroll down the left column to the list of apps and tap Mail.

3. Scroll down the Mail screen to the Composing section and tap Signature.

4. Tap All Accounts to create a signature for use with all your email accounts.

5. Tap Per Account to create a signature for a specific email account.

6. Tap within the text box (or the text box for a specific account), delete the default signature, and type a new one.

Settings — ①

	Mail	— ②
	Contacts	
	Calendar	

COMPOSING

Always Bcc Myself

Mark Addresses   Off >

Increase Quote Level   On >

Signature   Sent from my iPad >   ③

Default Account   iCloud >

Messages created outside of Mail will be sent from this account by default.

④ ⑤

All Accounts   ✓

Per Account

Sent from my iPad

⑥

>>>Go Further
SIGNATURES

Your email signature should be used to tell your recipients something about you. It can contain useful or fun information.

Many people use their signatures to display additional contact information, such as phone number or Twitter handle. Others display their job title or professional qualifications in their signature.

A signature doesn't have to be serious, however. Some people end their emails with a favorite quotation, or even a personal statement of some sort. Just keep it short—nobody wants to read a six-line signature in every email they receive from you!

Sending and Receiving Messages

The whole point of the Mail app is to let you send and receive email messages to and from your friends and family. (And any other person or organization who uses email, as well.) To that end, it's relatively easy to use—just like most other email apps and services.

Select an Inbox

If you've configured the Mail app for more than one email account, you have more than one inbox to deal with. The Mail app includes inboxes for each account you use, as well as a master inbox (All Inboxes) that displays messages from all your accounts in a single place. There's also a VIP inbox, which lists messages from people you've decided are very important.

(1) Tap the Mail icon to open the Mail app. (If you have unread email, you'll see a number on the Mail icon, which signifies how many messages you have waiting.)

② Tap All Inboxes to view all your incoming messages from all accounts.

③ Tap the name of an account to view messages from that specific account.

④ Tap VIP to view messages from your most important contacts.

Mailboxes	Edit
② All Inboxes	2 >
③ iCloud	1 >
Gmail	1 >
④ ★ VIP	ⓘ >

>>>Go Further
ADDING A VIP

To add a person to the Mail app's VIP list (their incoming messages automatically appear in the VIP inbox), tap to open the VIP inbox and then tap Add VIP. You now see a list of all your contacts; tap the name of the person you want to add to your VIP list.

Read a Message

Reading a message in the Mail app is subtly different depending on how you hold your iPad. When you hold the device horizontally, you see a split screen, with inbox contents on the left and the selected message on the right. When you hold the device vertically, so the screen isn't quite as wide, you see only the selected message; the inbox list slides offscreen to give more room to the selected message.

In this and the following tasks, I show you how Mail works in horizontal mode—which works best for reading emails.

1 From within the Mail app, tap the inbox you want to view. The left column slides offscreen to reveal all the messages in this inbox.

2 Unread messages are displayed in bold; messages you've read appear in normal type. Each message displays the sender's name and/or email address, the date received, message subject, and the first line or so of the message. Tap the message you want to read; the selected message header is shaded.

Mailboxes	Edit

⊟ All Inboxes	2 >
⊠ iCloud	1 >
⊠ Gmail	1 >
★ VIP	ⓘ >

1

〈 iCloud **Inbox** Edit

🔍 Search

● **Fred Miller** 2:28 PM
Sign up date
Mike, do you know when the sign up
date is the next session? I need to get...

Michael Miller 2:19 PM
Monthly meeting
Everybody, just a reminder that the
monthly meeting is coming up next Th...

📎 **Fred Miller** 2:16 PM
Pics
Mike: Here's a great pic from last
weekend. We had a blast! Fred

2

3 The selected message displays on the right side of the screen. (Or, if the iPad is held vertically, it fills the entire screen.) The name of the sender appears at the top, with the message subject beneath that. The text of the message fills the bottom of the message pane; if this message is in reply to a previous message, the previous message is "quoted" beneath that.

4 If the sender has attached photos to the message, those photos are automatically downloaded and displayed within the message text. (If a photo is not automatically displayed, tap the Download link to display it.)

Sender Recipient(s) Subject Trash

From: Fred Miller
To: Michael Miller >   FM Hide

Sign up date
Today at 2:28 PM

Mike, do you know when the sign up date is the next session? I need to get Hayley signed up but not sure how much time we have.

Fred

Date/time received Message **3**

From: Fred Miller
To: Michael Miller >   FM Hide

Pics
Today at 2:15 PM

Mike:

Here's a great pic from last weekend. We had a blast!

Fred

4

Reply to a Message

When you reply to an email message, the original message is "quoted" beneath your reply.

(1) Open the original message and then tap the Reply icon at the top of the screen.

(2) Tap Reply to open the Reply pane.

(3) The original sender is listed as the recipient in the To field, and the subject is also automatically filled in (although you can edit the subject, if you want). Enter your reply into the main text box.

(4) Tap Send to send your reply to the original sender.

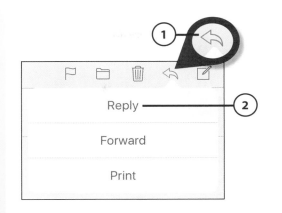

Create and Send a New Message

Writing and sending a new email message is similar to replying to an existing message. All you need to know is who you're sending it to!

(1) From within the Mail app, tap the New Message icon at the top-right corner of the screen. This displays the New Message pane.

2 Tap within the To field and start typing the name or email address of the intended recipient.

3 As you type, the Mail app displays matching names from your contacts list. If this person is listed there, tap their name.

Contacts

Learn more about your contacts and the Contacts app in Chapter 10, "Managing Your Contacts."

4 Alternatively, tap the + icon to display the Contacts pane, and select the recipient from that list.

5 If you're sending an email to someone not in your contacts list, continue entering the person's email address manually.

6 Add another recipient by tapping again within the To field and repeating steps 3 to 5.

7 Add Cc or Bcc additional recipients by tapping Cc/Bcc and adding the desired names.

Cc and Bcc

Cc stands for *carbon copy*, and sends a copy of your message to additional recipients. Bcc stands for *blind carbon copy*, and sends a copy of your message to additional recipients but hides their names and addresses from the main recipients.

Cancel	New Message	Send

To: Fred Miller

Cc/Bcc, From: millerwriter@icloud.com

Subject:

Sent from my iPad

8 Tap within the Subject field and enter the subject of this email.

9 Tap within the main text box and enter your email message.

10 Tap Send to send the message.

Attach a Photo to a Message

The Mail app lets you attach photos and other files to your email messages. This makes it easy to share pictures with your friends and family.

Attachments

A file of any sort attached to an email message is called an *attachment*.

1 From within the Mail app, tap the New Message icon to create a new message.

2 Beneath the New Message pane, tap the camera icon. (To attach a different kind of file, tap the paperclip icon instead.) The Photos pane displays.

3 Tap the photo album that contains the photo you want.

4 Tap to select the photo you want to attach.

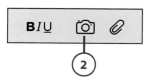

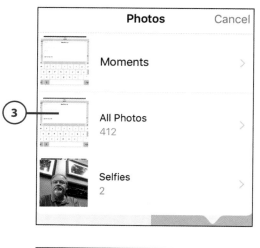

It's Not All Good

Keep It Small

Many digital photos, especially ones you take with your iPad camera, can create fairly large image files. If an image file is too large, your email service (or your recipient's email service) may reject it. For this reason, the Mail app may prompt you to resize any large photo you attach. If you're so prompted, choose a new size before proceeding.

(5) Tap Use. The photo is added to your new message.

(6) Tap the camera icon to attach another picture.

(7) Complete your email as normal and tap Send.

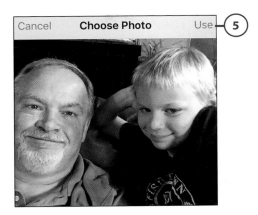

It's Not All Good

Unwanted Attachments

If you receive an attachment via email that you weren't expecting—especially from someone you don't know—do *not* tap to open it! Attachments can contain viruses and other malware that can infect or damage your iPad. Unwanted file attachments, and the emails they come attached to, should be deleted!

Delete a Message

When you're done reading a message you may want to delete it. You may even want to delete a message before you read it, if it's from some entity you don't want to hear from. Fortunately, you can delete messages from the inbox itself, or from the reading pane.

1. To delete a message after you've read it, display the message and then tap the Trash icon.

2. To delete one or more messages from the inbox, tap Edit.

3. Tap to select the message(s) you want to delete.

4. Tap Trash.

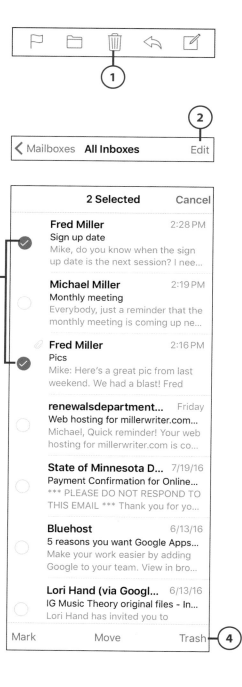

Organize Messages in Files

What do you do with your old messages after you've read them? You may want to delete some of them (and you just learned how), but you may want to keep some around for future reference. Instead of letting old messages clog up your inbox, create folders to organize and store your old messages.

1. From the Mailboxes list, tap Edit.

2. Tap New Mailbox. (The Mail app refers to folders as *mailboxes*.)

3. Tap within the Name field and enter a name for this new folder/mailbox.

4. Tap Mailbox Location.

5. Tap the account where you want to store this folder.

6. You can also select a master folder for this new folder; the new folder then becomes a sub-folder within that folder.

| Mailboxes | Edit | ① |

| New Mailbox | ② |

| Cancel | **New Mailbox** | Save |

③ Name

MAILBOX LOCATION

④ ⟩

‹ New Mailbox **Mailbox Location**

⑤ ☁ iCloud

📁 Deleted Items

📁 Junk E-mail

⑥ 📁 Receipts

📁 Sent Items

📁 Shoes

8 Gmail

📁 [Gmail]

📁 Important

📁 Starred

(7) Tap Save.

(8) Tap Done. The new folder/mailbox is now created.

(9) Move an email message to a folder by opening the message and then tapping the folder icon at the top of the screen.

(10) Tap the folder you want to move this message to. The message is moved to that folder.

Cancel	**New Mailbox**	Save —(7)

Meetings ⊗

MAILBOX LOCATION

☁ iCloud >

	Mailboxes	Done —(8)

⚐ 🗀 🗑 ↩ ☑

(9)

‹ Accounts	**iCloud**	Cancel

✉ Inbox

📄 Drafts

✈ Sent

🗙 Junk

🗑 Trash

🗂 Archive

🗀 Deleted Items   2

🗀 Junk E-mail

(10)— 🗀 Meetings

🗀 Receipts

🗀 Sent Items

🗀 Shoes

11 Tap a folder/mailbox in the Mailboxes pane to view the contents of that folder/mailbox.

Mailboxes	Edit
ICLOUD	⌄
⊠ Inbox	
▯ Drafts	
◁ Sent	
⊠ Junk	
🗑 Trash	
▭ Archive	
▭ Deleted Items	2 >
▭ Junk E-mail	>
▭ Meetings	>
▭ Receipts	>
▭ Sent Items	>
▭ Shoes	>

11 Receipts

Deal with Junk Email (Spam)

One of the more annoying things about email is the amount of junk email, or spam, you sometimes receive. Fortunately, the Mail app includes a spam filter that attempts to identify junk email and automatically send it to a special Junk E-mail folder.

1 View messages in the spam folder by going to a given account in the Mailboxes pane and tapping Junk.

ICLOUD	⌄
⊠ Inbox	
▯ Drafts	
◁ Sent	
⊠ Junk	
🗑 Trash	

1 Junk

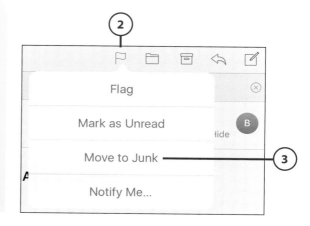

2 Send a message you've received to the Junk E-mail folder by opening the message and tapping the Flag icon.

3 Tap Move to Junk.

>>>Go Further
OTHER EMAIL APPS

Although Apple's Mail app is a very good email app, and it's included free with your iPad, there are other email apps available for your use. If you use a different email service, such as Gmail or Outlook.com, you may want to use the specific app for that service instead. You can find apps for most of the major email services in Apple's App Store; just search by the name of your email service.

In this chapter, you learn how to manage contacts on your iPad for email, messaging, and video chatting.

→ Using the Contacts App
→ Viewing and Contacting Your Contacts

Managing Your Contacts

When you use the Mail app to send an email to someone, you can enter that person's email address manually. That's not a big deal. Unless you send a lot of emails to that person, of course, in which case re-entering that same email address each time gets pretty annoying.

It's also annoying to try to remember the email address of each and every person you communicate with. Or their phone numbers. Or their street addresses. If you have a lot of friends and family, all that information becomes overwhelming.

In the real world, you might keep people's names and addresses in a physical card file or address book. On your iPad, you can do the same thing, by storing all their key information in the Contacts app. It's a lot easier to have the Contacts app remember all these names and addresses than trying to do it yourself!

Using the Contacts App

The Contacts app is preinstalled on your new iPad. You use the Contacts app to store the names, email addresses, street addresses, phone numbers, and other important information of the people you contact most often.

Add a New Contact

To add a new contact to the Contact app, all you need to know is that person's name and any contact information about that person.

1 Tap the Contacts icon to open the Contacts app. All your existing contacts are listed in alphabetical order.

2 Tap the + icon to display the New Contact panel.

3 Enter the person's first and last name into the First and Last fields. (If you're entering a company or organization, enter that entity's name into the Company field.) Past this point, any information you enter is optional—that is, you only need to enter the contact's name.

4 Tap the + next to Add Phone and enter the contact's phone number.

5 The Contacts app assumes this is the person's home phone number. If this is not the case, tap Home and then select another type of phone from the list—Work, Mobile, and so forth.

6 Add another phone number by tapping the + next to Add Phone and repeating steps 4 and 5.

7 Tap the + next to Add Email, and enter the contact's email address.

8 Scroll down, tap the + next to Add Address, and enter the contact's address.

9 Add other information by tapping the + next to that field and then entering the appropriate data.

10 Include a photo of this person (if you have one) by tapping Add Photo and selecting a picture from your iPad photo library.

11 Tap Done to save the contact.

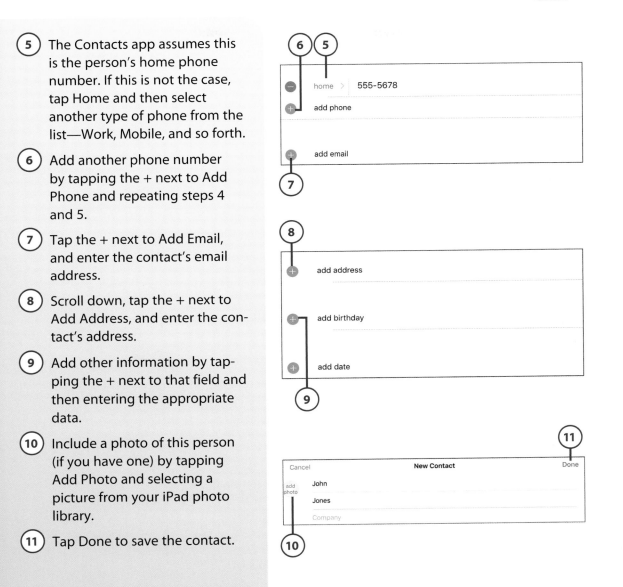

>>>*Go Further*
IMPORT CONTACTS

Although you can manually enter new contacts into the Contacts app, you can also import any existing contacts you have in other apps. This way you don't have to re-enter information you may have entered previously.

You do this by enabling contact sharing with those apps that have their own contacts, such as the Facebook and Mail apps. You do this from your iPad's Settings page.

Start by going to the Settings page and tapping Contacts. Then make sure the Contacts Found in Apps switch is on. (If not, tap it on.) You can then import contacts from within your individual app settings.

For example, to import your Facebook friends, tap Facebook in the left column, go to the Allow These Apps to Use Your Accounts section, and then tap on the Contacts switch. (It may be enabled by default.) To import Twitter contacts, tap Twitter in the left column and then tap Update Contacts.

If you have Gmail contacts or contacts from another email account, you can import these contacts by tapping Mail in the left column. Tap Accounts, select the email account, and make sure that the Contacts switch is tapped on.

Edit a Contact

Sometimes you may want to add new information about a given contact, or change existing info.

(1) From within the Contacts app, tap the name of the contact you want to edit.

Dennis **Hauser**
Dennis **Hauser**
Leslie **Higbee**
J
Ellie McFadden **Jacobson**
John **Jones** ——— **(1)**

2 Tap Edit.

3 Tap within any field you want to edit and make the necessary changes.

4 Tap Done.

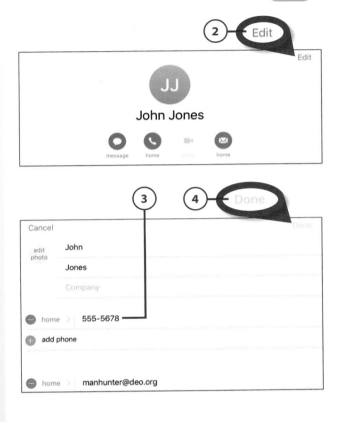

Delete a Contact

You can also delete contacts you're no longer interested in.

1 From within the Contacts app, tap the name of the contact you want to delete.

2 Tap Edit.

3 Scroll down to the bottom of the contact information and tap Delete Contact.

4 When asked to confirm this deletion, tap Delete Contact.

Consolidate Contacts from Multiple Sources

When you import contacts from various sources, you might end up with multiple entries for a single person. Let's say, for example, that you've manually entered Bob Smith's contact information, but also imported that person's info from Facebook and Gmail. You end up with three entries in the Contacts app for Bob Smith, with lots of duplicated information.

What you need to do is to consolidate these multiple contacts into a single contact—what Apple calls a *unified contact*. You do this by "linking" all the individual contacts together.

Automatic Linking

The Contacts app might attempt to automatically link contacts that it thinks are similar. You'll probably still need to manually link some contacts, however.

(1) From within the Contacts app, tap to select one of the contacts you want to link.

(2) Tap Edit.

(3) Scroll to the bottom of the screen and tap Link Contacts. This displays your entire contacts list.

Brett **Miller**

Fred **Miller** ——————————— (1)

Fred **Miller**

Melissa and Andy **Miller**

Edit —(2)

LINKED CONTACTS

⊕ link contacts... ——————— (3)

4 Tap the other contact you want to link.

5 You now see information about the other contact. Tap Link to return to the original contact screen.

6 Tap Done.

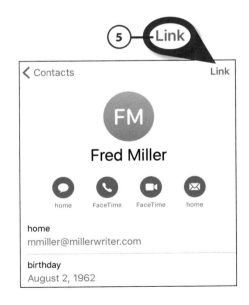

Viewing and Contacting Your Contacts

The Contacts app displays the names of all your contacts in the left column onscreen. When you select a contact, information for that person or entity is displayed on the right side of the screen.

Display a Contact

By default, your contacts are listed in alphabetical order by last name.

(1) From within the Contacts app, on the left side of the screen, tap a letter on the right edge of the list to display all contact names that start with that letter.

(2) Tap a contact name to display that contact's information on the right side of the screen.

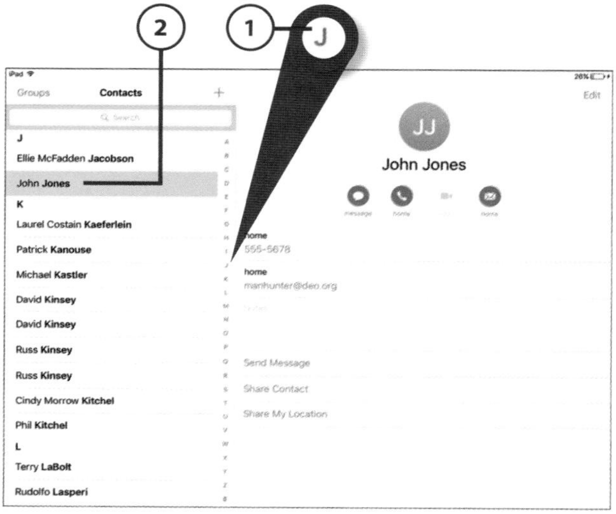

Search for a Contact

If you have a lot of names in your contacts list, it might be quicker and easier to search for a specific person instead of scrolling through all your contacts.

(1) From within the Contacts app, tap within the Search box. Use the onscreen keyboard to begin typing the person's first or last name.

(2) As you type, the Contacts app displays matching names. Tap to select the contact you want.

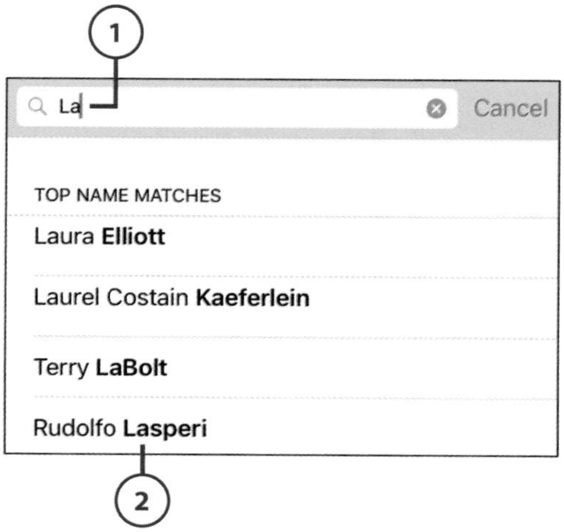

Change How Contacts Are Displayed

By default, your contacts are sorted by last name, but displayed as first name then last name, like this:

Bob Smith

You can change the way your contacts are both sorted and displayed.

1. Tap the Settings icon to display the Settings page.

2. In the left column, tap Contacts.

3. Tap Sort Order.

4. Select either Last, First (the default) or First, Last.

5. Tap Contacts to return to the previous screen.

6. Tap Display Order.

7. Select either First, Last (the default) or Last, First.

8. Tap Contacts to return to the previous screen.

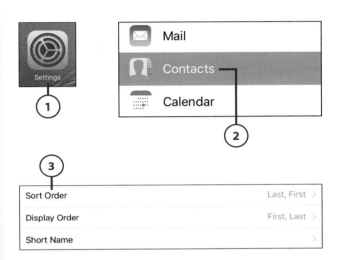

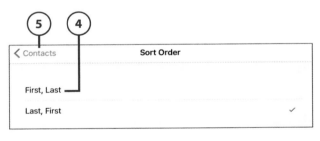

(9) Tap Short Name.

(10) Make sure the Short Name switch is in the on position.

(11) Tap how you want the app's "short names" to display. (Short names are used when space onscreen is at a premium.)

Sort Order	Last, First >
Display Order	First, Last >
Short Name	>

(9)

(10)

Short Name	
First Name & Last Initial	
First Initial & Last Name	
First Name Only	✓
Last Name Only	

Short names are sometimes used to fit more names on screen. Chinese, Japanese, and Korean names are not affected by this setting.

(**11**)

Contact a Contact

Many apps—including Mail, Messages, and FaceTime—use your contacts list to help you easily email or message your contacts. You can also send email to, message, or call (via FaceTime) a person directly from the Contacts app.

(1) From within the Contacts app, tap to select the person you want to contact.

A
Debbie & Troy **Albright**
Barry **Allen**
Pastor **Andrea**

(1)

2 Tap the Mail icon to send an email to this person. (The icon might say "Home" or "Work," if you've specified that person's home or work email address.)

3 Tap Message to send a text message to this person.

4 Tap the FaceTime Call or Call icon to initiate a FaceTime voice call with this person.

5 Tap FaceTime Video or Video icon to initiate a FaceTime video call with this person. (This icon is grayed out if the person isn't currently online and capable of receiving FaceTime calls.)

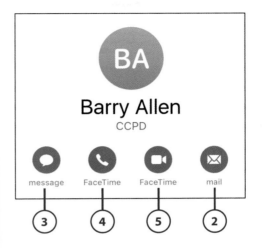

FaceTime and Messaging

To learn more about FaceTime and text messages, turn to Chapter 11, "Video Chatting and Texting."

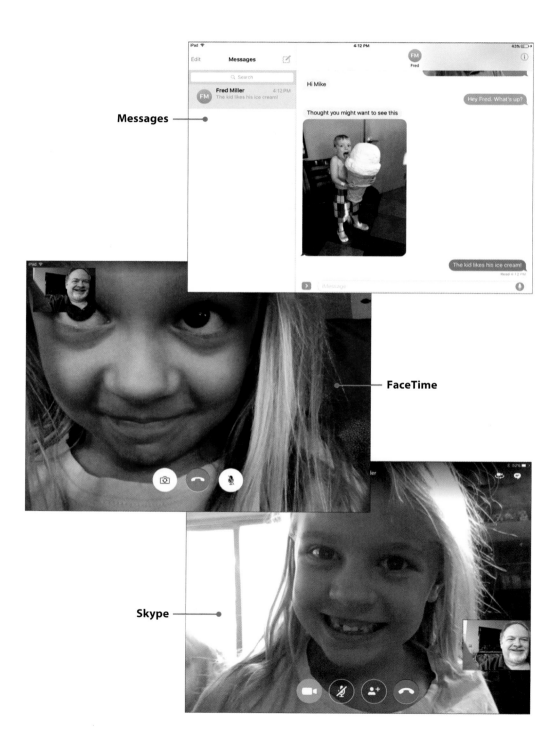

Messages

FaceTime

Skype

In this chapter, you learn how to communicate with friends and family using the Messages, FaceTime, and Skype apps.

→ Text Messaging with the Messages App
→ Video Chatting and More with FaceTime
→ Calling Other Friends with Skype

Video Chatting and Texting

You've learned how to communicate with friends, family, and businesses with email. But email is slow (relatively) and not at all like having a conversation in real time.

For that, we turn to text messaging and video chatting. Text messaging, using the iPad's Messages app, is great for sending short thoughts and notes. Video chatting, using the FaceTime or Skype apps, is better when you want one-on-one, face-to-face conversation.

Text Messaging with the Messages App

Let's start with text messaging, like you do on your phone. On your iPad, you use the Messages app to send text messages over Wi-Fi via Apple's iMessage service. Your messages can include photos, videos, and other files you attach to the basic text.

>>>*Go Further*

iMESSAGE

The Messages app utilizes Apple's iMessage service, which connects Apple devices via Wi-Fi. (It also connects iPhones via cellular service, if they're not connected to a wireless network.) iMessage is a lot like phone-based SMS/MMS text messaging, but is an Apple-only service.

At present iMessage is not available to users of Windows computers or Android phones or computers. Nor can you use iMessage to contact cell phone users via their text message services; you can only connect to other iPad and iPhone users via the Messages app.

Send and Receive Text Messages

The Messages app lets you send text messages to any of your friends and family who have an iPad, iPhone, or Mac computer. It's as easy as tapping out a message on the onscreen keyboard and then tapping the Send button.

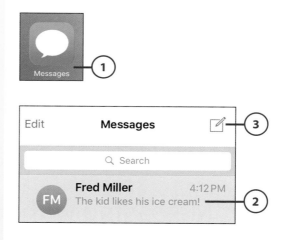

1. Tap the Messages icon to open the Messages app.

2. Previous conversations are listed in the left column. Tap a conversation to send another message to this person.

3. Tap the Compose icon to start a new conversation.

4 Tap in the To field and use the onscreen keyboard to begin entering the name or email address of the person you want to talk with.

5 As you type, the Messages app displays a list of matching people from your contacts list. Tap the name of the person you want to text with or finish entering the email address of the person.

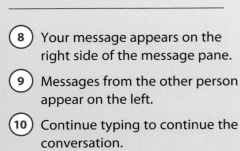

Group Messages

To send a message to a group of people, enter multiple names into the To box. Everyone listed here will receive and be able to respond to your message—and all subsequent responses.

6 Type your message into the iMessage box.

7 Tap the blue Send icon.

Emoji

To include an emoji character in your text, tap the Emoji (smiley face) button on the onscreen keyboard and make a selection from there.

8 Your message appears on the right side of the message pane.

9 Messages from the other person appear on the left.

10 Continue typing to continue the conversation.

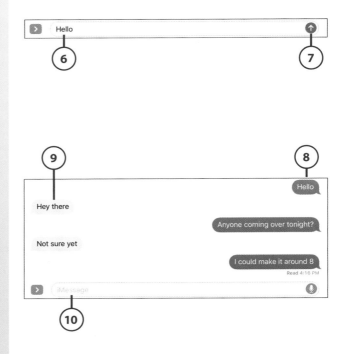

Send an Audio Message

Instead of sending a plain text message, you can record and send a short audio message. Just tap the Record button and start talking!

1 From within the Messages app, resume an existing conversation or start a new conversation and enter the recipient's name into the To field.

2 In the iMessage box, press and hold the microphone icon.

3 Begin talking. While you talk, make sure you keep pressing the microphone icon. You see the waveform of your voice in the iMessage box.

4 When you're done talking, lift your finger from the screen.

5 Tap the Play button to hear what you recorded.

6 Tap the Send button to send the recording to the other person.

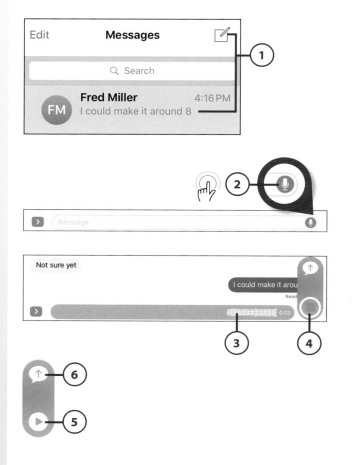

Send a Video Message

Just as you can record and send short audio messages, you can also record and send short (ten-second max) video messages, using your iPad's front-facing FaceTime camera.

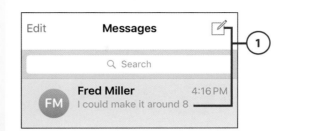

1. From within the Messages app, resume an existing conversation or start a new conversation and enter the recipient's name into the To field.

2. Tap the right arrow next to the iMessage box. (You don't have to tap this if you see three icons next to the box instead.)

3. This displays three new icons. Tap the center icon to display the video/scribble panel at the bottom.

(4) Tap the camera icon. This expands the panel and activates the FaceTime camera.

(5) Look into the camera and tap the red Record button. Start talking!

(6) When you've talked for ten seconds, the recording automatically stops. You can stop the recording sooner by tapping the Record button again.

(7) You now see the video you recorded. If you like it, tap the blue Send button.

(8) If you don't like the video, tap the Back button and try again, or tap the down arrow at the top right to return to the conversation.

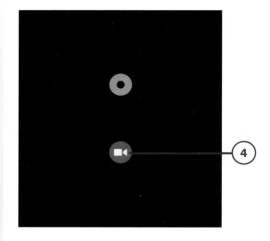

9 Tap the middle icon again to redisplay the onscreen keyboard.

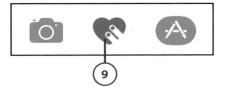

Send a Scribble

The Messages app also lets you scribble or draw onscreen and send that scribble to the person you're talking to.

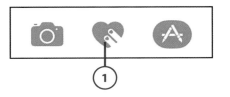

1 From within a conversation, expand the icons to the left of the iMessage box and tap the center icon to display the video/ scribble panel at the bottom.

2 Tap the round color icon to display the available colors.

3 Choose a color.

4 Use your finger to draw onscreen.

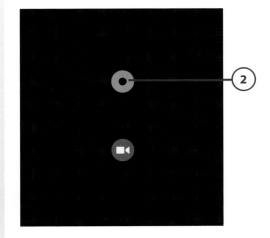

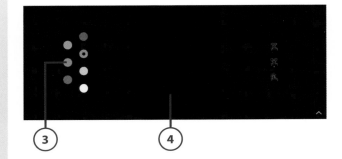

⑤ When you're done scribbling, tap the blue up arrow to send the scribble.

Send a Photo

Just as with phone-based MMS (multimedia messaging), you can send photos to people you're messaging in the Messages app. You can send photos stored in your iPad's photo library, or take a new photo (like a selfie) and send it.

① From within a conversation, expand the icons to the left of the iMessage box and tap the camera icon to display the photo panel at the bottom.

② Tap Photo Library to send a photo stored on your iPad.

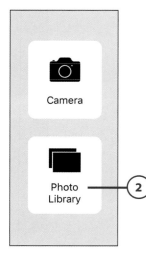

(3) Tap the album that contains the photo you want to send.

(4) Tap the desired photo.

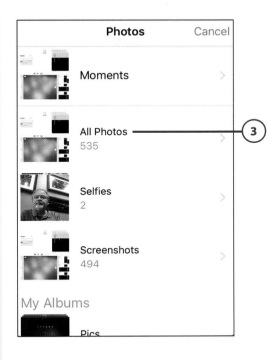

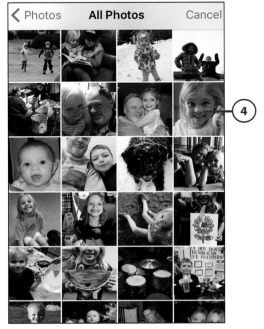

(**5**) Tap Use. The photo is added to the conversation pane.

(**6**) Tap the Send icon to send the photo to the person you're texting with.

(**7**) Tap Camera to send a new photo.

(**8**) Tap the camera icon to switch from the rear camera to the front camera.

(**9**) Aim your iPad and tap the big round icon to take the picture.

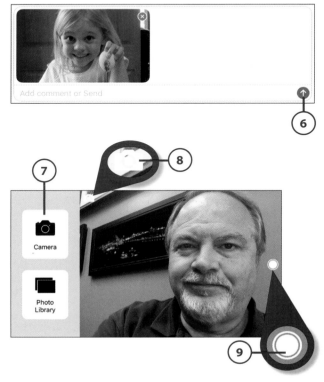

Take a Video

You can also use this screen to take a video instead of a still photo. Just tap Video and then press the red button to start recording.

(10) You see the picture you took in the conversation pane. If you like it, tap the send icon. (If not, tap the X to delete it.) The picture is now sent to the person you're texting with.

Video Clips

The Messages app includes a number as preselected short video clips that you can send to your friends. Tap the third ("A") icon to display and select available clips to send.

Video Chatting and More with FaceTime

Text messaging is nice, but sometimes you want a face-to-face conversation with someone. Maybe you're snowbirding down south while your grandkids are still in school up north. Maybe your siblings live in a different part of the country than you do. Maybe you or one of your family members is stuck at home and you just want to check in or keep in touch.

When a text message or phone call isn't good enough, use Apple's FaceTime app to video chat in real-time with your friends and family. All you need is your iPad—and its built-in camera and microphone. Every call you make is free!

Start a Video Chat

You can use FaceTime to video chat with anyone who has an iPad or iPhone that includes a front-facing camera.

1) Tap the FaceTime icon to open the FaceTime app.

2) You see yourself, via your iPad's front-facing FaceTime camera. Overlaid on the left side of the screen is a list of people with whom you've recently chatted. Tap Video at the top of this pane.

3) To chat again with one of the people listed, tap their name.

4) To chat with someone new, enter that person's name, email, or phone number into the text box. (Alternatively, tap the + icon to select a person from your contacts list.)

5) As you type, matching contacts are displayed. Those that are online and available to chat have a bright camera and/or phone icon next to their names. Select the person you want from this list, or finish typing the person's email address or phone number.

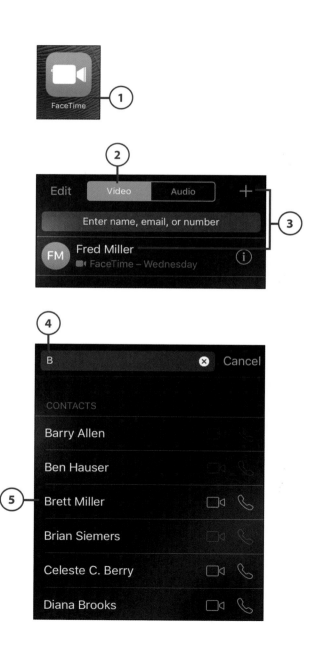

6 FaceTime dials the other person.

7 If that person is available and answers, you see that person onscreen. A small thumbnail in the top-left corner of the screen displays what the other person is seeing (You). Have a nice conversation!

8 Tap the screen to show the control buttons at the bottom.

9 Tap the Mute button to mute the sound. Tap the button again to resume normal conversation.

10 Tap the Flip button to switch from front-facing to rear-facing camera.

11 Tap the red End button to end the chat.

Fred Miller

connecting...

You

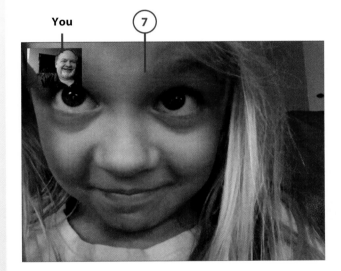

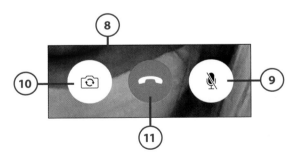

Answer a Video Chat Request

Just as you can call others via Face-Time, they can also call you. How do you answer a video call? By pressing a button and talking, of course!

① When someone calls you via FaceTime, your screen changes to the FaceTime screen and you see two icons at the bottom. Tap Accept to accept the call. (Tap Decline to not answer.)

② Your call starts—so start talking!

③ Tap the screen to display the control buttons at the bottom.

④ Tap the End button to end the chat.

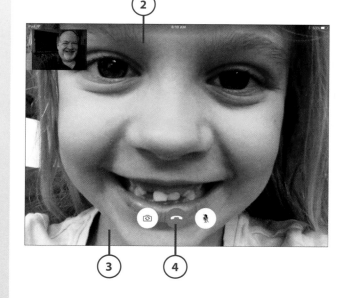

Make an Audio Call

FaceTime also lets you participate in audio calls—like phone calls but from your iPad to other Apple devices. This is good if you just want to talk and don't need to see the other person, if you're not quite presentable enough to show yourself to the other person, or if you're talking to someone who doesn't have a front-facing camera in their device.

(1) From within the FaceTime app, tap Audio at the top of the left pane.

(2) Enter or select the person you want to call.

(3) FaceTime dials the other person. If that person is available and answers, you see the FaceTime controls onscreen. Start talking!

(4) Tap the Mute button to mute the sound. Tap the button again to resume normal conversation.

(5) Tap the FaceTime button to turn this audio call into a video call.

(6) Tap the red End button to end this call.

Calling Other Friends with Skype

As convenient and easy-to-use as FaceTime is, it only lets you call people who have Apple devices. How can you chat with friends and family who have Samsung or Nexus smartphones or tablets, or Windows PCs?

The answer is to use Skype, a similar video-calling service that operates across all platforms. There are Skype apps not only for Apple's iPad and iPhones, but also for Android phones and tablets, Windows and Mac computers, and Xbox One game systems.

Bottom line, you can use Skype to video chat (and voice chat and text message) with just about anyone using just about any type of device. And, like FaceTime, your user-to-user calls are free.

Not Always Free

Skype is free when you're calling another Skype user, via your Skype accounts. Skype charges if you use the Skype service to dial a traditional telephone number. (Which you can do, for audio calls.)

Log into Skype

To use Skype, you must download the Skype app from Apple's App Store (it's free) and have a Skype account (also free). You can create a new Skype account or sign in with an existing Microsoft ID (but not an Apple ID).

(1) Tap the Skype icon to launch the Skype app.

2 The first time you launch the Skype app you're prompted to either sign in with your Skype name or email or create a new account. If this is your first time using Skype, tap Create Account and follow the onscreen instructions.

3 If you already have a Skype account (maybe you've used it before on another device), enter your Skype login information and tap the right arrow.

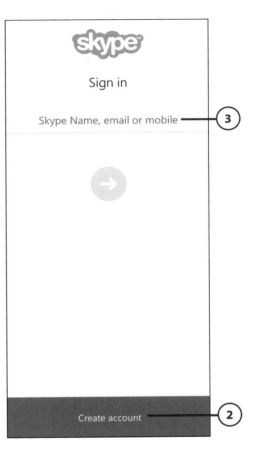

Add Contacts

To call someone on Skype, that person has to be added to your Skype contacts list. (This is separate from your normal iPad contacts list.) You have to invite someone to be a contact, and they need to accept your invitation.

(1) From within the Skype app, tap the Contacts icon to display the Contacts pane. All contacts you've previous listed are displayed here.

(2) Tap the Add icon to add a new contact via the Add Contact pane.

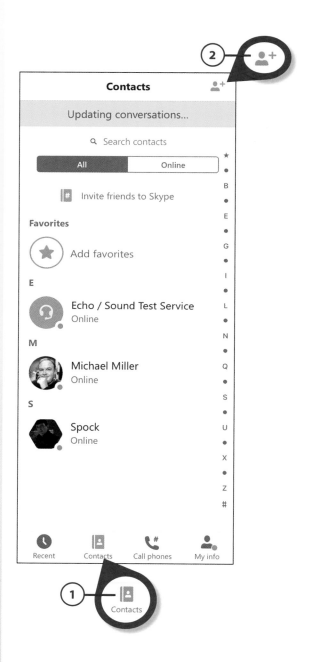

(**3**) Make sure the People tab is selected. (You probably don't want to talk to one of Skype's automated "bot" callers.)

(**4**) Enter the person's real name, Skype name, or email address into the Search box.

(**5**) Skype displays a list of matching names. Tap the person you want to contact.

(**6**) Tap the Send Contact Request button. This person is sent a contact request via Skype and can either accept or decline.

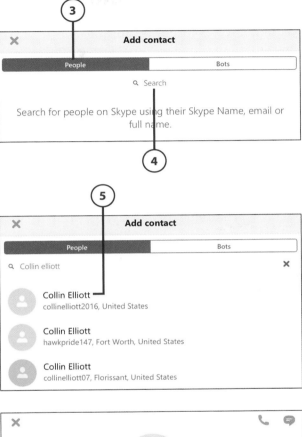

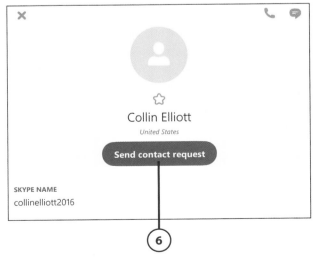

Make a Video Call

Video chatting on Skype is similar to video chatting with FaceTime. Just make sure the other person is online and signed into the Skype service.

(1) From within the Skype app, tap the Contacts icon to display the Contacts pane.

(2) Tap the name of the person you want to call. (Anyone currently online and signed into Skype has a green dot next to their name.) This displays the conversation pane for that person on the right side of the screen.

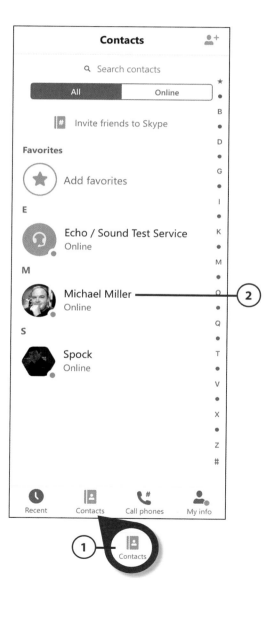

3 Type into the Type a Message Here box to text message this person.

4 Tap the Phone icon to initiate an audio call.

5 Tap the Video icon to initiate a video call.

6 Skype dials the other person. If he accepts your call, the screen changes and you see this person fullscreen on your iPad. (Your thumbnail appears in the lower-right corner of the screen.) Start talking!

5 **4**

8:11 AM

● Michael Miller
Online

Wednesday 2:46 PM

You and **Michael Miller** are now contacts.
You have shared your contact details

Call, 3min 55s

Type a message here

3

6

You

(7) Tap the screen to show the command buttons at the bottom.

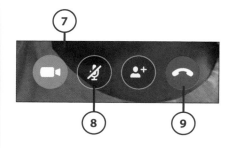

(8) Tap the Mute button to mute the audio. Tap this button again to return to normal conversation.

(9) Tap the red End button to end this call.

>>>Go Further
FACETIME OR SKYPE?

FaceTime and Skype are similar services. Which should you use?

In my opinion, FaceTime is a little easier to use than Skype, probably because it works within the Apple infrastructure. If you're talking to someone who owns an Apple device (iPhone, iPad, or Mac computer), FaceTime is the obvious way to go.

On the other hand, if you want to talk to someone who *doesn't* have an Apple device, FaceTime simply isn't an option. Skype's the one to choose here, and it works just fine.

Facebook

Pinterest

Twitter

LinkedIn

In this chapter, you learn how to share your thoughts and experiences online via Facebook, Pinterest, Twitter, and other social networks.

→ Understanding Social Networking
→ Using Facebook on Your iPad
→ Using Pinterest on Your iPad
→ Using Twitter on Your iPad
→ Using LinkedIn on Your iPad

12

Getting Social with Facebook, Pinterest, and Other Social Networks

Social networking is all the rage. We're talking online communities like Facebook, Pinterest, and Twitter, places where you can go to share what you're doing with your online friends, and find out what they're up to, too.

If you've never used a social network before, it's a whole new world to explore—and you can do it from the comfort of your iPad. If you have used Facebook or another social network, you need to install the appropriate app(s) on your iPad and learn how they work.

Understanding Social Networking

A *social network* is an Internet-based service that hosts a community of users and makes it easy for those users to communicate with one another. Social networks enable users to share experiences and opinions with one another, and thus keep in touch with friends and family members, no matter where they're located.

The goal of a social network is to create a network of online "friends," and then share your activities with them via a series of message posts. These posts are short text messages, sometimes called *status updates*, which can be viewed by all your friends on the site. A status update can be text only, or contain photos, videos, and links to other web pages.

Your online friends read your posts, as well as posts from other friends, in a continuously updated stream. On Facebook, this stream is called the *News Feed* (other sites call it different things), and it's the one place where you can read updates from all your online friends and family; it's where you find out what's really happening.

There are many social networks on the Internet, and Facebook is the largest and most popular among users of all ages, including older users. Other social networks popular among those 50+ include LinkedIn, Pinterest, and Twitter.

More About Social Media

Learn more about Facebook, Pinterest, Twitter, and other social networks in my companion book, *My Social Media for Seniors*, available online and in bookstores everywhere.

Using Facebook on Your iPad

With more than one billion users worldwide, chances are many of your friends and family are already using Facebook. This leading social network was launched by Mark Zuckerberg while he was a student at Harvard in 2004. Facebook (originally called "thefacebook") was originally intended as a site where college students could socialize online. Sensing opportunity beyond the college market,

Facebook opened its site to high school students in 2005, and then to all users over age 13 in 2006.

Although Facebook started as a network for college students, today it's the social network of choice, especially for older users. In fact, half of all people aged 65 or older who are online make Facebook their hub for online social activity—and browse the site for at least an hour each day.

People of all ages use Facebook to connect with current family members and reconnect with friends from the past. If you want to know what your friends from high school or the old neighborhood have been up to over the past several decades, chances are you can find them on Facebook.

In addition, Facebook helps you keep your friends informed about what you're doing. Write one post and it's seen by hundreds of your online "friends." It's the easiest way I know to connect with almost everyone you know.

Like all the social networks discussed in this chapter, Facebook is completely free to use. You access Facebook from its iPad app, which you can download from Apple's App Store.

Navigate Facebook's iPad App

The first time you launch the Facebook app, you're prompted to either sign into an existing account (if you have one) or create a new account. Follow the onscreen instructions to proceed from there.

Whenever you open the Facebook app, you see the News Feed screen. The News Feed is where you view status updates from all your Facebook friends, and it looks different depending on how you're holding your iPad.

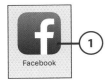

Facebook

1 Tap the Facebook icon to launch the Facebook app.

(2) In portrait mode (held vertically), you see the normal screen with no additional sidebars. All the navigation icons are at the bottom of the screen; tap News Feed to display the News Feed.

(3) In landscape mode (held horizontally), you see the News Feed on the left with a sidebar on the right side of the screen that displays upcoming events, the Chat panel (with favorite friends listed), trending topics, and more. Scroll down the screen to view more updates in the News Feed; refresh the News Feed by pulling down from the top of the screen and then releasing.

(4) Tap the down arrow in the top-right corner to access app settings.

(5) When a person you know sees you on Facebook, she might send you a friend request. You have to be friends with someone on Facebook to see their posts in the News Feed. To view your friend requests, tap the Requests icon.

(6) Tap the Notifications icon to view notifications from Facebook.

(7) Tap the More icon to view your favorite pages and groups, and to configure Facebook settings.

Pages and Groups

In addition to posts from individuals, Facebook also offers official "pages" from companies and celebrities, as well as topic-specific groups. You can "like" a public page to receive posts from that page, or join a group to post and receive messages from other members of that group.

Read and Respond to Posts

The messages people post to Facebook are called *status updates* or *posts*. You read and respond to posts from your friends on the News Feed screen.

1. From the News Feed screen, tap the Like icon to like a post. Tap and hold the Like icon to choose from a range of responses, from Love to Sad to Angry.

2. Tap the Comment icon to comment on a post.

3. Tap the Share icon to share a post.

4. Tap the poster's name to view that person's Timeline page. (The Timeline page serves as a person's home base, displaying his personal profile, posts he's made, and photos he's uploaded.)

5. If the post includes a photo, tap the photo to view it full screen.

Dinah Lance
Yesterday at 3:38 PM

Can you believe what that guy said?

Like   Comment   Share

Dinah Lance
Just now

Here's something cute -- grandson Jackson out for a walk.

Like   Comment   Share

6 If the post includes a video, tap the video thumbnail to begin playback. (Some videos may play back automatically when you scroll to them.)

7 If the post includes a link to another web page, tap the link or thumbnail to view that page on a new screen.

Michael Miller
Tuesday at 1:49 PM · 🌐

We were watching some old home videos last night and stumbled across this one from November of 2010. This is granddaughter Hayley, then about 2 years old (she's 8 now), discovering the video camera and showing us all she knows. Then as now, Hayley is whipsmart and a bit of a showoff. Then again, she has (and had) plenty to show off. This is really cute -- enjoy!

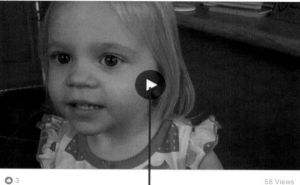

👍 3   58 Views

👍 Like   💬 Comment   ➤ Share

6

Michael Miller
Tuesday at 11:07 AM · 🌐

Ross Macdonald is my favorite genre writer, and one of my favorite writers, period. I agree that he's the best of the holy trinity of crime writers, and arguably the most influential. If you've never read any Lew Archer novels, now is the time to get started. Archer is a tough private dick with the sensitive soul of a poet. They're more than crime fiction, they're stories that wrap around you and make you think and feel.

Why you should get reacquainted with mystery novelist Ross Macdonald

Ross Macdonald's work — once thought of as better than Chandler's or Hammett's — has been revived for a new generation of readers by the Library of America, which has published two vol...

seattletimes.com/entertainment/...

👍 2   2 Comments

👍 Like   💬 Comment   ➤ Share

7

Post a Status Update

You create new status updates from the Facebook app's News Feed screen. The status updates you post are displayed on your friends' News Feeds.

1. In the What's on Your Mind? box, tap the Status icon to display the Update Status pane.

2. Type the text of your message into the What's on Your Mind? area.

3. Tap Photo/Video to include a photo or video with your post.

4. Tap Live Video to shoot live video and share with your friends.

5. Tap Check In to include your location in your post.

6. Tap Feeling/Activity to tell others how you feel or what you're doing.

7. Tap the Tag Friends icon to tag another person in your post.

8. Change who can see the post by tapping the Privacy button beneath your name.

9. Tap Post to post the status update.

More About Facebook

Learn more about Facebook in my companion book, *My Facebook for Seniors*, available online and in bookstores everywhere.

Using Pinterest on Your iPad

Facebook isn't the only social network that may interest you. Pinterest is a newer, different type of social network with particular appeal to middle-aged and older women—although there are a growing number of male users, too.

Unlike Facebook, which lets you post text-based status updates, Pinterest is all about images. The site consists of a collection of virtual online boards that people use to share pictures they find interesting. Users "pin" photos and other images to their personal message boards, and then they share their pins with online friends.

You can pin images of anything—clothing, furniture, recipes, do-it-yourself projects, and the like. Your Pinterest friends can then "repin" your images to their boards—and on and on.

Like Facebook, Pinterest is totally free to use. You access Pinterest from the Pinterest app.

View and Repin Pins

You can download the Pinterest app, for free, from Apple's App Store. The first time you launch the app, you're prompted to either sign into an existing account (if you have one) or create a new account. Follow the onscreen instructions to proceed from there.

1. Tap the Pinterest icon to launch the Pinterest app. You see a variety of pins.

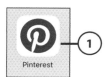

2 The pins in your feed include items pinned by people you follow, as well as recommended pins from Pinterest. Tap a pin to view it full screen.

3 Press and hold a pin to display the command icons.

4 Keep your finger pressed to the screen and move it to the Pin It icon to repin this item to one of your boards.

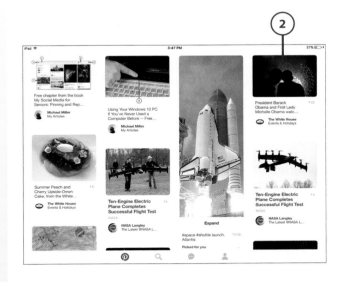

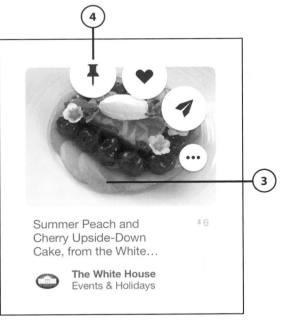

Summer Peach and
Cherry Upside-Down
Cake, from the White…

The White House
Events & Holidays

5 Accept or edit the current description of the item.

6 Scroll down and select which board you want to pin to (or tap Create a Board to pin to a new board). The item is then pinned to that board.

Not Always Welcome

Some websites don't want people to pin their images, and code their pages to prohibit pinning. If you try to pin from one of these pages, you get a message that no pinnable images have been found. If you happen to pin an image that some entity owns and doesn't want you to pin, they can ask Pinterest to take down the pin. (Legally, Pinterest says it's not responsible for any copyright claims for items pinned to its site.)

Pin from a Website

Many Pinterest users find images outside of Pinterest to pin to their boards. When you see an image on a website, you can easily pin it to a Pinterest board.

1 From the Safari web browser, navigate to the web page that contains the image you want to pin and then tap the Share button in the browser to display the Share panel.

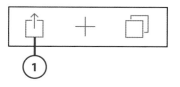

2 Tap Pinterest to display the Pick an Image panel. (If you don't see the Pinterest icon, tap More to display it.)

3 You see thumbnails of all the images on that web page. Tap the thumbnail you want to pin.

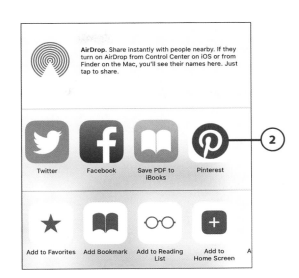

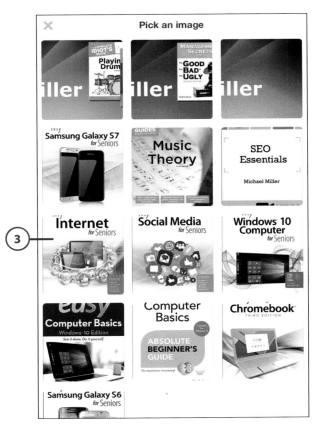

(**4**) Accept or edit the description for this pin.

(**5**) Tap the board you want to pin to (or tap Create a Board to pin to a new board). The selected image is pinned to that board on Pinterest.

More About Pinterest

Learn more about Pinterest in my companion book, *My Pinterest*, available online and in bookstores everywhere.

Using Twitter on Your iPad

You may have heard of Twitter, even if you haven't used it yourself. It's one of the more popular social media out there, although it isn't that widely used by those 50 and up. It's most popular among users in their twenties and thirties.

Twitter is kind of like Facebook, but with only posts—called *tweets*—and no groups or pages or any of that. Tweets are short posts (140 characters or less), kind of like text messages, although they can include photos, videos, and links to pages on the Web.

As happens with the other social networks, you identify people you want to follow, then you see all of their tweets in your feed. People who follow you see your tweets in their feed.

Read Tweets

Twitter is completely free to use. You have to sign up to use it, however, which you can do from the Twitter app, available for free from Apple's App Store.

(1) Tap the Twitter icon to open the Twitter app.

(2) Tap the Home icon to display your feed. Tweets from people you follow are listed here.

(3) To "like" a tweet, tap the heart icon.

(4) To retweet a tweet (that is, post it to the people who follow you), tap the retweet icon, then tap Retweet.

Create a New Tweet

Tweets can be a maximum of 140 characters long. You can include photos, videos, and web links in your tweets.

(1) From the Twitter app, tap the New Tweet icon at the top of the screen.

(2) Use the onscreen keyboard to enter the text for your tweet. Remember to make it no more than 140 characters long!

(3) To tweet a photo or video, tap the camera icon and then select a photo stored on your phone. (The photo or video doesn't count toward the 140-character limit.)

(4) Tap the Tweet button to post your tweet.

Hashtags

Twitter encourages the use of *hashtags* in their tweets. A hashtag is a word or phrase (with no spaces between words) preceded by the hash (#) character, like this: **#hashtag**. Use hashtags to link your tweet to other tweets with the same hashtag; click a hashtag to see other tweets with that hashtag.

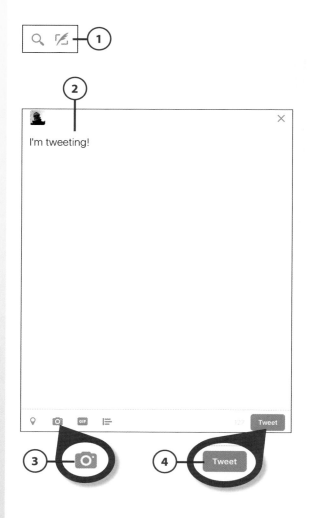

Using LinkedIn on Your iPad

LinkedIn is a social network with a business bent. It's designed primarily for business professionals, and it's a good way to keep in touch with others in your profession, including people you've worked with in the past. LinkedIn is particularly useful if you're in the market for a new job; it's easy to make new contacts and do your business networking online.

Navigate the LinkedIn App

Like all the other social networks, LinkedIn is free to use; all you have to do is create an account and enter a little information about yourself. You access LinkedIn on your iPad from the LinkedIn app, which is available for download (for free) from Apple's App Store.

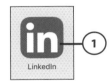

1. Tap the LinkedIn icon to open the LinkedIn app.

2. Tap Home to view posts from people you follow.

3. Tap My Network to connect with other users and view suggestions of people to follow.

4. Tap Messaging to exchange private messages with other LinkedIn users.

5. Tap Notifications to view recent activity from the people you follow.

6. Tap Me to view and edit your own personal profile on the LinkedIn site.

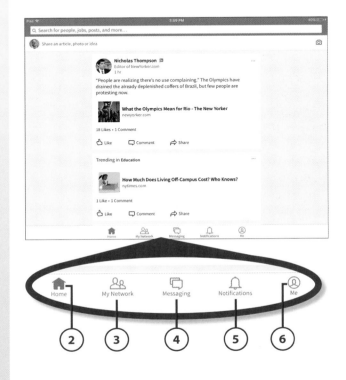

Create a New Post

You can share notes, articles, photos, and more with the people you're linked to on LinkedIn.

1. From the app's Home screen, tap within the Share an Article, Photo, or Idea box to display the Share screen.

2. Enter the text of your message within the text box.

3. Tap the Link icon to include a link to a web page or article.

4. Tap the Photo icon to include a photo with your post.

5. Tap the Share button to post your update.

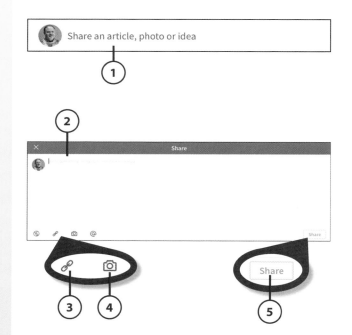

>>>Go Further

PRIVACY ON SOCIAL NETWORKS

It's important, when using any social network, to be aware of your privacy. It's easy to think of Facebook or any social network as a personal diary, but it's not. These social networks are extremely public; when you post a message or photo, it could be viewed by millions of people you don't even know.

If you value your privacy, you want to configure your settings on each network so that what you post is seen only by select people. Ideally, you want only your friends to see what you post; that means changing the posting privacy options from public to another more private setting. In addition, some networks (such as Facebook) let you adjust your privacy on a post-by-post basis. This way you could post something that you want your family members to see but don't want to show to co-workers or other friends.

How you adjust a network's privacy settings differs from network to network. In the Facebook app, for example, tap the Menu button (down arrow) at the top-right corner and then tap Privacy Shortcuts; everything you need to configure, privacy-wise, is listed there.

Of course, the best way to keep some things private on a social network is to not post them at all. You're old enough to know when to be discreet; resist the urge to post private information, private thoughts, and photos that ought to stay private. If you don't post 'em, nobody'll see 'em.

Finally, never, ever post your private contact information on a social network—or anywhere, online, for that matter. If you don't want strangers calling you up or showing up at your door, don't share your phone number or street address with them. In addition, never post about going out of town (or even out on the town); it's not unheard of for burglars to troll the social networks so they'll know when a house is empty and ripe for the looting.

Bottom line: Be careful out there!

Calendar app

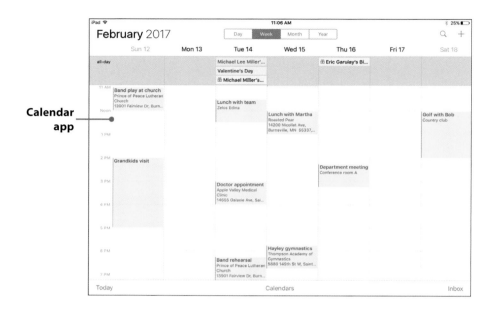

Reminders app

In this chapter, you learn how to use the iPad's Calendar and Reminders apps to manage your schedule and to-do lists.

→ Using the Calendar App
→ Using the Reminders App

13

Staying Organized with Calendar and Reminders

Sometimes it's tough to keep track of your time. How are supposed to juggle all the various things you're supposed to do—appointments, events, and everything that's on your to-do list?

Fortunately, you can use your iPad to help you manage just about everything on your schedule. Use the Calendar app to manage your appointments and events, and the Reminders app to track all the items on your to-do list.

Using the Calendar App

Apple's Calendar app was included with your iPad. Use the Calendar app to track everything you have on your schedule—what the app calls *events*.

View Events

You can view your calendar by day, week, month, or year.

(1) From the Home screen, tap the Calendar icon to open the Calendar app.

(2) Tap the Day tab to view a daily schedule. Scroll down to view times later in the day.

(3) Swipe the calendar to the left to view the next day.

(4) Swipe the calendar to the right to view the previous day.

(5) Tap a specific date at the top of the calendar to view events for that day.

(6) Tap a specific event on the calendar to view details about that event.

(7) Tap Delete Event to delete the selected event.

(8) Tap the Week tab to view all events this week.

(9) Swipe the calendar to the left to view the next week.

(10) Swipe the calendar to the right to view the previous week.

(11) Tap an event to view details about that event.

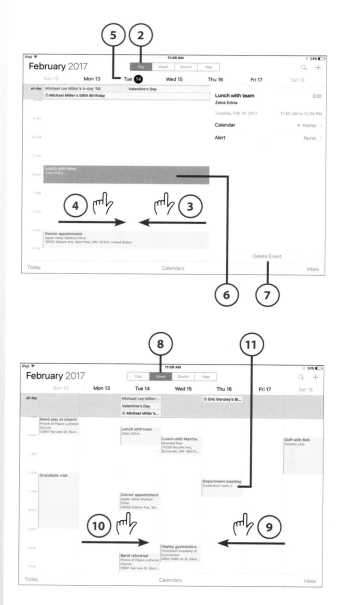

12 Tap the Month tab to view all events this month.

13 Scroll down the page to view events in the future.

14 Tap an event to view details about that event.

15 Tap the Year tab to view a yearly calendar.

16 Tap within a given month to view that monthly calendar.

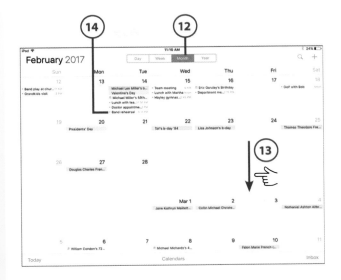

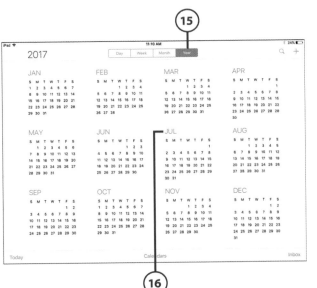

Add a New Event

By default, the Calendar app imports important dates from your contacts list—birthdays, anniversaries, and the like. It also creates events for major national holidays. (These show up in color shading.)

The real value of the Calendar app, of course, is evident when you add your own events to the calendar. You can add events for meetings, parties, sports games—you name it.

(1) From within the Calendar app, navigate to the day, week, or month you want and then tap the New (+) icon.

(2) Tap within the Title field and add the name of this event.

(3) Tap within the Location field and enter the location of this event. (This information is optional; the more detail you include—such as the street address—the better.)

(4) If this event lasts all day, tap on the All-Day switch. Otherwise...

(5) Tap the Starts field to expand the panel.

6 Use the spin control to select the date of the event.

7 Use the spin control to select the start time of the event. (The date, hour, minutes, and AM/PM controls spin separately.)

8 If necessary, select the appropriate time zone for the event.

9 Tap the Ends field to select the end date and time for the event.

10 If you need to travel to this event, tap Travel Time and add the appropriate travel time.

11 Tap Add to add this event to your calendar.

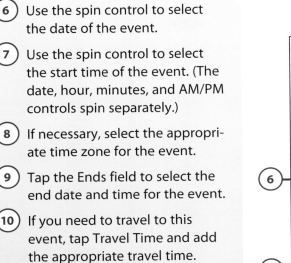

Cancel	New Event	Add

| Starts | Jan 4, 2017 | 11:00 AM |

	Mon Jan 2	9	58
	Tue Jan 3	10	59
6	**Wed Jan 4**	**11**	**00** **AM**
	Thu Jan 5	12	01 PM
	Fri Jan 6	1	02

8 Time Zone	Chicago >
9 Ends	12:00 PM
Repeat	Never >
10 Travel Time	None >

Create a Recurring Event

Some events repeat. For example, you might have a standing golf match every Saturday morning, or a neighborhood meeting the first Monday of each month. Fortunately, the Calendar app lets you create recurring events.

1 From within the Calendar app, create a new app as normal and then tap the Repeat field.

All-day	◯
Starts	Jan 4, 2017 11:00 AM
Ends	12:00 PM
1 Repeat	Never >
Travel Time	None >

(2) Tap how often this event recurs—Every Day, Every Week, Every 2 Weeks, Every Month, or Every Year.

(3) If the occurrence is more complex, tap Custom.

(4) Tap Frequency to select how often the event recurs—Daily, Weekly, Monthly, or Yearly.

(5) Tap Every to determine how the event recurs—every 1, 2, 3, or so days, weeks, months, or years.

(6) If you selected Weekly frequency, select which day(s) of the week this event recurs.

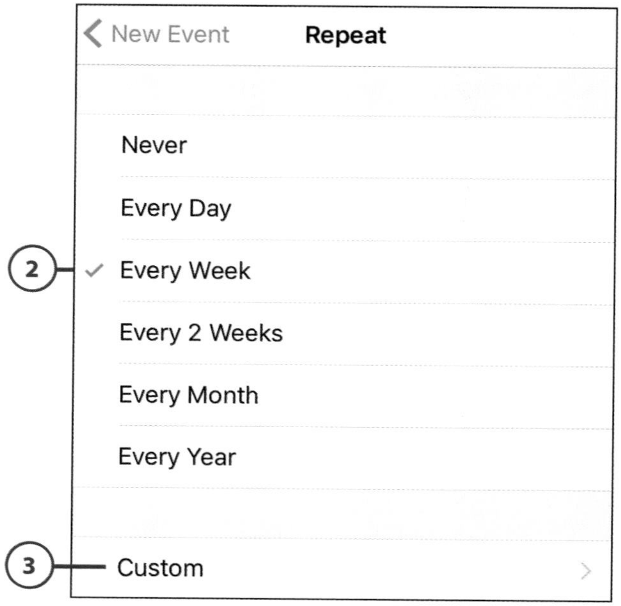

⟨ New Event   **Repeat**

Never

Every Day

(2) ✓ Every Week

Every 2 Weeks

Every Month

Every Year

(3) Custom   ⟩

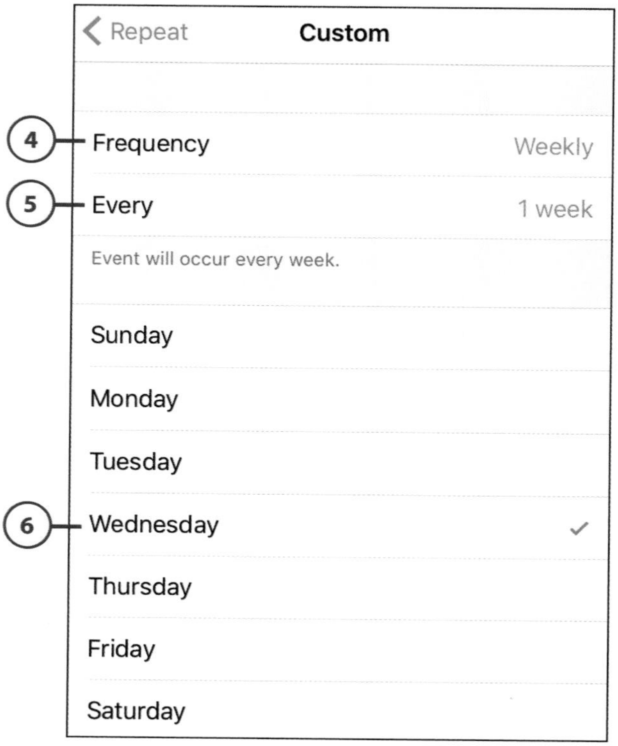

⟨ Repeat   **Custom**

(4) Frequency   Weekly

(5) Every   1 week

Event will occur every week.

Sunday

Monday

Tuesday

(6) Wednesday   ✓

Thursday

Friday

Saturday

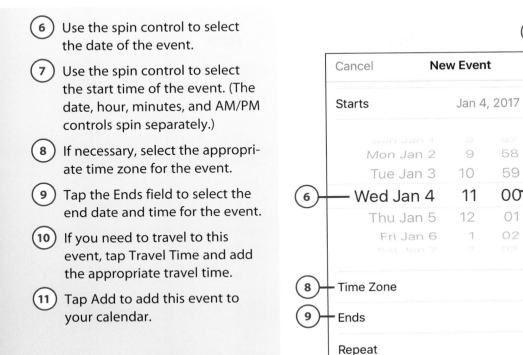

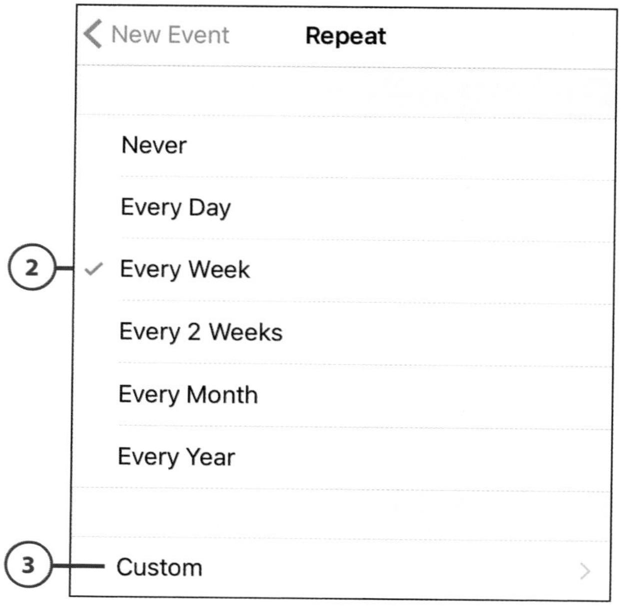

Never

Every Day

(2) ✓ Every Week

Every 2 Weeks

Every Month

Every Year

(3) Custom   >

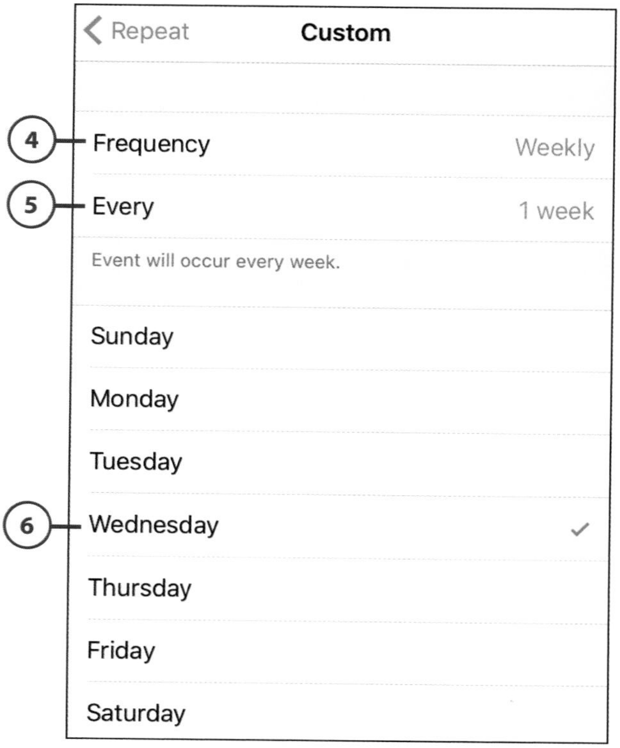

< Repeat   Custom

(4) Frequency   Weekly

(5) Every   1 week

Event will occur every week.

Sunday

Monday

Tuesday

(6) Wednesday   ✓

Thursday

Friday

Saturday

(7) If you selected Monthly frequency, select which day(s) of the month this event recurs. *Or...*

(8) Tap On The and select which day(s) you want (First Sunday of the month, Second Thursday of the month, and so forth).

(9) If you selected Yearly frequency, select which month(s) of the year and days of the week this event recurs.

(10) Tap the back arrow to return to the Repeat panel, then again to return to the New Event panel.

❮ Repeat	**Custom**	
Frequency		Monthly
Every		Month
Event will occur every month.		
Each		✓
On the...		

1	2	3	4	5	6	7
8	9	10	11	12	13	14
15	16	17	18	19	20	21
22	23	24	25	26	27	28
29	30	31				

❮ Repeat	**Custom**		
Frequency			Yearly
Every			Year
Event will occur every year.			

Jan	Feb	Mar	Apr
May	Jun	Jul	Aug
Sep	Oct	Nov	Dec

Days of Week

(11) Tap the End Repeat field, unless the event is ongoing. (If it's ongoing—that is, if it doesn't have a set end date—don't tap End Repeat, and skip steps 12 and 13.)

(12) Tap On Date.

(13) Use the spin controls to select the last date this event occurs. (If the event is ongoing, skip steps 11 through 13.)

(14) Tap the back arrow to return to the New Event panel and finish creating the event. Tap Add when done.

Repeat	Yearly >
End Repeat	Never >

New Event   **End Repeat**

Never

On Date   ✓

October	1	2019
November	2	2020
December	3	2021
January	4	2022
February	5	2023
March	6	2024
April	7	2025

Create an Alert for an Event

Sometimes you want to be notified when an event is coming up. Maybe you need a full day to prepare for a big event, or just a five-minute reminder to let you know what you need to do next. You can add alerts to any event you create in the Calendar app.

(1) From within the Calendar app, create a new app as normal and then tap the Alert field.

Alert	None >
Show As	Busy >

(**2**) Tap when you want to be alerted, anywhere from at the time of the event to 1 week before. Your iPad displays an alert for this event at the designated time.

❮ New Event	**Alert**
None	
At time of event	
5 minutes before	
(2)— 15 minutes before	
30 minutes before	
1 hour before	
2 hours before	
1 day before	
2 days before	
1 week before	

Invite Others to an Event

Some events are personal. Others are quite public, involving lots of other people. (We're talking meetings, parties, and the like.) With the Calendar app you can invite your friends and family to new events you create, so they'll have these events on their calendars, too.

 (**1**) From within the Calendar app, create a new app as normal and then tap the Invitees field.

Calendar	● Home ❯
(1)— Invitees	None ❯

2. From within the Add Invitees panel, tap the To field and enter the name or email address of the person you want to invite.

3. Alternatively, tap the + to display and select from people in your contacts list.

4. This person is added to the invite list. Repeat steps 2 and 3 to add more invitees.

5. Tap Done. Each invitee is sent an email inviting them to your event.

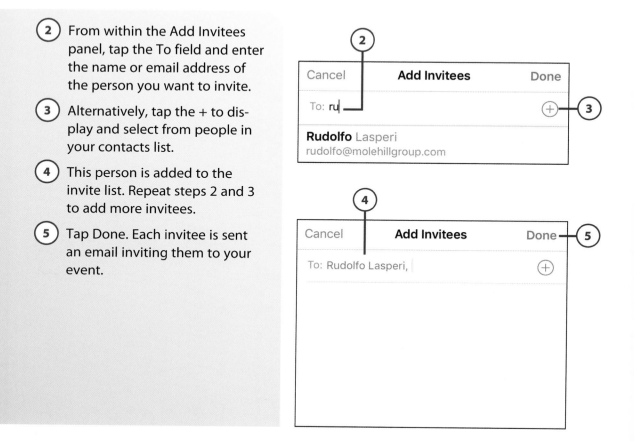

Using the Reminders App

I have trouble remembering things. Always have—it's not an age thing. As such, I can use all the help I can get to help me track all the various things I need to do.

Apple's Reminders app, included with your iPad, lets you create a digital to-do list containing all the various tasks and chores you need to remember. Add an item to the Reminders list and you'll be prompted (or nagged, as the case may be) to complete that task.

View and Manage Your Reminders

By default, upcoming and past-due reminders are displayed in the Reminders widget on your iPad's Search screen. You can also review them all in the Reminders app itself.

(1) From the Search screen, tap a reminder to view it in the Reminders app. *Or…*

(2) From the Home screen, tap the Reminders icon to open the Reminders app.

(3) Tap Reminders to view items you have not yet completed.

(4) Tap Scheduled to view items you want to complete by a given date.

(5) Tap the circle next to a given item to mark that item as completed.

Change the Order

To change the order of the items in your reminders list, tap Edit at the top of the list and then tap and drag any item to a new position.

Add a New Reminder

Adding a new item to your reminders
list is as easy as adding a new event
to your calendar.

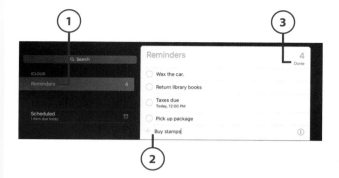

(1) From within the Reminders app,
tap Reminders.

(2) Tap next to the + within the
reminders list and enter the
item you need reminding of.

(3) Tap Done.

(4) To add an item that has a set
completion date, tap Scheduled.

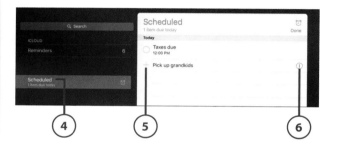

(5) Tap next to the + within the
scheduled list and enter the
item you need reminding of.

(6) Tap the Information (i) icon to
display the Details pane.

(7) Tap the Alarm field and select a
day and time for the completion
of this item.

(8) If this is a high-priority item,
go the Priority section and tap
from one to three exclamation
marks (!).

(9) Tap Done.

Details	Done
Pick up grandkids	
Remind me on a day	
Alarm	Wed, 8/17/16, 12:00 PM
Repeat	Never >
Priority	None ! !! !!!
Notes	

>>>*Go Further*

USE SIRI

Instead of entering events and reminders manually, you can use Siri to create new items for both the Calendar and Reminders apps.

To add a calendar event, activate Siri and speak as much information as you know about the event. Say something like, "Schedule a meeting Monday at 3:00 at the Mounds Conference Center" or "Create an event on Tuesday the 29th at 4 pm."

To add a reminder, activate Siri and speak about the task. Say something like, "Remind me to pick up milk on the way home" or "Remember to pay the rent on the first of the month."

Delete a Reminder

As you've seen, it's easy enough to mark an item as completed; when completed, the item no longer shows in the Reminders list. But what about items that you haven't completed and don't want to show any more? Fortunately, they're easy to delete.

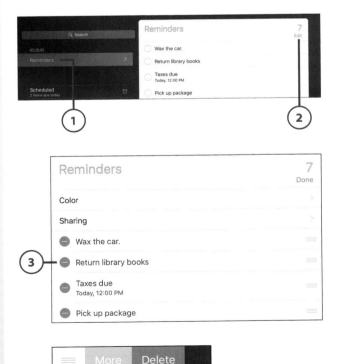

1. From within the Reminders app, tap Reminders.

2. Tap Edit at the top of the reminders list.

3. Tap the red – next to the item you want to delete. The event slides left and you see additional controls.

4. Tap Delete. The item is deleted.

iBooks app

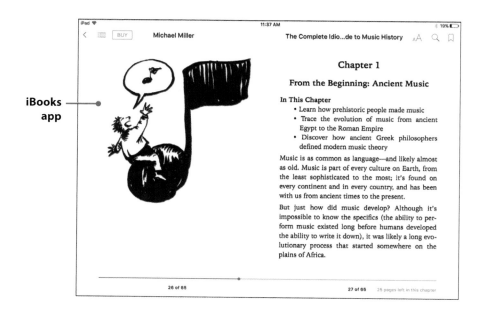

News app

In this chapter, you learn how to use your iPad to read various types of publications.

→ Reading eBooks on Your iPad
→ Reading News Stories with the News App

14

Reading eBooks, Magazines, and Newspapers

Your iPad is a great device for reading. You can use your iPad, and the appropriate apps, to read books, newspapers, magazines, and other articles—all in electronic format, all in the palms of your hands.

Reading eBooks on Your iPad

Electronic books, also known as eBooks, are a convenient way to read your favorite books. You can store multiple eBooks on your iPad and read any of them whenever and wherever you want. No more bulky paper books to haul around; no more losing your place among the dog-eared pages. Everything fits on and is viewed on your iPad.

Apple's iBooks app is preinstalled on your new iPad. You use the iBooks app to purchase eBooks from Apple's iTunes Store—and to read those eBooks you purchase.

Find and Purchase Books with the iBooks App

Before you can read eBooks with iBooks, you have to buy something to read—which you do directly from the iBooks app, from Apple's iTunes Store.

1. From the iPad's Home screen, tap the iBooks icon to open the iBooks app.

2. Tap Featured to view books featured in the iTunes Store.

3. Tap NYTimes to view books on the *New York Times* bestseller list.

4. Tap Top Charts to view top books in various categories.

5. Tap Top Authors to view books by best-selling authors.

6. Tap Categories to view and select a category and see the best-selling titles in that category.

7. Type within the Search box to search for books by title or author.

8. Tap a book to view more details.

9. Tap Sample to download a short sample of this book.

10. Tap the price button to purchase the book; the button changes to a Buy Book button.

11. Tap the Buy Book button.

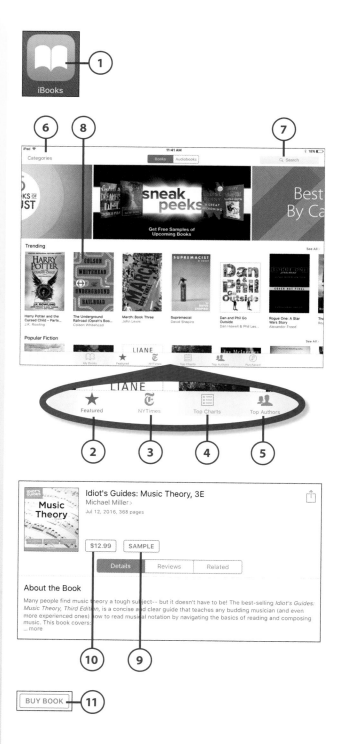

12 You're prompted to sign into the iTunes Store with your Apple ID. Enter your password and click OK to complete the purchase using the payment method you've previously supplied. (If you haven't yet provided a payment method, you're prompted to do so now.)

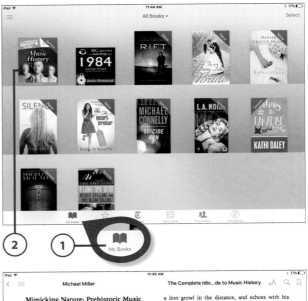

Sign In to iTunes Store

Enter the password for your Apple ID "millerwriter@icloud.com".

Password

Cancel　　　　OK

12

Read a Book with the iBooks App

All the books you've purchased are downloaded to your iPad and displayed on the My Books screen.

1 From within the iBooks app, tap My Books to view the books and samples you've purchased.

2 Tap a book cover to open that book.

3 Swipe from right to left (or tap the right side of the screen) to turn to the next page.

4 Swipe from left to right (or tap the left side of the screen) to turn to the previous page.

5 Drag the slider at the bottom of the page to move to another section in the book.

Mimicking Nature: Prehistoric Music

Let's be up-front about it: no one knows who or where the first music was made. It may have been a caveman pounding out a beat on a hollow log; it may have been a cavewoman mimicking a nearby bird whistle while cooking dinner over the communal fire. Wherever or whatever it was, it was probably something very simple, at least compared to our modern notion of music.

The Sincerest Form of Flattery

The earliest music likely developed in response to the natural sounds that early humans heard all around them. Imagine a prehistoric man standing on the African veldt, listening to the sounds of insects and animals all around him, communicating with one another via a variety of sounds. Have you ever heard a noise and tried to mimic it? Imagine, then, to imagine our prehistoric man hearing a locust clicking its welcome and answering by making a clicking sound with his own mouth. He hears

a lion growl in the distance, and echoes with his own growl. And when he hears a bird singing to its flock, our ancient friend does his best to imitate that bird call, by whistling the notes of its song.

It's a short step from imitating bird songs to creating uniquely human music, no matter how simple that music may be. But it's clear that the earliest music was an imitation of natural sounds, and thus shared similar tonality, patterns, and repetition to those sounds. In other words, our prehistoric musicians weren't whistling anything too complex; it's likely that the first snippets of music were short, simple and repeated over and over. This simple music may even have been used for the same purposes that other animals vocalized their sounds—to establish territory, to warn of danger, and to attract mates.

This earliest music, produced by humans in preliterate cultures, is called *primitive* or *prehistoric music*. The prehistoric era of music runs from at least 50,000 B.C.E. to about 4000 B.C.E.—when humans began to record their history in writing.

6 Tap the Fonts icon to change the look and feel of the page.

7 Tap the right A to make the text larger. Continue tapping to make the text even larger.

8 Tap the left A to make the text smaller. Continue tapping to make the text even smaller.

9 Tap Fonts to display and select a different font for the book's text.

10 Tap one of the colored circles to change the display theme for the book pages.

11 Tap off the Auto-Night Theme switch if you don't want the screen to change in low-light conditions. (Leave it on for better reading in bed at night.)

12 Tap on the Scrolling View switch if you'd prefer to scroll through instead of flip through pages.

13 Tap the Search (magnifying glass) icon to display the Search box.

14 Type within the Search box to search for a given word or phrase within this book.

15 Tap the Bookmark icon to bookmark this page in the book.

16 Tap the Contents icon to view the book's table of contents.

17 Tap the left-arrow icon to return to the My Books screen.

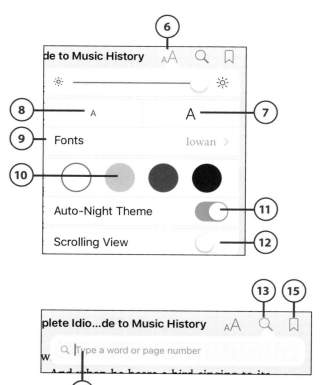

>>>*Go Further*

LISTENING TO AUDIOBOOKS IN iBOOKS

In addition to reading eBooks, you can also use the iBooks app to listen to audiobooks on your iPad. To purchase an audiobook, tap the Featured or Top Charts tabs and tap to select Audiobooks at the top of the screen. You can then purchase and download any audiobook just as you would an eBook.

To listen to an audiobook, tap that book on the My Books page. Use the playback controls at the bottom of the screen to pause or resume playback, skip 15 seconds back or forward, and even change the speed of the playback.

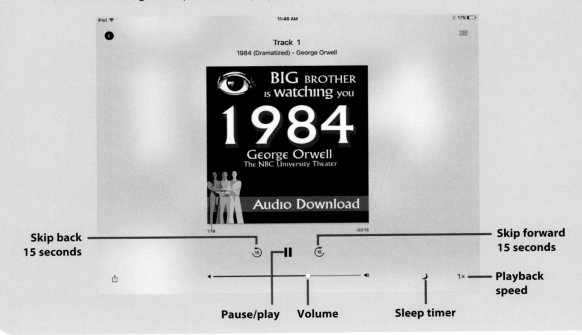

Skip back 15 seconds · Skip forward 15 seconds · Pause/play · Volume · Sleep timer · Playback speed

Find and Purchase Books with the Kindle Book Browser

Apple provides its iBooks app for reading eBooks, but let's be honest—when you think about books and booksellers, Apple is not the first company that comes to mind. When you want a larger selection of eBooks, you might want to check out Amazon, the world's largest online bookstore, and Amazon's Kindle eReader app. You can download the Kindle app (it's free) from Apple's App Store.

Amazon Account

When you first launch the Kindle app, you're prompted to sign into your existing Amazon account. Do so and the app will remember who you are. If you don't yet have an Amazon account, tap Are You New to Kindle? and follow the onscreen instructions from there.

(1) From the iPad's Home screen, tap the Kindle icon to launch the Kindle app. You see your book library.

(2) Tap the Amazon icon to open Kindle's Book Browser and identify books you'd like to purchase.

(3) Tap Cloud to view all books you've purchased. (Book purchases are not automatically downloaded to your iPad; they're stored online in the "cloud" until you're ready to read them.)

(4) Tap Device to view those books that are stored on your iPad.

(5) Tap the Search (magnifying glass) icon to search for a specific book in your library.

(6) Tap the book you want to read. (If the book was in the cloud, it is now automatically downloaded to your iPad.)

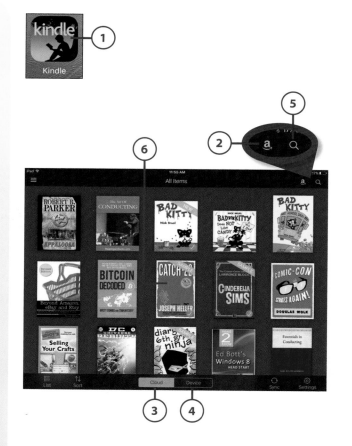

7 Swipe from right to left (or tap the right side of the screen) to turn to the next page.

8 Swipe from left to right (or tap the left side of the screen) to turn to the previous page.

9 Tap anywhere on the screen to display Kindle's page view.

10 Drag the slider at the bottom of the screen to move to another section of the book.

11 Tap the View Options (font) icon to change font size, font type, color scheme, and more.

12 Tap the Bookmark icon to bookmark the current page.

13 Tap the Search (magnifying glass) icon to search within this book.

14 Tap a page to return to reading view.

15 Tap the Menu icon to display the menu pane.

Free eBooks Online

Some eBooks are free. Amazon, Barnes & Noble, and the iTunes Store offer some older books for free download. If you're an Amazon Prime member, you get a variety of free eBooks as part of that subscription. You can also find many free eBooks at your local library—ask your librarian how to access them.

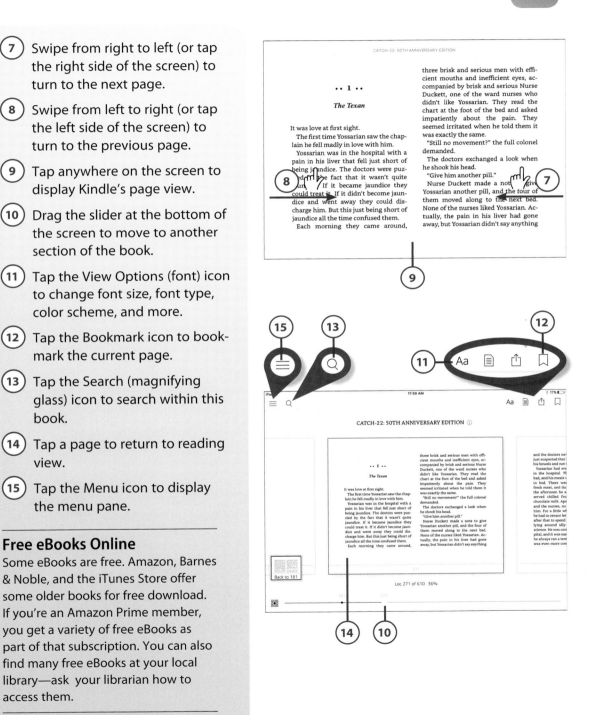

(16) Tap Library to return to your book library.

(16)— Library ⌂

About This Book

Cover

Table of Contents

Beginning

Location...

Sync
Sync to Furthest Page ⟳

It's Not All Good

No In-App Purchases

Unlike with the iBooks app, you can't purchase books from within the Kindle or Nook apps. That's because Apple doesn't allow third parties to sell books directly from within the Kindle app. (Well, they do, but they require the retailers to share their profits with Apple—which Amazon and Barnes & Noble don't really want to do.)

Instead, you have to make your purchases from the retailer's website, using the Safari web browser. In the case of Amazon, you can use the Kindle Book Browser to identify the eBooks you want to buy, and add those books to a shopping list or wish list. You then switch to the Safari web browser to actually make the purchase from the Amazon website. After you've purchased a book, it shows up in the Kindle app for reading.

It's much the same with Barnes & Noble's Nook app. You can't purchase books from within the app, so you have to go to the retailer's website (www.bn.com) and make your purchases there. All eBooks you purchase automatically display within the Nook app.

Read a Book with Barnes & Noble's Nook App

Amazon may be the largest online bookstore, but Barnes & Noble (B&N) is the largest physical bookseller in the United States. B&N also has a healthy online presence, and offers the Nook eReader app for reading eBooks you purchase from their online store.

Barnes & Noble Account

When you first launch the Nook app, you're prompted to sign into your existing Barnes & Noble account. Do so and the app will remember who you are. If you don't yet have a Barnes & Noble account, go to www.bn.com and create a new account there.

1. From the iPad's Home screen, tap the Nook icon to launch the Nook app. You see your book library.

2. Tap the book you want to read. (If you haven't yet opened the book, it is now automatically downloaded to your iPad.)

3. Swipe from right to left (or tap the right side of the screen) to turn to the next page.

4. Swipe from left to right (or tap the left side of the screen) to turn to the previous page.

5. Tap anywhere on the screen to display the toolbar at the top of the screen and the slider at the bottom.

(6) Drag the slider at the bottom of the screen to move to another section of the book.

(7) Tap the Text Options (font) icon to change font size, font type, theme, and more.

(8) Tap the Contents icon to display the book's table of contents, bookmarks, and annotations.

(9) Tap the back arrow to return to your book library.

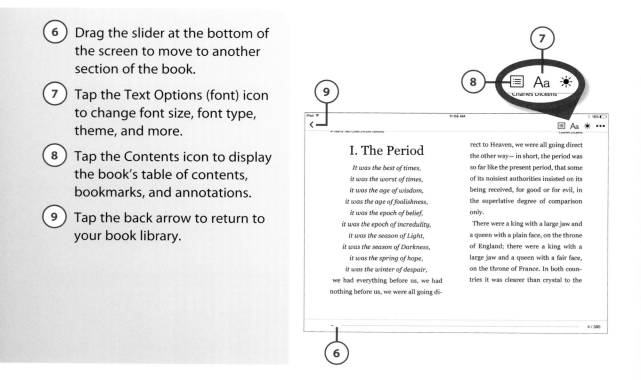

Reading News Stories with the News App

Books aren't the only things you can read on your iPad. You can also read online newspaper and magazine articles, using Apple's News app.

The News app aggregates stories from a variety of news sources, based on your reading habits. You see stories about topics you're most interested in, from those sources you like the best.

Personalize What News You Receive

When you first launch the News app, you're prompted to select news sources (Apple calls them Channels) you'd like to include in your news feed. A handful of sources are already listed, just in case you don't have any preferences yet. You can select additional news sources now or do so at any later time.

(**1**) From the iPad's Home screen, tap the News icon to launch the News app.

(**2**) Tap Explore at the bottom of the screen.

(**3**) You now see a side scrolling list of available news sources. Tap the + for each source you'd like to include in your news feed.

(**4**) As you select news sources, the News app figures out what you like and don't like, and adds sources and topics to the Recommended for You Section. Tap the + for any source or topic here you'd like to include.

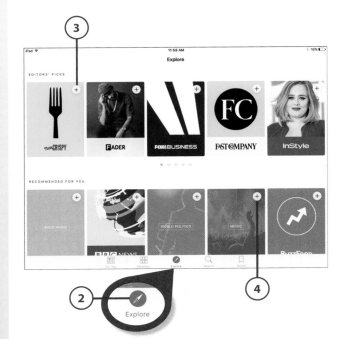

Read News Stories

The News app assembles stories based on the sources and topics you select, and then fine-tunes those selections based on what you actually read over time. Stories are displayed on the main For You page.

1. From within the News app, tap For You to view stories in your news feed.

2. Stories are organized by news source and topic. Scroll down the screen to view additional sources and topics.

3. Tap the Favorites icon to view all your news sources.

4. Tap a source to view all stories from that source.

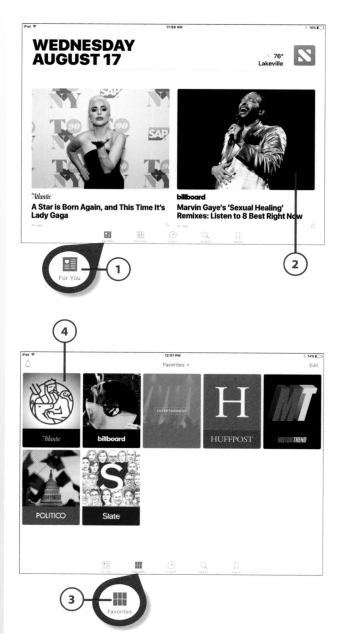

5. Tap a story to read it.

6. Tap the Font icon to change the size of the onscreen text.

7. Tap the Bookmark icon to bookmark this story.

8. Tap the Like (heart) icon to like this story.

9. Top the Don't Like icon to dislike this story.

10. Tap the Share icon to share this story via instant message, email, or social media.

11. Tap the back arrow to return to the previous screen.

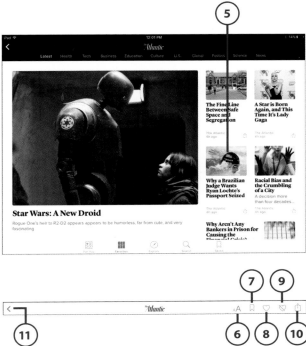

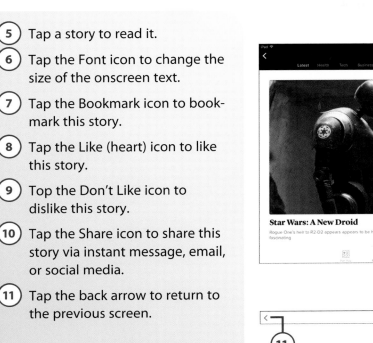

>>>Go Further

FINDING OTHER NEWSPAPERS AND MAGAZINES ONLINE

The News app is what some call a *newsreader*, which is a type of app or website that aggregates news articles from a variety of sources in a personalized manner. Apple's News app is only one such newsreader; there are other popular newsreader apps available (most for free) in the App Store, including Feedly, Flipboard, and Newsify. Go to the App Store and browse the News category or search for newsreaders for more.

Of course, you can always go directly to the source for your news, sports, financial, and weather information. Most local newspapers, television stations, and radio stations have websites that offer a variety of local news. The big cable news networks (CNN, Fox News, and MSNBC) all have robust websites, as do the major network news organizations (ABC, CBS, and NBC). Most magazines offer at least some of their articles on the web, and there are a variety of web-only news sources, as well. Just use the Safari web browser to access these sites—and use Google to search for specific sites in which you're interested.

In this chapter, you learn how to use your iPad to shoot photos and videos, and then edit and share what you shot.

→ Shooting Digital Photos
→ Viewing and Editing Your Photos
→ Shooting and Editing Videos
→ Sharing Photos and Videos

15

Shooting, Editing, and Sharing Photos and Videos

Your iPad is much like an iPhone or other smartphone in terms of the features it offers. (But with a much bigger screen, of course.) This is especially true when it comes to photography, as your iPad features two built-in cameras—one facing outward and one pointing toward your face. You can use these cameras to shoot still photos and videos, and then use various apps to edit and share those items with others.

Shooting Digital Photos

Yes, you can use your iPad to shoot digital photos. You can take a picture of anything in front of you, or switch to the front-facing FaceTime camera and take a picture of yourself. (That's called a *selfie*.) You use the iPad's screen to preview the picture, then aim the camera at whatever it is you're shooting and press the Shutter button. You can then edit the pictures you take to crop them, rotate them, adjust brightness and color, and even apply filters for special effects.

Launch the Camera App

Since you never know when a good photo op will present itself, Apple offers three different ways to quickly launch your iPad's camera.

(1) From the iPad's Home screen, tap the Camera icon.

(2) From any screen, swipe up from the bottom to display the Control Center and then tap the Camera icon.

(3) From the Lock screen, swipe from right to left. (That's right—you don't have to unlock your iPad to use the camera!)

Camera

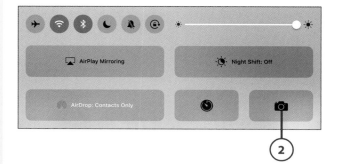

Take a Picture

When it comes to taking pictures with your iPad, you can shoot in the 16:9 aspect ratio that mirrors the iPad screen or in a square format better suited for some types of web uploads (such as your profile picture in Facebook). Use the rear-facing iSight camera to take pictures of things in front of you or (as discussed in the next task) the front-facing FaceTime camera to take selfies.

(1) Open the Camera app and make sure the rear-facing camera is selected. If not, tap the Switch button.

(2) Hold your iPad vertically to take a portrait photo, or horizontally to take a landscape photo. The onscreen controls rotate accordingly.

(3) Tap Photo in the lower right to shoot 16:9 ratio photos.

(4) Tap Square in the lower right to shoot square photos.

(5) To enable HDR photos, which provide higher contrast results, tap to enable the HDR button.

HDR

HDR stands for *high dynamic range*, which combines the results of three photos automatically shot in rapid succession (with different exposure settings) to create more detail in high-contrast photos.

(6) To use the timer (good if you want to include yourself in the shot—set the timer and run around in front of the camera!), tap the Timer button and select either a 3- or 10-second timer. The timer activates when you press the Shutter button.

(7) Drag the zoom slider on the left side of the screen to zoom into a shot. Alternatively, expand two fingers onscreen to zoom in.

(8) Optionally, tap the subject of the photo onscreen to focus on that person or object. This displays a box around the selected area, and an Exposure slider; drag the slider up to increase the exposure (makes the shot brighter) or down to decrease the exposure (darkens the shot).

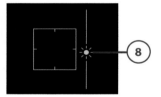

Auto Focus and Exposure

Your iPad's iSight camera includes auto focus and auto exposure, which uses face-recognition technology to identify the subject of the picture and focus and set exposure automatically. You can override these automatic controls by tapping to select a person or object onscreen different from the one your iPad selects.

(9) Use the iPad's display to aim the camera and compose your picture, then press the Shutter button to take the photo. Alternatively, press either Volume button on the side of your iPad to take the picture.

(10) Tap the preview thumbnail to view the picture you just took.

Burst Shots

To take a series of rapid-fire ("burst") shots, press and hold the Shutter button. Release the button to stop shooting. (Not available on older iPad minis.)

>>>Go Further
CONFIGURING THE CAMERA APP

Your iPad's Camera app works just fine "out of the box," as it were, but there are a few options you can configure to personalize the way it works. To configure the Camera app, tap the Settings icon on any Home screen, then select Photos & Camera in the left column.

Here are a few of the settings you might want to change:

- Enable iCloud Photo Sharing to upload and share your photos online.

- In the Camera section, tap on the Grid switch to display an onscreen grid, to help you better compose your photos.

- By default, the iSight camera records video at 1080p HD resolution, with a frame rate of 30 fps. This works fine in most instances, but if you want to record at a slightly lower resolution (which creates smaller files and saves space on your device), tap Record Video and select 720p HD at 30 fps.

- When you shoot HDR photos, the Camera app by default stores all three photos used to create the final HDR photo. If you'd rather save on storage space, tap off the Keep Normal Photo switch in the HDR section.

Take a Selfie

Use the front-facing FaceTime camera on your iPad to take selfies of yourself. (Is that redundant?) When you use the FaceTime camera, you have fewer shooting options available—for example, you can't shoot HDR photos, or zoom into the shot.

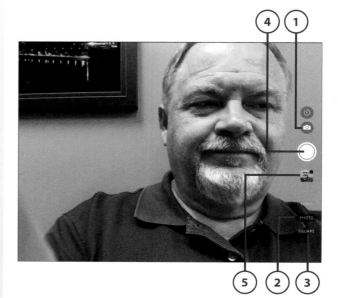

(1) Open the Camera app and tap the Switch button to switch to the front-facing FaceTime camera. Rotate the iPad vertically to take a portrait picture (most common for selfies) or horizontally to take a landscape photo.

(2) Tap Photo to take a 16:9 ratio photo.

(3) Tap Square to take a square photo. (Great for profile pictures on many websites.)

(4) Smile at the camera (and look at your smiling face onscreen), then press the Shutter button to take the picture.

(5) Tap the preview thumbnail to view the selfie you just took.

Screen Capture

To take a screenshot of what's currently displayed on your iPad's screen, simultaneously press and release the Sleep/Wake and Home buttons on your iPad. Screenshots are stored in the Photos app or iCloud Photo Library.

Take a Panoramic Photo

Apple's Camera app also lets you take panoramic photos that include a wide expanse not normally captured in a single photo. To create a panoramic photo, you shoot multiple photos from left to right, then the Camera app digitally stitches them together.

Panoramic photos are great for capturing outdoor landscapes, as well as "panning" a room indoors.

Panoramic photo

1. From within the Camera app, make sure the iSight (rear-facing) camera is selected, then tap Pano in the lower-right corner.

2. Hold the iPad vertically (portrait mode) and tap the Shutter button. (If you hold the iPad horizontally, the Photos app takes a vertical panoramic photo that stretches from the bottom to the top.)

(3) As directed onscreen, move or pan the iPad slowly in the direction of the arrow. The progress of your pan appears in an inset over the main display.

(4) Tap the Shutter button when you're done panning.

>>>Go Further
AN iPAD CAN'T REPLACE YOUR CAMERA

I'm going to show my prejudice here. While the iPad includes a camera (two of them, actually), and many people use it to shoot photos and videos, it really isn't a camera. It's a tablet.

A camera is a smaller device that you can hold in one hand. Traditional cameras are dedicated devices that only take photos (and sometimes videos) and include lenses and sensors that are optimized for that task. One can even argue that your smartphone functions like a camera; while the phone's lens and sensor might not be as sophisticated as those found in dedicated cameras, it is small and takes pretty good pictures.

Your iPad, however, is not small. You can't hold it in one hand. Yes, it takes pictures. (Surprisingly good ones, too.) But it's a really big and awkward device, at least when it comes to photography. When you want to shoot a picture or video, you have to hold up this clunky rectangular thing that's as big as your head. It looks weird, it doesn't feel comfortable, and it can block people behind you from seeing whatever it is you're shooting.

In short, I don't think iPads should be used for cameras, unless you're in a situation where that's all you have. I think you're better off pulling out your smartphone, compact digital camera, or digital SLR. All of these devices are a lot smaller and more convenient than shooting with your iPad—and, in the case of dedicated cameras (not smartphones) you'll get better picture quality, too, thanks to their more advanced lenses and sensors.

I fully realize that all of my protesting is probably for naught. Many, many people use their iPads to capture pictures and videos, and all my bloviating in opposition won't change that behavior one iota. So be it. But even though I show you how to take photos and videos with your iPad, you won't see me doing it. There are too many better options available.

Viewing and Editing Your Photos

While the iPad may be a little inconvenient as a day-to-day digital camera, it's actually pretty good for viewing and editing photos. The large screen, combined with handy touchscreen operation, makes it easy to look at the photos you've taken and make minor changes to them, if necessary.

You use Apple's Photos app to both view and edit your photos. In fact, you can use the iPad's Photos app to view and edit not only pictures taken with your iPad, but also photos taken by any of your Apple devices. When you use the iCloud Photo Library, all photos you take with your iPad *and* iPhone are automatically uploaded and stored online, and available to all your Apple devices. So take a picture with your iPhone and edit it with your iPad—it's the best way to use both devices!

View Your Photos

You can view photos you've just taken from within the Camera app or from Apple's Photos app.

(1) From within the Camera app, tap the preview thumbnail to display the photo full screen. (Tap Camera to return to the camera to shoot some more photos.) Or…

(2) From the Home screen, tap the Photos icon to open the Photos app.

(3) You can let the Photos app organize your photos, by "smart" groups, or you can organize them yourself, in albums. To view the app's smart groups, tap Photos.

(4) The largest type of smart group is called a Year; this simply organizes your photos by year taken. The next smallest group is called a Collection, which is typically a group of photos that share a time range or topic in common. The smallest group is called a Moment, which is typically photos within a Collection taken on a given date. The heading of a given screen indicates which type of smart group you're viewing. To move to the next smallest smart group, tap a Year or Collection.

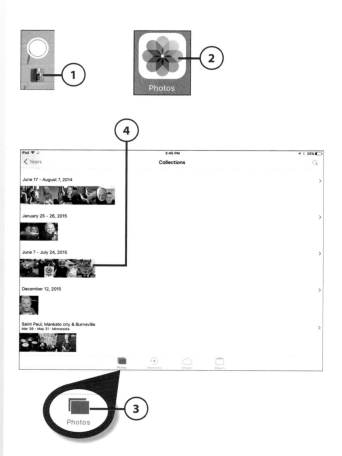

5 To move to the next largest group, tap the back button at the top of the screen.

6 Tap Memories to view photos and videos curated by the Photos app into collages and short videos.

7 Tap a memory to view it.

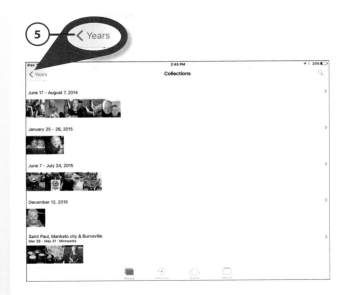

(8) Tap Shared to view photos from this and other devices stored in the iCloud Photo Library.

(9) Tap to view a specific photo.

(10) Tap Albums to view your photos organized by album.

(11) Tap an album to view the photos stored within.

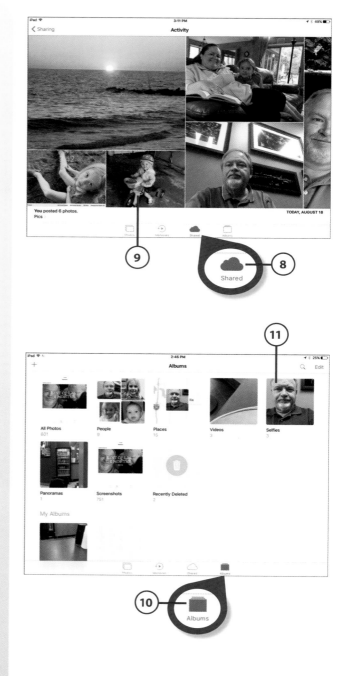

12 Tap to view a specific photo.

13 Tap the heart icon to add this photo to your Favorites album.

14 Tap the trashcan icon to delete the photo.

15 Additional photos in this group or album are displayed as thumbnails in a strip along the bottom of the screen. Drag the strip left or right to see additional photos.

16 Tap the back arrow to return to the previous group or album.

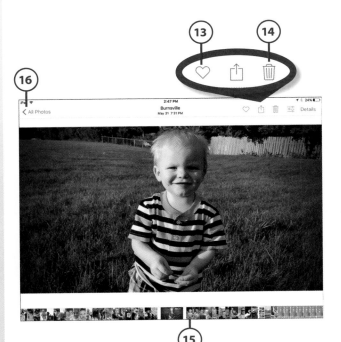

>>>*Go Further*

USING THE iCLOUD PHOTO LIBRARY

While you can store your photos (up to 1,000 of them, anyway) locally on your iPad, you can store many more photos online in Apple's iCloud Photo Library. When you enable the iCloud Photo Library on your device, all photos and videos you shoot are automatically uploaded to and stored on Apple's iCloud online storage service.

You can then access your photos and videos from any connected computer or device, just by going to the iCloud website (www.icloud.com) and logging in with your Apple ID. Any edits or changes you make to the stored photos are visible on all your devices.

To enable iCloud Photo Library storage, tap the Settings icon, select iCloud, then tap Photos. On the next screen, tap on the iCloud Photo Library switch, and you're ready to go.

(Note that if you use the iCloud Photo Library, you no longer use the iTunes software to synchronize photos and videos between your iPad and your computer.)

Organize Photos in Albums

The Photos app does a good job automatically organizing your photos into smart groups. That said, you might want to organize your photos your own way, by creating virtual photo albums to group photos by type, activity, location, and so forth.

(1) From within the Photos app, tap Albums to display your existing albums. (If you're within a given album, tap the back arrow to return to the main Albums screen.)

2 Tap an album to view the photos stored within.

3 Tap the + icon to create a new album.

4 From the New Album panel, enter a name for this album.

5 Tap Save.

6 You're prompted to add photos to your new album. Tap to select those photos you want to add. (You can select multiple photos; as you select each photo, a blue check mark appears on each item you select.)

7 Tap Done. The selected photos are added to your new album.

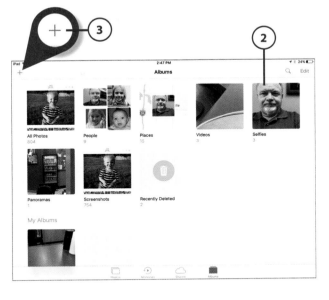

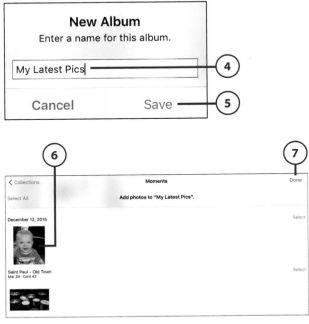

8 To add additional photos to an album, open the group or album that contains the photo(s) you want to add.

9 Tap Select.

10 Tap Add.

11 Tap to select the photos you want to add.

12 Tap Done.

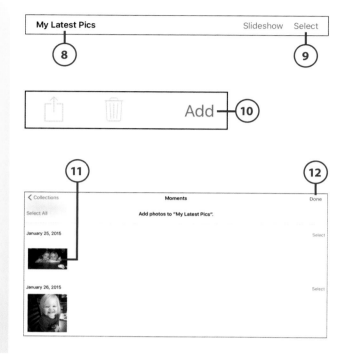

Slideshows

The Photos app enables you to play a slideshow of photos from any given album. Just open the album, then tap Slideshow in the top-right corner of the screen.

>>>Go Further
WORKING WITH SMART ALBUMS

The Photos app in iOS 10 includes several "smart" albums that are automatically filled with appropriate photos, as best as the app can determine.

Let's start with the People album. This album uses facial recognition technology to identify and include photos that have people's faces in them. It also groups photos by like faces, so that all photos of a given person should be grouped together. Tap a group to view all photos of that person. You can add more people to the People album by tapping the Add People tile.

The Places album attempts to organize your photos by where they were taken. (That's if your iPad knows this; you have to take a photo with your device's location services enabled for this to work.) Open the Places album and you see a map of the U.S. with one or more places pinpointed; tap a location to view photos taken at that location. (And if the grouping is too vague—for example, all photos taken within a state are grouped together—just zoom into the map to display more local locations.) If the map is too confusing to you, tap Grid to display location photos in a traditional grid listing.

The Photos app also groups photos by type, so you'll see albums for Selfies, Panoramas, Screenshots, and the like. Just tap an album to view its contents.

People album

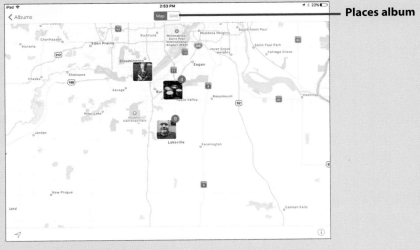

Places album

Crop and Straighten a Picture

Not every picture you take is perfect. Fortunately, digital pictures can be easily edited. You use the Photo app to make any necessary corrections to your photos.

1. From within the Photos app, open the photo you want to edit.

2. Tap the Edit button to display the editing screen.

3. Tap the Crop button.

4. To crop the picture, tap the Crop button and then drag the corners of the screen until you like what you see.

5. To rotate the picture 90 degrees counterclockwise, tap the Rotate button at the top of the screen.

6. To straighten or rotate the picture in smaller increments, drag your finger on the rotation dial until the picture is as you like it.

7. Tap Done when you're satisfied with the results. Or...

8. Tap Cancel to undo your changes and return to the original photo.

Apply Auto-Enhance

Sometimes a picture doesn't look quite right, but you don't want to do a lot of manual fine-tuning to fix it. In these instances, use the Photo app's Auto-Enhance control and let the app do the fixing for you. Auto-Enhance adjusts brightness, contrast, color, and other controls to try to make your picture look better.

1. From within the editing screen for a photo, tap the Auto-Enhance (magic wand) button.

2. If you like what you see, tap Done.

3. If you don't like the results, tap the Auto-Enhance button again to turn off the auto enhancement.

Apply a Filter

Another easy way to change the way a picture looks is to apply a photo filter. The Photos app comes with more than a half-dozen filters that can change the mood of a picture.

1. From within the editing screen for a photo, tap the Filters button.

(2) You now see the available filters. Tap a filter to apply it to your photo.

(3) If you like this filter, tap Done.

(4) If you don't like this filter, select another or tap Cancel.

Adjust Brightness and Color

The Photos app also offers more traditional editing controls you can use to enhance your photos—brightness and contrast (what the app calls Light), color saturation (Color), and more.

(1) From within the editing screen for a photo, tap the Adjustments button.

(2) Tap Light to adjust brightness.

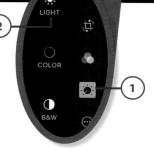

3 Scroll down to make the picture darker; scroll up to make it brighter.

4 To more precisely adjust brightness characteristics, tap the More button.

5 Tap to adjust any of the following characteristics: Brilliance, Exposure, Highlights, Shadows, Brightness, Contrast, and Black Point.

6 Use the slider to adjust the selected adjustment.

7 Tap the More button to return to the previous screen.

8 Tap Color to adjust color saturation (how much color there is in the photo).

9 Scroll down to remove the color from the picture; scroll up to increase the color level.

10 To more precisely adjust color characteristics, tap the More button and then tap to adjust any of the following characteristics: Saturation, Contrast, and Cast (tint).

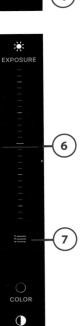

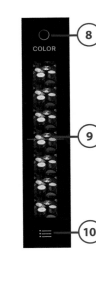

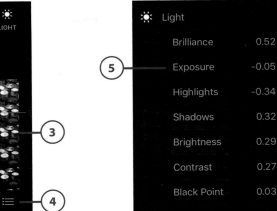

11   Tap the B&W button to turn your picture into a black-and-white photo, and make appropriate adjustments.

12   The Photos app removes all color from your photo. Use the slider to adjust the look of the black-and-white picture.

13   To more precisely adjust black-and-white characteristics, tap the More button and tap to adjust any of the following characteristics: Intensity, Neutrals, Tone, and Grain.

14   Tap Close to close out the current control, and then tap Done when you're done editing. (Or tap Cancel to undo your changes and return to the original photo.)

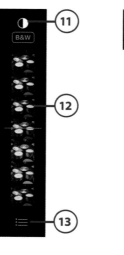

Revert to Original

When you make changes to a photo, the Photos app keeps a copy of the original photo. You can discard any changes and revert back to the original photo at any time by re-opening the photo for editing and tapping Revert in the top-right corner. When prompted, tap Revert to Original, and that's what you get.

Mark Up a Photo

You can also, if you want, "mark up" a photo by drawing on it or adding text to the picture.

(**1**) From within the editing screen for a photo, tap the More button.

(**2**) Tap Markup.

(**3**) Tap the Pen button to draw on the photo.

(**4**) Tap the Color button to select the pen color.

(**5**) Tap the Size button to select the size of the pen point.

(**6**) Drag your finger across the screen to draw.

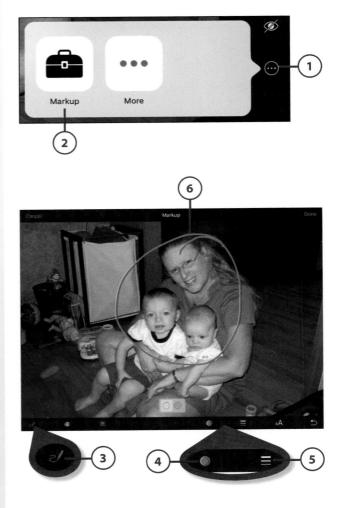

7 To magnify a part of the screen, tap the Magnify button. This places a magnification circle on the screen.

8 Drag the magnification circle to the position you want.

9 Drag the blue selection point to make the circle bigger or smaller.

10 Drag the green selection point around the edge of the circle to magnify the contents.

11 Tap the Text button to add text to the photo. This places a text box on the screen.

12 Double-tap the text box to display the onscreen keyboard, and then type the text you want.

13 To change the text color, tap the text box, select Edit, and tap the Color button and make a new selection.

14 To change the size and other characteristics of the text, select the text box and then tap the Font button. Tap to select a different font family. Use the slider to change the size of the text. Or tap one of the alignment buttons to change how the text is aligned (left, center, justified, or right).

15 Tap Done when you're done.

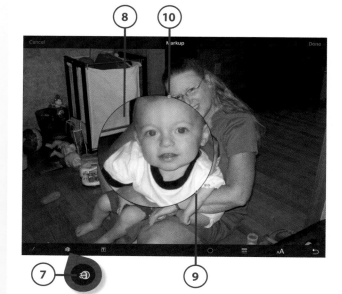

Shooting and Editing Videos

The rear-facing and front-facing cameras in your iPad can also be used to shoot videos. That means you can shoot videos of family gatherings, vacations, sporting events, and more—even selfie videos of yourself!

Shoot a Video

Shooting a video with your iPad is almost as easy as shooting a still photograph.

(1) Tap the Camera icon to open the Camera app.

(2) Tap Video in the lower-right corner of the screen.

(3) Tap the Switch button to switch between the rear-facing (iSight) and front-facing (FaceTime) cameras.

(4) Hold your iPad vertically to take a portrait video, or horizontally to take a landscape video. The onscreen controls rotate accordingly.

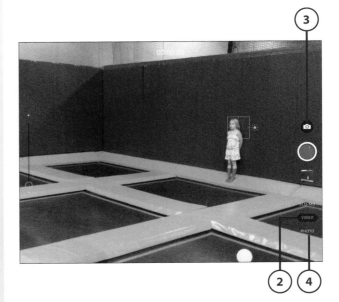

Widescreen Videos

Most videos are shot in landscape format, which requires you to hold your iPad horizontally. This is the orientation used by all movies and TV shows; it produces a 16:9 ratio widescreen picture, which fits perfectly on your TV screen.

(5) Drag the zoom slider on the left side of the screen to zoom into a shot. Alternatively, expand two fingers onscreen to zoom in.

(6) Optionally, tap the subject of the video onscreen to focus on that person or object. This displays a box around the selected area, and an Exposure slider; drag the slider up to increase the exposure (makes the video brighter) or down to decrease the exposure (darkens the video).

(7) Use the iPad's display to aim the camera and compose your picture and then press the red Record button to start recording. Alternatively, press either Volume button on the side of your iPad to initiate recording.

(8) As you record, the elapsed time is displayed at the top of the screen. Tap the Record button again to stop recording.

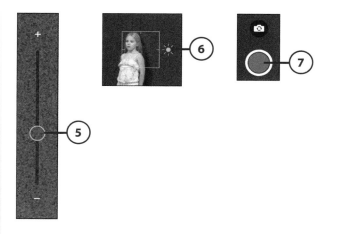

>>>*Go Further*
SLO MO AND TIME-LAPSE VIDEOS

The Photos app enables you to take two special types of videos. You can shoot video for slow-motion playback or record a series of still photographs as a time-lapse video.

To shoot in slow motion, select Slo Mo as the recording type. Your video is then shot at a super-fast 120 frames per second (fps). When a fast fps video is played at a normal (30 fps) frame rate, you get crystal-clear slow motion. You select which parts of your video to play in slow motion when you edit the video.

To record a time-lapse video, you have to keep your iPad perfectly still over the period of time you're shooting. Select Time-Lapse as the recording type, tap the Record button, and the Camera app starts capturing individual shots. Tap Record again to end the recording, and the individual shots are compiled into a short video.

Trim a Video

After you've shot a video, you can trim the beginning and end to make the video shorter and focus on the important parts. You can do this editing from within the Camera or Photos apps.

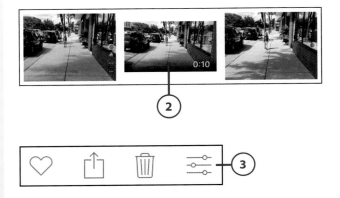

(1) After you've shot the video in the Camera app, tap the thumbnail to display the video playback screen. Or…

(2) From within the Photos app, tap to open the video you want to trim.

(3) Tap the Edit button.

4 In the series of thumbnails (called a *timeline*) beneath the video, touch and drag either of the arrows until a yellow border appears in the timeline.

5 Drag the yellow left and right arrows until you've selected the portion of the video you want to keep. (Everything outside the yellow selected section will be trimmed.)

6 Tap the Play button to play the selected (yellow) section of the video.

7 Tap Done when you're done.

>>>Go Further
iMOVIE

If you want to further edit a video you've shot, you can use the iMovie app, which is included with your iPad. This is a powerful yet easy-to-use app that lets you create *projects* that include multiple video clips, photos, music, and more.

When you create a new project, you select which elements you want to include, then add them to the project's timeline. You can select various project themes that determine the final look and feel, add fades between elements (and at the start and finish), apply filters, and more. If you're so inclined, check it out!

Sharing Photos and Videos

When you take a photo or video that you like, you might want to share it with friends and family. Fortunately, the Camera and Photos apps both make it easy to share your pics and vids via text message, email, social media, and more.

Share via Text Message

You can share photos and videos with your contacts via the Messages app.

1. From within the Camera or Photos app, open the item you want to share and then tap the Share button.

2. Tap Message to display the New Message pane.

3. Enter the name of the person you want to share with into the To field. (You can enter multiple people if you want.)

4. The photo or video is added to conversation. Tap within the item to add a text message.

5. Tap Send to send the message.

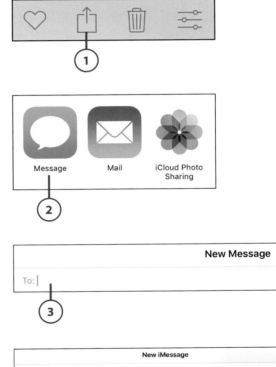

Share via Email

You can also send a photo or video to any of your contacts via email, using your iPad's Mail app.

1. From within the Camera or Photos app, open the item you want to share and then tap the Share button.

2. Tap Mail to display the New Message pane.

3. Tap within the To field and enter the names or email addresses of the intended recipients.

4. Tap within the Subject field and enter a subject for this email.

5. Tap within the main text area and enter any accompanying message.

6. Tap Send to send the email.

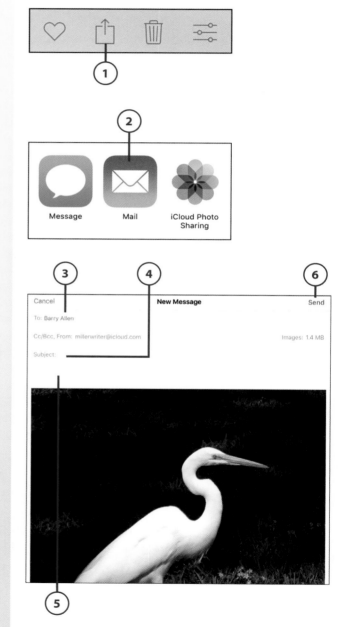

Share via Facebook

If you're on Facebook or other social media, you can also post a photo or video to that social network. This example uses Facebook, but the steps are similar if you're posting to Twitter or other networks.

(1) From within the Camera or Photos app, open the item you want to share and then tap the Share button.

(2) Tap Facebook to display the Facebook pane.

(3) Tap within the Say Something About This Photo (or Video) field and enter the text of your post.

(4) Tag any friends or locations in this photo or video, if you want.

(5) Tap the right arrow to select your privacy options—who you want to see this post.

(6) Tap Post to post this photo or video as a new status update.

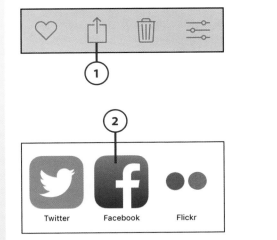

Twitter   Facebook   Flickr

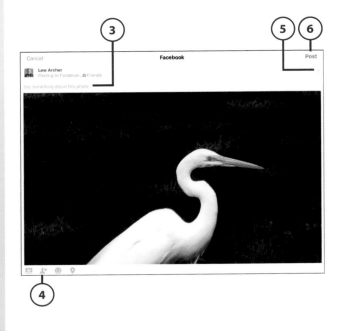

Cancel   **Facebook**   Post

Lew Archer
Posting to Facebook, Friends

Say something about this photo

>>>*Go Further*

OTHER SHARING OPTIONS

Your iPad offers several other ways to share your photos and videos.

If you've enabled iCloud photo sharing, and created shared folders for your friends and family members, you can upload your photos and videos to a shared folder. Just open the photo or video, tap the Share button, and then tap iCloud Photo Sharing. You can add a comment to accompany this item and select which shared album you want to post to.

When it comes to videos, many people like to post their videos to YouTube, the world's largest video sharing community. (Chapter 17, "Watching TV Shows, Movies, and Other Videos," covers watching YouTube videos.) If you have a YouTube account, it's easy to post your videos directly from your iPad. Just open the video, tap the Share button, and then tap YouTube. You're prompted to supply a title and other information for the video, and then you can begin uploading. When the uploading is complete, anyone on YouTube can view it.

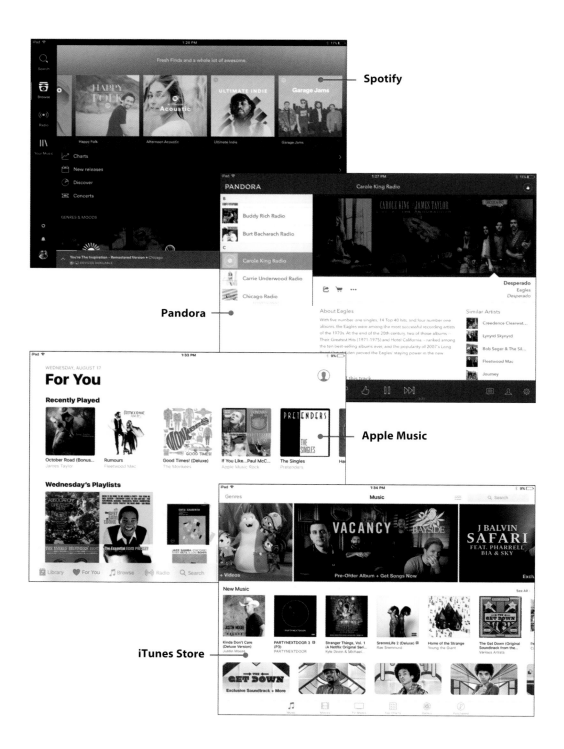

Spotify

Pandora

Apple Music

iTunes Store

In this chapter, you learn how to listen to
music on your iPad.

→ Listening to Streaming Music

→ Buying and Playing Music from the iTunes Store

Listening to Music

If you like to listen to music, you're in luck. Your iPad is a versatile music playback system that lets you listen to the music you love wherever you happen to be. You can purchase and download music direct to your iPad, or stream just about any song in the world over your iPad if you have an Internet connection.

Listening to Streaming Music

The way we listen to music has changed over the years. When I was growing up, I could listen to music over AM or FM radio, or buy LPs and singles to play on my record player. Later generations listened to audio-cassettes on their portable Walkman devices or purchased albums on digital compact discs. Still later generations learned how to download music from the Internet, either legally (through the iTunes Store) or illegally (via the infamous Napster).

Today, digital downloads are being supplanted by the concept of streaming music services. These services, such as Pandora and Spotify, stream huge music libraries (tens of millions of tracks) over the Internet direct to any connected device—including your iPad. All you need is an Internet connection, and just about any song you want is available for your listening pleasure. There's nothing to buy, and nothing to download to your device.

Free—or Not

Most streaming music services offer some type of free listening level, typically supported by commercials. If you want to get rid of the commercials (and gain more control over what you listen to), paid subscriptions are available.

Listen to Pandora

The most popular streaming service today is Pandora. With Pandora, you specify a song or artist or genre you like, and the service builds a custom playback "channel" based on your selection. For example, if you really like James Taylor, you can create a James Taylor Radio channel. Although you can't specify which specific songs for Pandora to play, you do get a lot of music similar to those songs or artists you like. (And Pandora fine-tunes your stations over time, based on which tracks you like or don't like.)

You listen to Pandora via the Pandora app, available for free from Apple's App Store. Basic Pandora service (with ads) is free; upgrade to Pandora One service ($4.99/month) to get rid of the ads. When you first launch the app, you're prompted to either sign up or log in, so do one or the other.

(1) From the iPad Home screen, tap the Pandora icon to launch the Pandora app.

2 All your existing radio stations are listed on the left. Tap a station to listen.

3 Tap the Pause button to pause playback. The button turns into a Play button; tap Play to resume playback.

4 Tap the Thumbs Up icon if you like a track; the radio station will be fine-tuned to play more tracks like this.

5 Tap the Thumbs Down icon if you don't like a track; it will now be skipped and the radio station fine-tuned to not play music like this.

6 Tap the Next button if the track is okay but you just don't want to listen to it now. The track will be skipped but it won't affect how Pandora fine-tunes your station.

7 Tap + Create Station to create a new station.

8 Use the onscreen keyboard to type in the name of a song, artist, or genre.

9 Pandora lists matching artists, tracks, and genres. Tap a selection to create that station, add it to your station list, and begin playback.

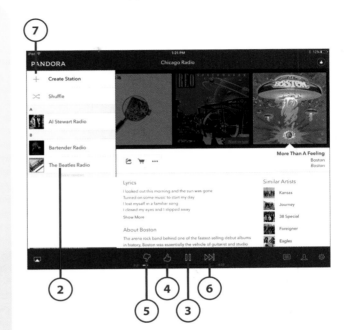

Listen to Spotify

The second most popular streaming music service is Spotify. Unlike Pandora, Spotify lets you specify individual tracks to listen to. You can also create your own playlists or let Spotify create personalized radio stations for you.

Basic Spotify service is free, but full of ads. To get rid of the ads, subscribe to Spotify Premium for $9.99/month.

You listen to Spotify via the Spotify app, which is available (for free) in Apple's App Store. The first time you launch the app you're prompted to either sign up or log in, so do so.

(1) From the iPad Home screen, tap the Spotify icon to launch the Spotify app.

(2) Tap Browse to browse through Spotify's music selections.

(3) Tap Charts to view the top music charts.

(4) Tap New Releases to view new music releases.

(5) Tap Discover to view new music recommended for you.

6 Scroll down the page to view popular musical genres and moods. Tap a tile to view playlists of that type.

7 Tap a tile to listen to that playlist.

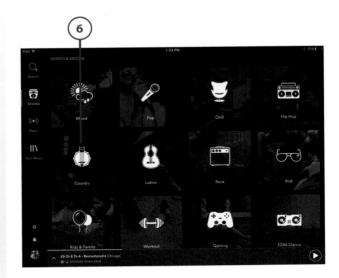

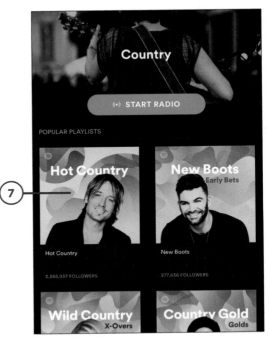

(8) Tap Search to search for specific songs or artists.

(9) Enter the name of the artist or track you want to listen to.

(10) Spotify lists artists and songs that match your search. Tap the music you want to listen to.

(11) This displays a playback panel on the right side of the screen. Tap Shuffle Play to play back songs in random order, or tap a specific song to play that song.

(12) Tap the bar at the bottom of the screen to display the currently playing screen.

(13) Tap the Pause button to pause playback. The Pause button changes into a Play button; tap Play to resume playback.

(14) Tap Shuffle to play back tracks in random order.

(15) Tap Back to listen to the previous track.

(16) Tap Forward to listen to the next track.

(17) Tap Repeat to repeat this track. (Tap this button again to stop repeating the thing.)

(18) Tap the down arrow to return to the home screen.

Listen to Apple Music

Not surprisingly, Apple offers its own streaming music service to compete with Spotify and Pandora. Unlike those services, Apple Music doesn't have a free level; you pay $9.99/month, after a free three-month trial.

You access Apple Music from the Music app on your iPad. To sign up for the service, tap the For You tab. When prompted, opt to get your three months free, choose which plan you want (Individual, Student, or Family), and proceed from there.

When you first log on, you're prompted to choose your favorite music, which you do by selecting those genres and artists you like best. Apple Music then fills up the For You tab with music it thinks you might like.

(1) From the iPad Home screen, tap the Music icon to launch the Music app.

(2) Tap For You to view recommended playlists, albums, and artists.

(3) Tap Browse to browse through new music.

(4) Tap Radio to listen to Apple Music's preprogrammed radio stations.

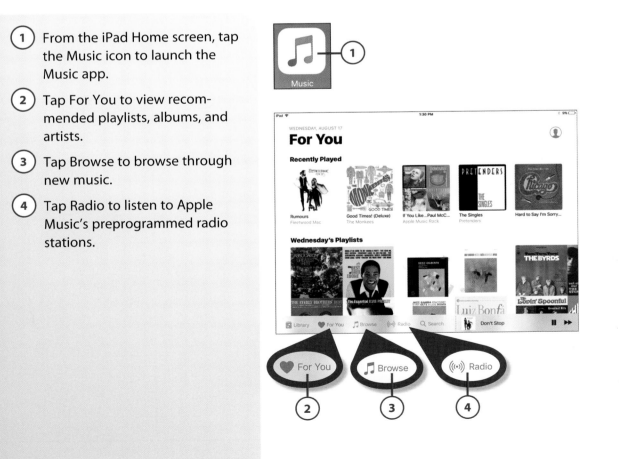

5 Tap Search to search for specific music.

6 Tap within the Search box.

7 Tap to select Apple Music. (If you select Your Library, you search only through the music you have stored on your iPad, not Apple Music's much larger online library.)

8 Enter the name of the artist or track you're looking for.

9 Apple Music displays a list of matching artists, albums, and songs. Tap to select the one you want.

10 Tap to listen to a given track, station, album, or playlist.

11 Playback now begins and playback controls are displayed in the bottom-right corner of the screen. Tap Pause to pause playback; tap Play to resume playback.

12 Tap Next to play the next track.

Music on YouTube

Many people also listen to music on YouTube, the popular video sharing site. Most major artists and record labels have official music videos on YouTube, and many individuals have created and uploaded so-called "lyric videos" (music with lyrics superimposed onscreen) for other songs. In short, there's a lot of music available on YouTube, and it's all available for free.

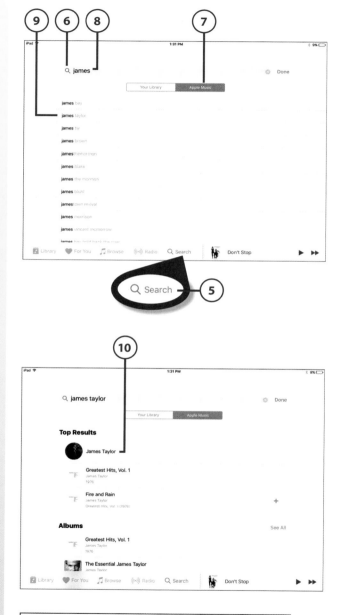

>>>*Go Further*
AMAZON PRIME MUSIC

Online retailer Amazon also offers a streaming music service, called Amazon Prime Music, in addition to all the digital music it has for purchase and download. This service is available for free to all Amazon Prime subscribers. (Amazon Prime offers free two-day shipping on qualifying purchases; a one-year subscription costs $99 and includes free access to the Prime Music service.)

Amazon Prime Music is a lot like Spotify and Apple Music. You get access to tens of millions of tracks for on-demand streaming, as well as artist-focused radio stations and your own user-created playlists.

What's unique about Amazon Prime Music is that it also gives you access to any music you've purchased from Amazon, on either CD or in MP3 format. It also integrates all the music currently stored on your iPad. Copies of your purchased tracks stream just like any other music in the Prime Music library, which means you can play any of your favorite music, even if it's not officially available for streaming on Amazon or other music services.

You access Amazon Prime Music from the Amazon Music app, available for free from Apple's App Store. Sign in with your existing Amazon Prime account, and you have access to everything that Amazon Prime Music offers. (If you don't yet subscribe to Amazon Prime, fire up the Safari web browser, go to www.amazon.com, and click Try Prime.)

Buying and Playing Music from the iTunes Store

While streaming music may be all the rage, many of us still prefer to own the music we like, so we can take and listen to it anywhere—even if there's no Internet connection handy. The way to do this on your iPad is to purchase digital music from Apple's iTunes Store, and then download your purchases to your iPad for playback.

Purchase Music from the iTunes Store

Apple offers tens of millions of individual tracks for purchase in the iTunes Store. Most tracks are priced from $0.99 to $1.29, which means it's affordable to build your own personal music library.

1. From the iPad Home screen, tap the iTunes Store icon to open the iTunes Store.

2. Tap the Music tab to view music available for purchase.

3. Tap Genres to brows music by genre.

4 Tap within the Search box and enter the name of a song, album, or artist.

5 iTunes displays a list of matching artists or music. Tap the one you want.

6 Tap the price button to purchase an album or track. The button changes to a Buy Song or Buy Album button.

7 Tap Buy Song or Buy Album and follow the instructions to enter your Apple ID and complete the transaction.

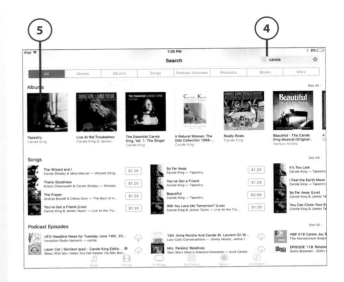

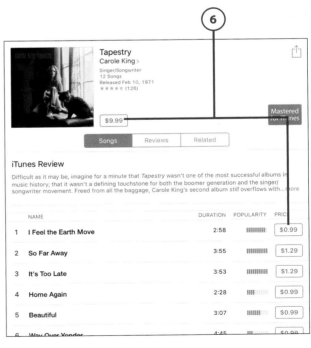

Play Your Tunes

When you purchase a track from the iTunes Store, that track is automatically downloaded to and stored on your iPad. You play this music with the iPad's Music app.

(1) From the iPad Home screen, tap the Music icon to open the Music app.

(2) Tap the Library tab to view all the music stored on your iPad.

(3) Tap Library to select how you view your music—Recently Added, Playlists, Artists, Albums, Songs, or Downloaded Music.

(4) If you select Artists or Albums, tap through to view individual tracks.

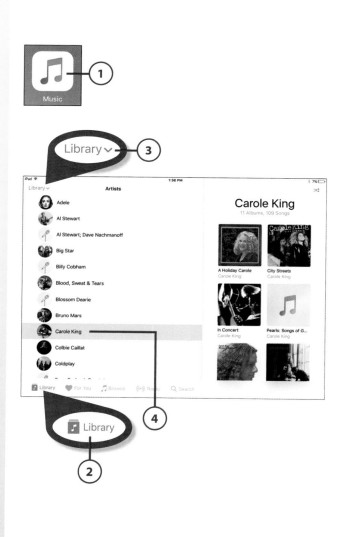

(5) Tap Shuffle All to play all tracks by this artist or in this album in random order.

(6) Tap a track to play that track.

(7) Playback controls appear in the lower-right corner of the screen. Tap Pause to pause playback; tap Play to resume playback.

(8) Tap Next to skip to the next track.

My Digital Entertainment for Seniors

If you want to learn more about digital music available on your iPad and elsewhere online, check out Que's companion book, *My Digital Entertainment for Seniors*, available on the AARP website or wherever books are sold. There's a lot more to listen to online if you know where to find it!

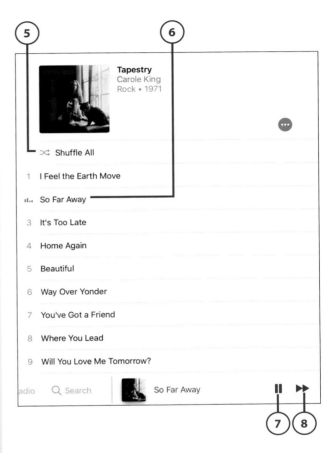

Netflix

Hulu

Amazon Video

iTunes Store

In this chapter, you learn how to use your iPad to watch movies, TV shows, and other videos.

→ Watching Netflix
→ Watching Hulu
→ Watching Amazon Video
→ Watching YouTube
→ Buying and Renting Videos in the iTunes Store

17

Watching TV Shows, Movies, and Other Videos

Your iPad is a great device for watching your favorite movies, TV shows, and other videos wherever you happen to be. Whether you're relaxing on your couch, sitting in a coffeehouse, or traveling cross country, just pull out your iPad and dial up what you want to watch—on Netflix, Hulu, Amazon Prime, and other video services.

(If you want to learn more about movies and TV shows available on your iPad and elsewhere online, check out Que's companion book, *My Digital Entertainment for Seniors*, available on the AARP website or wherever books are sold. There's a lot more to watch online if you know where to find it!)

Watching Netflix

Most of the video you watch on your iPad is *streaming video*. This is video that streams in real time, over the Internet, from a streaming video service. Of course, you can also purchase and download movies and TV shows to your iPad for future viewing (which is covered later in this chapter). But most people these days watch their video entertainment via streaming video. There's nothing to download; just press "play" and you're ready to watch.

The most popular streaming video service today is Netflix. (You've probably heard of it.) Netflix offers a variety of movies, past and current TV shows, and original programming, all for a flat $9.99/month.

Use the Netflix App

You watch Netflix programming via the Netflix app, which you can download for free from Apple's App Store. The first time you launch the app you're prompted to either sign into an existing account, if you have one, or sign up for a new account. Do so.

1 From the iPad's Home screen, tap the Netflix icon to launch the Netflix app.

2 Netflix lets you create multiple viewer profiles. If you've created more than one profile, they're displayed on the Who's Watching? screen. Tap the profile you want to use.

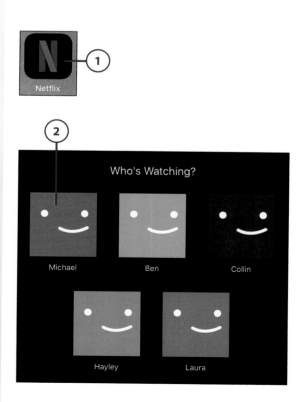

3 On the Netflix home screen, scroll down to see various sections—Popular on Netflix, Trending Now, Watch It Again, Top Picks, and so forth.

4 Tap the Menu icon to view programming by category—TV Shows, Action & Adventure, Comedies, Dramas, and so forth.

5 Tap the Search (magnifying glass) icon to display the Search page and search for specific programming.

6 Tap the program or movie you want to watch.

7 If you selected a television show, you see a detail panel for that show. Tap the Seasons down arrow to display all episodes from a given season.

8 Tap a thumbnail to start watching that episode.

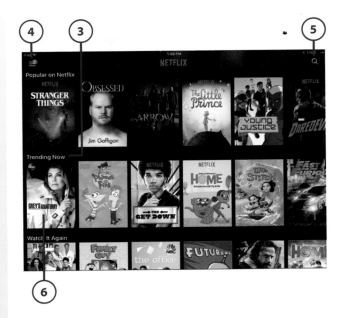

9 If you selected a movie, you see the detail panel with information about that movie. Tap the Play icon to begin watching.

10 Tap the screen to display the controls at the bottom of the screen. Tap the Pause button to pause playback; the button changes to a Play button. Tap Play to resume playback.

11 Drag the slider (sometimes called a "scrubber") to move to another point in the program.

12 Tap the Back (10) icon to skip back 10 seconds.

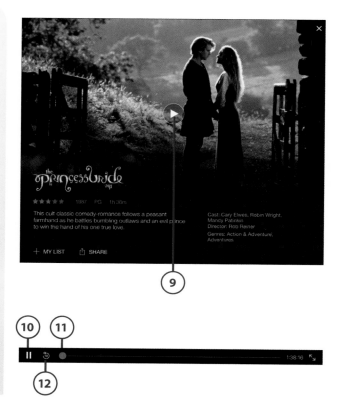

Watching Hulu

Hulu is a streaming video service known for offering recent episodes of network and cable programming. It's a great service for cable cord cutters, as you can watch just about any TV program within a few days of its original airing. (Hulu also offers a selection of movies and original programming.)

Like Netflix, Hulu is a subscription-only service. The Limited Commercials plan costs $7.99/month (as the name implies, you see commercials in your programs), while the No Commercials plan (commercial free, naturally) costs $11.99/month. (These prices are good if you sign up on Hulu's website; try to sign up via iTunes, and you might pay a surcharge for that privilege.)

Use the Hulu App

You watch Hulu from the Hulu app, which you can download for free from Apple's App Store. The first time you launch the Hulu app you're prompted to either sign into an existing account, if you have one, or create a new account. Do whichever you need to do.

(1) From the iPad's Home screen, tap the Hulu icon to launch the Hulu app.

(2) Scroll down Hulu's home screen to view picks and recommendations.

(3) Tap the Menu button to view available programming by type—TV, Movies, Originals, Kids, and so forth.

(4) Tap the Search (magnifying glass) icon to search for specific programming.

(5) Tap a thumbnail to watch that particular program or movie.

(6) If you selected a TV program, scroll down to view episodes by season.

(7) Tap to watch a given episode.

8. If you selected a movie, tap the Play icon to begin watching.

9. Tap the screen to display the playback controls. Tap the Pause button to pause playback; tap Play to resume playback.

10. Drag the slider/scrubber to move to a different point in the program.

11. Tap the Back (10) icon to skip back 10 seconds.

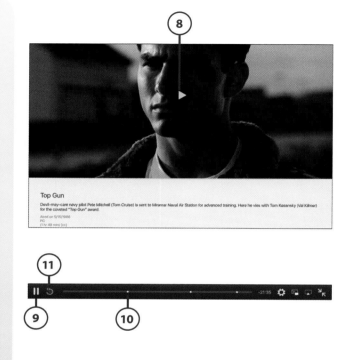

Widescreen Video

Because movies and TV shows are shot wider than they are tall (especially with true widescreen programming), the best way to watch movies on your iPad is to hold your device horizontally, in landscape mode.

Watching Amazon Video

You may know Amazon as a popular online retailer. But Amazon is also in the streaming video business, with its Amazon Video service. Like Netflix and Hulu, Amazon Video offers a variety of movies, TV programs, and original programming.

You watch Amazon Video from the Amazon Video app, which you can download for free from Apple's App Store. You can purchase or rent individual programs, episodes, and movies, or subscribe to Prime Video ($8.99/month) and get many—but not all—programs for free. (Not all shows and movies are available for free with Prime; you still have to purchase them separately.)

Amazon Prime

Amazon Prime Video is both separate from and a part of Amazon Prime, the service that gives you free shipping on most Amazon orders. It's separate in that you can subscribe separately; the $8.99/month Prime Video subscription just covers video streaming, not physical shipping. However, if you go with a full Amazon Prime subscription ($10.99/month or $99.99/year), you not only get free shipping on your Amazon purchases, you also get a full Prime Video membership. Depending on how much shopping you do at Amazon, that might be the best deal.

Use the Amazon Video App

The first time you launch the Amazon Video app you're prompted to sign in with your Amazon account. Do so if you have one; if you don't yet have an Amazon account, you need to go to Amazon's website and create one.

1 From the iPad's Home screen, tap the Amazon Prime icon to launch the Amazon Prime app.

2 Tap the Home tab to view Amazon Video's Home screen.

3 Tap the TV Shows tab to view only TV shows.

4 Tap the Movies tab to view only movies.

5 Scroll down the page to view suggestions by type.

6 Tap the Search box to search for specific shows or movies.

7 Tap to select the item you want to watch.

8 If you selected a TV show, tap to select a season.

9 Tap the Play icon for the episode you want to watch.

10 If you selected a movie, tap Watch Now to watch now.

You own this TV season

The Flash
★ ★ ★ ★ ★ (1,502) **IMDb** 8.2/10   X-Ray

Watch Episode 24

Add To Watchlist

Following the defeat of Barry Allen's arch-nemesis Eobard Thawne (aka Reverse Flash), Team Flash quickly turned their attention to the singularity swirling high above Central City, consuming everything in its path. Armed with the heart of a hero and the ability to move at

+ Read More

Season 1   Season 2

⌄ 1. The Man Who Saved Central City

⌄ 2. Flash of Two Worlds

⌄ 3. Family of Rogues

Interstellar
PG-13 ★ ★ ★ ★ ★ (32,698) **IMDb** 8.6/10   X-Ray

Prime

Watch Now

Download

Add To Watchlist

Play Trailer

From director Christopher Nolan (Inception) comes the story of ex-pilot Cooper (Matthew McConaughey), who must leave his family and Earth behind to lead an expedition beyond this galaxy to discover whether mankind has a future among the stars.

Movie Details

Director:
Christopher Nolan

Duration:
2 hours 49 minutes

Captions:
English

Studio:
Paramount Pictures

Release Year:
2014

11 Tap to display the playback controls. Tap Pause to pause playback; tap Play to resume playback.

12 Tap the Back icon to skip back 10 seconds.

13 Tap the Forward icon to skip forward 10 seconds.

14 Drag the slider/scrubber to move to another point in the program.

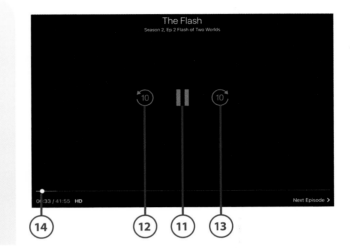

Watching YouTube

Online video isn't all movies and TV shows. YouTube is a video sharing community where regular people, like you and me, can upload and share their home movies and other videos. There's also a lot of more professional content on YouTube, including lots of music videos and educational videos.

Unlike Netflix, Hulu, and Amazon Video, YouTube is completely free. You do get subjected to a fair number of commercials, however, so be prepared for that.

If you want to take advantage of all of YouTube's features, including your own personal playlists and favorites, you need to sign in with your personal account—either a YouTube-specific account or a Google account, both free.

Use the YouTube App

You can watch YouTube from within the Safari web browser or, even better, from the YouTube app. You can download the app, for free, from Apple's App Store. The first time you launch the app you're prompted to sign in to your account or continue as a guest. Make your choice to continue.

1. From the iPad's Home screen, tap the YouTube icon to launch the YouTube app.

2. Tap the Home tab to view YouTube's Home screen.

3. Tap the Trending tab to view trending (popular) videos.

4. Tap the Subscriptions tab to view videos from channels you've subscribed to.

5. Tap the Account tab to view or edit your account information.

6. Scroll down the Home screen to view recommended videos of various types.

7. Tap the Search (magnifying glass) icon to search for specific videos.

8. Tap a thumbnail or title to view that video.

9. The video starts playing automatically. Tap the screen to display the playback controls.

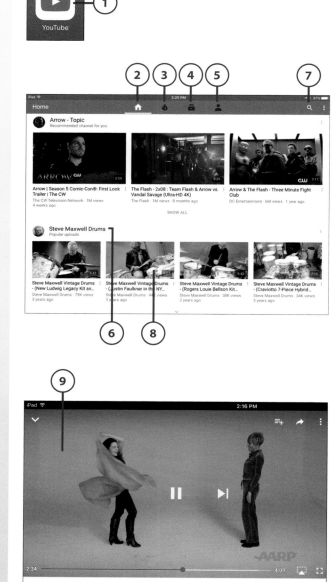

YouTube Ads

Some YouTube videos roll an advertisement before the video itself. In some instances, you can tap Skip Ad to skip the ad after the first few seconds. In other instances, you have to watch the entire ad before the video begins.

10 Tap Pause to pause playback. Tap Play to resume playback.

11 Tap the Next icon to advance to the next recommended video.

12 Drag the slider/scrubber to move to a different point in the video.

13 Tap the Fullscreen icon to display the video full screen. (Tap the icon again to return to the normal YouTube page.)

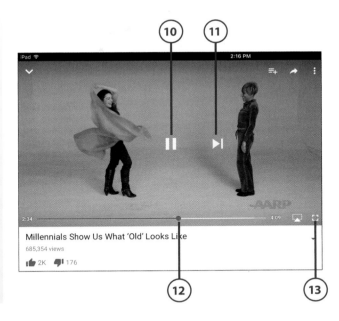

Buying and Renting Videos in the iTunes Store

You can also buy and rent movies and TV shows from Apple's iTunes Store. These items are stored in your iCloud account, so you can buy a movie on one Apple device (like your iPad) and watch it on another (like your iPhone). You can even opt to download the items you purchase to your iPad, so you can watch when you don't have an Internet connection.

Rent Versus Purchase

Items you purchase from the iTunes Store are yours to watch however many times you want. Items you rent (which costs less, naturally) are available to watch for 30 days after purchase. Once you start watching, you have 24 hours to finish.

Rent or Purchase a Video

You can purchase and rent videos directly from the iTunes Store app or from your iPad's Videos app. This example uses the Videos app.

1. From the iPad's Home screen, tap the Videos icon to launch the Videos app.

2. Tap Store to open the iTunes Store.

3. Tap Movies to shop for movies.

4. Tap the movie you want to watch.

5. Tap the Buy button to purchase the movie.

6. Tap the Rent button to rent the movie for a 30-day period.

7 Tap TV Shows to shop for television programs.

8 Tap the program you want to watch.

9 Tap the top price button to purchase all the episodes in the selected season.

10 Tap an individual price button to purchase the selected episode.

Season Pass

For some current television programs, you can purchase a season pass that enables you to watch each new episode as it's available. For more information, look for the Season Pass section in the program's description.

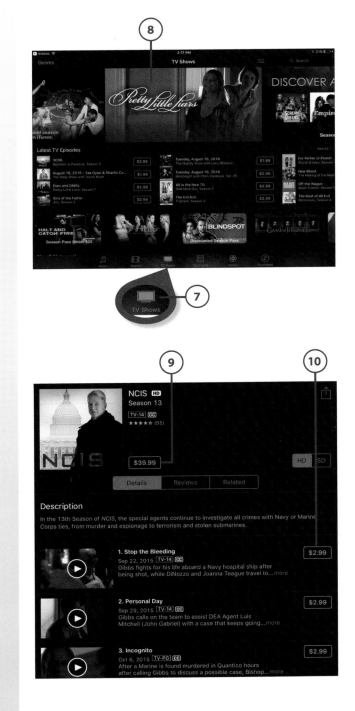

Watch a Video

Once you've rented or purchased a video, you can watch it from the Videos app.

1. From the iPad's Home screen, tap the Videos icon to launch the Videos app.

2. Tap Rentals, Movies, or TV Shows to display items of that type.

3. Tap the show or movie you want to watch.

4. If you selected a movie, tap the Play button to begin playback.

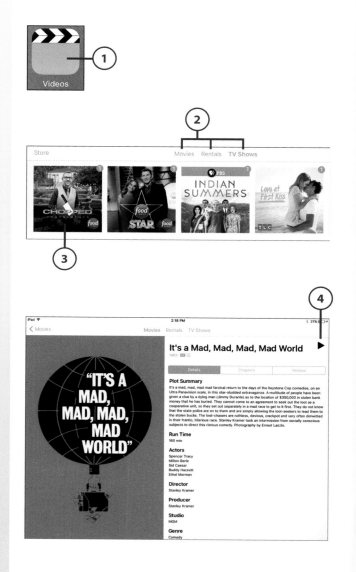

5 If you selected a television show, available episodes are displayed. Tap the episode you want to watch.

6 The selection begins to play. Tap the screen to display the playback controls and then tap Pause to pause playback. Tap Play to resume playback.

7 Press and hold the Fast Forward button to fast-forward.

8 Press and hold the Fast Backward button to go backwards.

9 Use the slider/scrubber at the top of the screen to move to a different point in the video.

10 Tap Done when you're done watching.

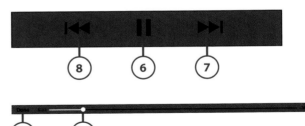

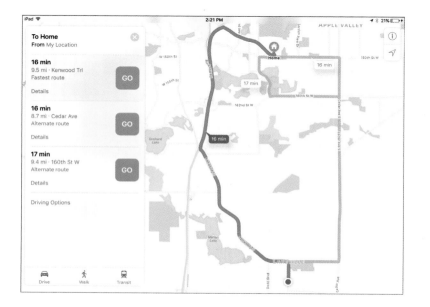

In this chapter, you learn how to use your iPad when you're traveling.

→ Traveling with the Maps App
→ Exploring Other Travel-Related Apps

Traveling with Maps and Other Travel Apps

Your iPad is a handy device when you're at home or out and about. It's even more handy when you're traveling—you can use the Maps app to generate maps and driving directions, and there are all sorts of other fun and useful travel-related apps you can use.

Traveling with the Maps App

Apple's Maps app can show you how to get just about anywhere from wherever you may happen to be. It displays maps of any location, as well as driving directions for how to get there.

Display a Map

The Maps app is, as the name implies a maps app. Enter any location—street address, intersection, major landmark—and it will generate a map of that location.

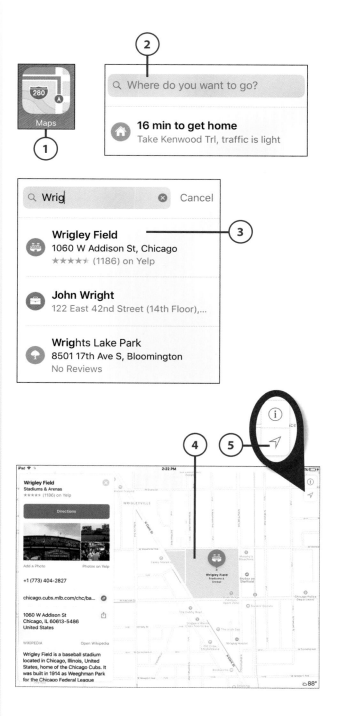

(1) From the iPad's Home screen, tap Maps to open the Maps app.

(2) Tap within the Where Do You Want to Go? panel and enter the location you want mapped. You can enter a street address (accompanied by city and state, if you like), intersection (10th and Main, for example), landmark (such as Brooklyn Bridge or Wrigley Field), or business.

(3) As you type, the Maps app displays suggested matches. Tap the one you want to map.

(4) The app now maps the location you entered, which is pinpointed in the middle of the map. Use your fingers to drag the map left, right, up, or down, or expand/pinch your fingers to zoom into and out of the map.

(5) Tap the Home (arrow) icon to return to (and map) your current location.

Getting Home

The Where Do You Want to Go? panel also tells you how many minutes it will take to get home, with the best route highlighted. (Assuming you've entered your home address into the Contacts app, of course.) Tap this item to display driving directions to your home.

Generate Driving Directions

One of the most useful aspects of the Maps app is to generate driving directions to a given location. It's good to know how to get to where you're going before you leave home!

(1) From within the Maps app, tap within the Where Do You Want to Go? panel and enter the address or description of the destination location.

(2) This location is now mapped, and a descriptive panel appears on the left side of the screen. Tap the Directions button.

3 Suggested routes are displayed. Tap the route you want to take; this route is now mapped onscreen in dark blue. (Alternate routes are in light blue.)

4 Tap the Go button for your selected route to display turn-by-turn instructions.

Walking and Mass Transit

Maps can generate directions if you're walking or taking mass transit. Just tap the Walk or Transit icons at the bottom of the directions panel to change your mode of transport.

5 Swipe right to left in the instructions pane to advance to the next step. Swipe from left to right to return to the previous step.

6 Tap End to return to the previous screen.

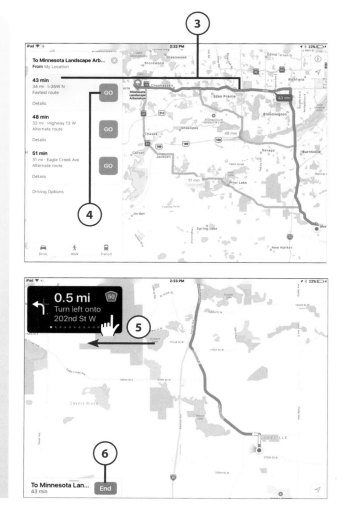

>>>Go Further
DIRECTIONS WHILE DRIVING

If you have an iPad with cellular connectivity, you can use the Maps app in your car to generate turn-by-turn directions while you drive. Because most iPads have only Wi-Fi connectivity, this isn't an option for most users. Instead, use the iPad to preview your route while you're still inside and connected to Wi-Fi. (You can always use the Maps app with your iPhone to guide you while you're driving.)

Exploring Other Travel-Related Apps

The Maps app isn't the only iPad app useful to travelers. Let's take a look at other travel-related apps you might want to consider.

Discover Travel Apps

Here are just a few of the many travel-related iPad apps in Apple's App Store. You can search for specific apps by name, or tap the Categories tab and select the Travel category to see all available apps.

1. Find and book hotel rooms, airline flights, rental cars, and more with the Airbnb, Expedia, Hotels.com, Hotel Tonight, Priceline, Travelocity, and similar apps.

2. Use the TripAdvisor app to learn more about what's available at a given destination—and book your travel plans, too.

3 Use a hotel chain's app to book lodging directly.

4 Use airline apps to book flights directly.

5 Use the Yelp app to find and read reviews for local restaurants—then use the OpenTable app to make a reservation online!

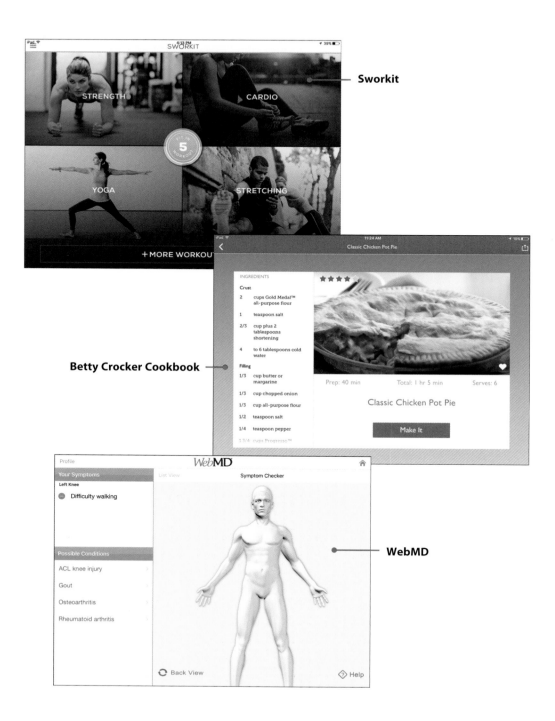

Sworkit

Betty Crocker Cookbook

WebMD

In this chapter, you discover a variety of health and fitness apps for your iPad.

→ Exploring Health and Fitness Apps
→ Exploring Food and Nutrition Apps
→ Exploring Medical Apps

19

Keeping Fit and Healthy

Many people use their tablets to help them manage their daily health and fitness needs. You can find workout and yoga apps, food and nutrition apps, even apps to help you find important medical information. These apps add more value to your iPad and can help you keep healthier!

And if you want to learn more about health options available on your iPad and elsewhere online, check out Que's companion book, *My Health Technology for Seniors*, available on the AARP website or wherever books are sold. There's a lot of good health-related information available online, if you know where to find it!

Exploring Health and Fitness Apps

When it comes to staying fit, nothing beats the combination of a healthy diet and a regular exercise routine. We'll cover diet-related apps in the next section, but for now let's focus on the fitness end of things.

Discover Exercise Apps

It's important to make sure you get enough exercise each day. You can use the following apps to track your daily exercise—and guide your workouts.

(1) Fitnet Live Coach (free with in-app purchases) offers a combination of video and live fitness workouts from your choice of coaches.

(2) Use the Seven app (free) to access 7-minute daily workouts.

(3) Sworkit (free) offers a variety of personalized video workouts, from 5 to 60 minutes long.

Finding Health and Fitness Apps

You can find all the health and fitness apps discussed in this chapter—and more!—in Apple's App Store. Launch the App Store app and search for a particular app by name, or browse the Food & Drink, Health & Fitness, and Medical categories.

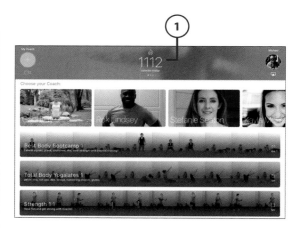

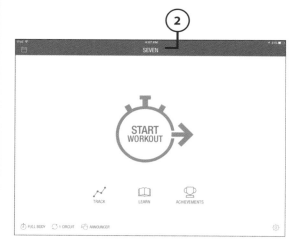

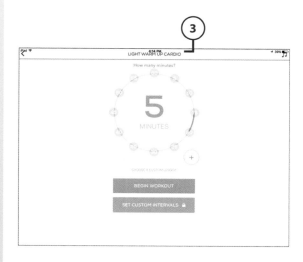

It's Not All Good

In-App Purchases

Many purportedly "free" apps offer in-app purchases for additional features or content. Just because you get an app for free doesn't mean it won't always cost you nothing!

Discover Yoga Apps

If a traditional physical workout is too… well, physical, then check out these Yoga apps for your iPad.

1. Daily Yoga (free) offers more than 100 yoga and meditation exercises, along with 500 yoga poses, guided meditation, and soothing music.

2. FitStar Yoga (free) lets you choose the duration and intensity of each session, and offers a variety of HD yoga videos.

(**3**) Simply Yoga (free and paid versions) offers 20-, 40-, and 60-minute workouts for both men and women.

>>>*Go Further*

HEALTHIER LIVING

In addition to the specific apps in the exercise and nutrition categories, there are also apps that look at healthier living in a more holistic fashion. These apps help you manage your diet, exercise, and other activities to lead a healthier lifestyle. Among the more popular of these healthy living apps are fitJourney (free) and Lifesum (free)—find them in the App Store!

Exploring Food and Nutrition Apps

When it comes to staying healthy, exercise is just part of the equation. You also need to watch what you eat—which you can do with these dieting and food apps.

Discover Dieting Apps

Use these apps to keep track of what you eat—and eat healthier!

1. My Diet Coach (free) helps you set diet goals, tracks your calorie intake, and motivates you with tips and photos.

2. MyFitnessPal's Calorie Counter & Diet Tracker (free) is an easy-to-use calorie counter with a huge database of more than 5 million different foods.

3. When you want to eat healthy, MyPlate Calorie Tracker (free) tracks everything you eat with a database of more than 2 million food items.

Discover Cooking and Recipe Apps

Whether you're trying to eat healthy or just want to spice up your dinner routine, check out these cooking and recipe apps, for all types of cuisine.

1. Use the Allrecipes Dinner Spinner (free) to access popular recipes from the 30 million members of the Allrecipes community—and watch more than 1,000 step-by-step cooking videos, too!

2. The Betty Crocker Cookbook app (free) offers more than 15,000 recipes inspired by the best-selling Betty Crocker cookbooks.

3. The Big Oven app (free) offers more than 350,000 recipes and lets you create your own menu plans and shopping lists.

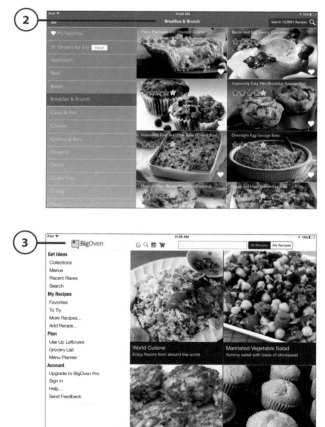

4 The Food Network in the Kitchen app (free) offers recipes from celebrity cooks such as Alton Brown, Guy Fieri, Bobby Flay, and Rachael Ray.

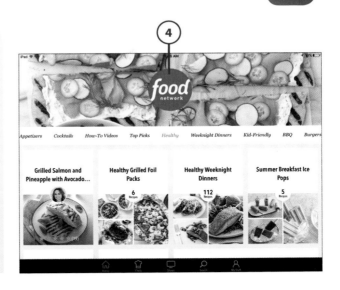

Exploring Medical Apps

There's a ton of medical services and information available on the Internet. The following apps let you access that information—and better track your own medical needs.

Discover Medical-Related Apps

The following apps let you access large online databases about medical conditions, symptoms, and medications. (You still should contact your own personal physician if you think there's something wrong, of course!)

1 The Complete Anatomy app (free) brings anatomy to life with tons of 3D interactive anatomy models. (Lots of paid extra content in this one.) Also popular: Essential Anatomy 5 ($24.99).

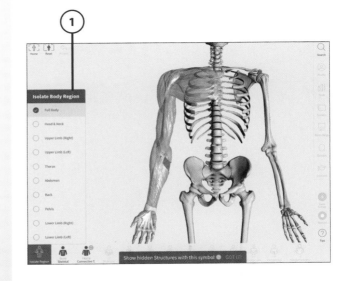

2 The Drugs.com Medication Guide app (free) lets you look up prescription drug information, identify any random pills you might have lying around the house, check drug interactions, and manage your own personal prescription records. Also popular: Formulary Search (free) and PocketPharmacist (free).

3 HealthTap (free) lets you get personal answers and advice regarding your healthcare questions, from more than 100,000 top U.S. doctors.

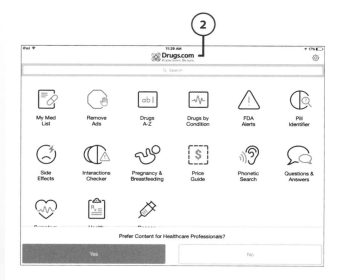

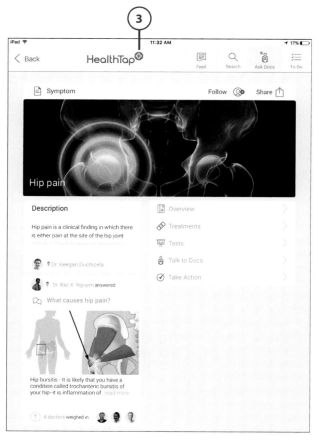

4 Medical Dictionary (free) is a medical dictionary app with more than 180,000 medical terms, 50,000 audio pronunciations, and 12,000 images.

5 The WebMD app (free) is a one-stop shop for everything medical, including a huge database of medical conditions, a symptom checker, medication reminders, drug information, first-aid essentials, and local health provider listings.

It's Not All Good

Don't Self-Diagnose

As tempting as it is to plug your symptoms into one of these medical-related apps and see what pops out, these apps should never replace the experience, knowledge, and advice you get from your own personal physician. Although these apps can be informative, they're not always accurate or complete. It's always best to consult with your own doctors—and use these apps to supplement, not replace, that information.

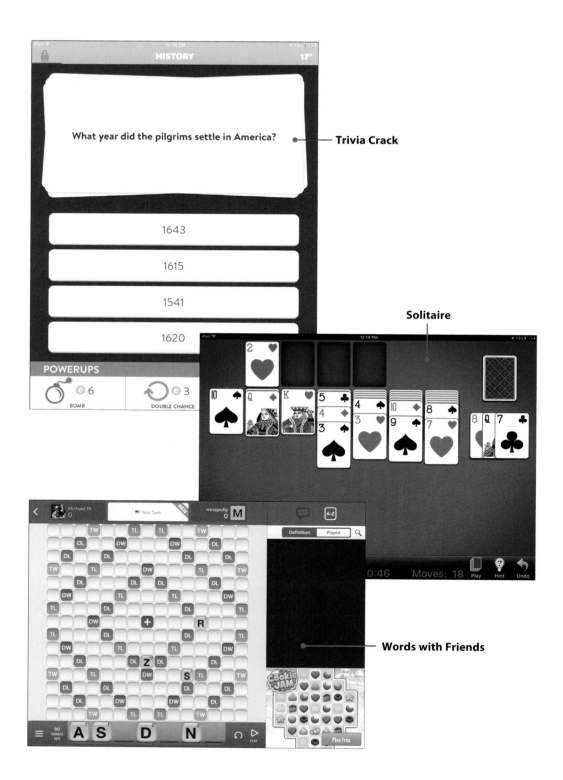

Trivia Crack

Solitaire

Words with Friends

In this chapter, you learn how to find and play games on your iPad.

→ Finding Games to Play
→ Discovering Popular Games

20

Playing Games

Yes, you use your iPad to send and receive emails and text messages, listen to music, watch videos, and read and post to Facebook and other social networks. You may even take a few photos or videos, or even do some real productive work.

But let's be honest. You also spend a fair amount of time on your iPad playing games. And if you don't, your kids or grandkids do. No need to hide it; the iPad is a great game-playing device, and there are lots of fun games you can play on it.

Finding Games to Play

A game is just a certain type of app. Just as you find regular apps for your iPad in Apple's App Store, that's also where you find the games you want to play on your iPad.

Download Games from the App Store

The App Store has a separate section just for games. It's easy to browse through the game categories or search for specific games to download.

1. From your iPad's Home screen, tap the App Store icon to open the App Store.

2. Tap the Categories icon to display all app categories.

3. Tap the Search box to search for specific games.

4. Tap Games to display a list of game categories.

5. Tap the type of game you want to browse—Action, Adventure, Arcade, and so forth.

6. Tap the game you want to play.

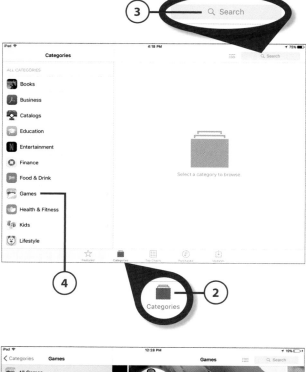

7. Some games are free. To download a free game, tap Get.

8. Many games cost money to play. To purchase a game, tap the price button, which becomes a Buy button.

9. Tap the Buy button.

10) When prompted, enter your Apple ID to pay for and complete the purchase.

Discovering Popular Games

What types of games can you find in the App Store? Apple organizes games by category, as you'll soon discover.

Action Games

Action games are those that emphasize physical challenges and require good hand-eye coordination. Popular action games for the iPad include Angry Birds, Bowmasters, Clash of Clans, Five Nights at Freddy's, and Star Wars: Commander.

Adventure Games

When you play an adventure game, you assume a starring role in some sort of episodic story. Popular adventure games include Criminal Case, MARVEL Contest of Champions, ROBLOX, and Zootopia Crime Files.

All that said, the most popular adventure game for the iPad or any device is Minecraft. This is a world-building game, where you use your block-like character to explore new environments, mine for resources, and build complex structures. The version of Minecraft for the iPad is Minecraft PE (Personal Edition), and while it might not be your thing, your grade school-aged children and grandchildren are probably already hooked.

Arcade Games

Arcade games for the iPad mimic the gameplay of classic coin-operated games, typically with state-of-the-art animation and operation. Popular arcade games for the iPad include Candy Crush Saga (and its endless variants), Farm Heroes Saga, Fruit Ninja, and Sonic Dash 2. You can also find some real, honest-to-goodness classic arcade games in the App Store, including Breakout, PAC-MAN (and Ms. PAC-MAN, too), and various variations of electronic pinball.

If you like classic arcade games, you should also check out a couple of vintage game collections. Atari's Greatest Hits includes paid access to more than 100 classic Atari 2600 and arcade games, including Asteroids, Centipede, and Missile Command. And the 80s Arcade Games pack offers authentic reproductions of Centipede, Defender, Donkey Kong, Joust, and more.

Board Games

Board games for the iPad are just like traditional board games, except you play them on your iPad screen, either by yourself (against the computer) or with others (over the Internet). Popular board games include The Game of Life, Mahjong, Monopoly, and YAHTZEE.

Card Games

There are many games for the iPad that mimic traditional physical card games. These include Canasta, Gin Rummy, Skip-Bo, and Solitaire.

Casino Games

Just about any game you can play in a casino is available in an iPad-friendly version. Popular casino games include Big Fish Casino, DoubleDown Slots & Casino, Jackpot Casino Slots, Poker Night 2, and Zynga Poker—Texas Holdem.

Dice Games

Yes, you can even play dice-driven games on your iPad, including Backgammon, Craps-Shooter, and Dice with Buddies.

Educational Games

If you have little ones around the house, you can keep them busy with fun educational games. The most popular include PBS KIDS Games, Elmo Loves ABCs, LEGO Juniors Create & Cruise, Letter Quiz, and Train Kit.

Family Games

For slightly older kids, check out these fun family games, including Despicable Me: Minion Rush, Disney Magic Kingdoms, Hay Day, and Where's My Water?

Music Games

Many games revolve around music creation and quizzes. In particular, check out Five Little Monkeys Jumping on the Bed, My Singing Monsters, Piano Tiles 2, and Rolling Sky.

Puzzle Games

These games require you to slide your tiles around until you solve or form a puzzle. Popular puzzle games for the iPad include Gummy Drop!, TETRIS, Toy Blast, and Wooden Block Puzzle.

Racing Games

Strap yourself in to race all sorts of virtual vehicles in CSR Racing 2, Extreme Car Driving Simulator, Offroad 4x4 Truck Trials, and Real Racing 3.

Role-Playing Games

These are even more involved adventure games, many of them with lots of shooting and violence. Popular games of this type include Assassin's Creed Identity, Dragon City Mobile, Game of War—Fire Age, and Mobile Strike.

Simulation Games

When you want to simulate some fun real-world activity or persona, check out games like Fishdom, Goat Simulator, My Talking Tom, and Plastic Surgery Simulator.

Sports Games

Just about every popular sport is represented in the App Store, including Madden NFL, NBA LIVE Mobile, Pixel Cup Soccer, R.B.I. Baseball, and WGT Golf Game.

Strategy Games

Strategy games require more thinking than action. The most popular include Clash Royale, Cooking Fever, King of Thieves, and Plants vs. Zombies.

Trivia Games

Who was the first actor to play James Bond? What is the longest river on Earth? What was the top boy band in the 1990s? Answer these and other questions in games such as Family Feud, Jeopardy!, Trivia Crack, and Wheel of Fortune.

Word Games

For many people, this is saving the best category for last. Word games let you put your word-building skills to the test, playing either solo or against other players. The most popular word games for the iPad include SCRABBLE, WordBrain, Words with Friends, and WordWhizzle.

It's Not All Good

In-Game Purchases

Many games strongly suggest that you pay money to get additional levels or resources. These in-game purchases can quickly add up, so think twice before tapping the "buy now" button in any given game.

Document in Pages app

Spreadsheet in Numbers app

Presentation in Keynote app

In this chapter, you learn how to use your iPad for business with key productivity apps.

→ Using Your iPad's Built-In Productivity Apps
→ Discovering More Productivity Apps

Getting Productive

It might not look like it, but your iPad is as powerful as many notebook computers. That means you can use your iPad for just about any office tasks from word processing to spreadsheets to presentations. You can also use your iPad to take notes and create illustrations. All you need are the right apps—and the right accessories, like a physical keyboard. (Learn more about iPad accessories in Chapter 23, "Accessorizing Your iPad.")

Using Your iPad's Built-In Productivity Apps

Your iPad comes with three apps that can help you be more productive in the office and beyond. These apps are Pages, for word processing; Numbers, for spreadsheets; and Keynote, for presentations. These free apps serve the day-to-day productivity needs of many users.

iPad Pro for Productivity

Productivity apps work even better if you have an iPad Pro. The Pro's larger screen, more powerful processor, and Smart Keyboard make office work as easy and intuitive as it is on a traditional notebook computer. If you want to take your work on the road (even if it's just to your local coffee shop), this is the combination for success.

Pages

The Pages app is a word processor, much like Microsoft Word, but optimized for use on the iPad. You can use Pages with your iPad's onscreen keyboard or, even better, use a wireless keyboard for faster and more accurate typing.

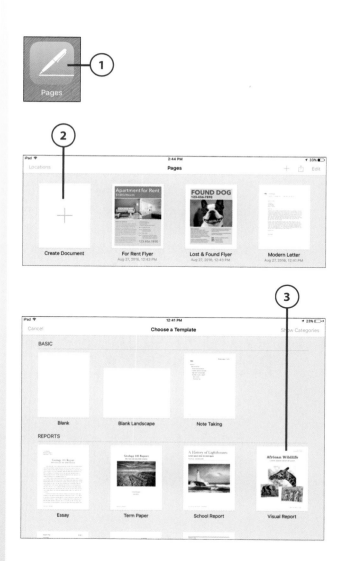

1. From the iPad's Home screen, tap the Pages icon to launch the Pages app.

2. You now see tiles for documents you've previously created. Tap one of these tiles to reopen an existing document, or tap the Create Document tile (or the + at the top right) to create a new document.

3. Tap to select a template for your new document.

4 Most documents include place-holder text as defined by the template you selected. Tap any block of placeholder text to replace that text with your own text, using the onscreen keyboard.

5 Tap the paintbrush icon in the toolbar to format the selected text.

6 Tap the Paragraph Style control to change the paragraph style.

7 Tap Font to change the font family.

8 Tap B to boldface text.

9 Tap I to italicize text.

10 Tap the − and + buttons to decrease or increase the size of the selected text.

11 Tap the + icon to insert a table, chart, shape, or picture.

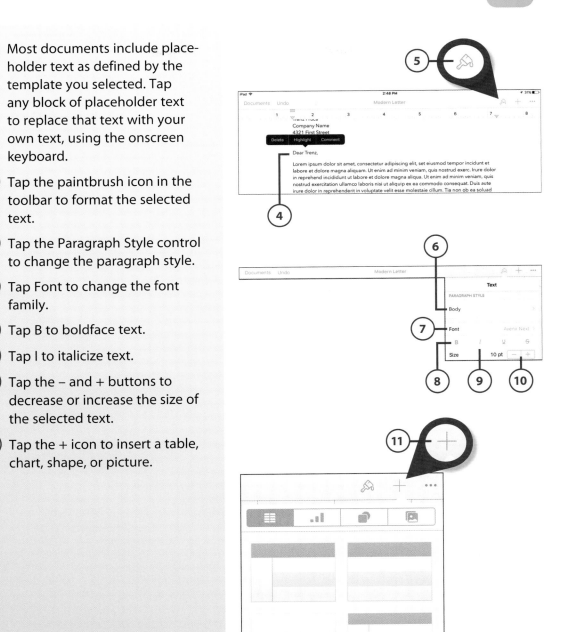

12 Tap the More icon to collaborate with others, send a copy of this document, print this document, and more.

10

More

Collaborate With Others

Send a Copy

Print

Find

Change Tracking

Stored in the Cloud

By default, all Pages, Numbers, and Keynote documents are stored in the cloud—in Apple's iCloud, to be specific. This means you don't have to manually save your work; all changes are saved automatically, as you make them. It also means that your documents won't fill up the limited storage on your iPad, and they will be available to any device connected to the Internet, via your iCloud account.

Numbers

You use the Numbers app to… well, to work with numbers. You can create spreadsheets in which you can enter and manipulate numerical data. It's great for creating budgets, expense reports, financial plans, and the like. You can perform all sorts of complex calculations and then display your results in attractive charts and graphs.

1 From the iPad's Home screen, tap the Numbers icon to launch the Numbers app.

1

2 You now see tiles for spreadsheets you've previously created. Tap one of these tiles to reopen an existing spreadsheet, or tap the Create Spreadsheet tile (or the +) to create a new spreadsheet.

2

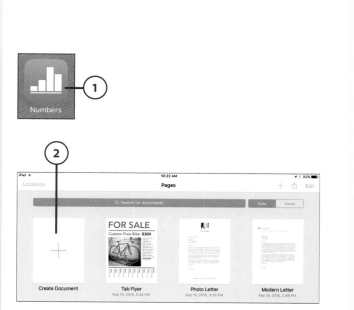

3 Tap to select the template you want to use for your new spreadsheet.

4 The new spreadsheet includes placeholder text and numbers entered into cells. Tap any cell to replace its placeholder contents with your own text and numbers, using the onscreen keyboard. (To select more than one cell, use your finger to drag any of the selection corners to include additional cells.)

5 Tap the paintbrush icon to format the selected cell(s).

Rows, Columns, and Cells

A spreadsheet consists of multiple *rows* (arranged down the left edge of the screen) and *columns* (arranged along the top of the screen). The intersection of any given row and column is called a *cell*; all the contents of a spreadsheet are contained in individual cells.

6 Tap the Table tab to format the selected cells as a table.

7 Tap the Cell tab to format the contents of the selected cell(s). You can apply text formatting (bold, italic, underline, strike-through); change text options (size, color, and font); apply cell fill color; add various types of borders; and opt to wrap long text in a cell, or not.

8   Tap the Format tab to format the numerical data in the selection. You can choose a general Number format, Currency format, Percentage, and so forth.

9   Tap the Arrange tab to move the selected element forward or backward on the page.

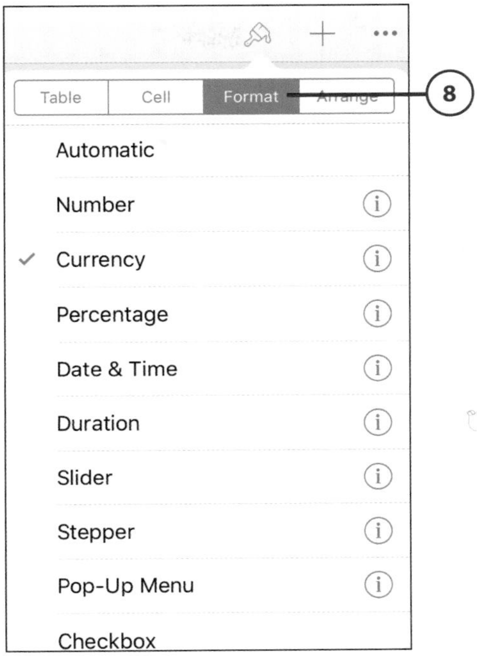

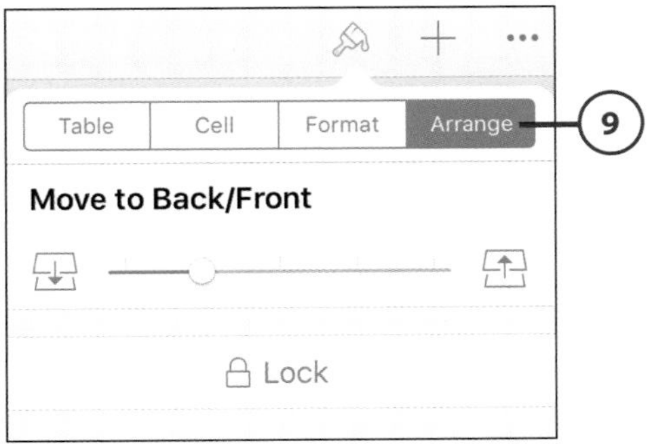

Table	Cell	Format	Arrange

Automatic

Number   ⓘ

✓ Currency   ⓘ

Percentage   ⓘ

Date & Time   ⓘ

Duration   ⓘ

Slider   ⓘ

Stepper   ⓘ

Pop-Up Menu   ⓘ

Checkbox

Table	Cell	Format	Arrange

Move to Back/Front

🔒 Lock

10 Tap the + icon to insert a table, chart, shape, or picture.

11 Double-tap a cell to enter a formula or function to perform a numerical calculation.

Formulas and Functions

You perform a calculation in a spreadsheet by entering a formula that may include the contents of specified cells. You can include built-in formulas, called functions, within your larger formulas. (Unfortunately, the whole concept of formulas and functions is much more involved than we can discuss in this chapter; tap More, Numbers Help to view coaching tips onscreen.)

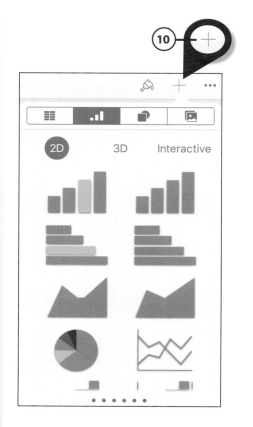

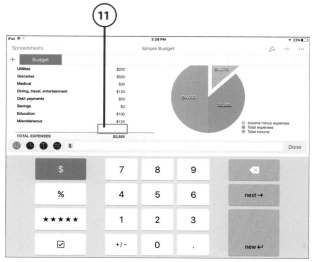

Keynote

When you need to put on a presentation to any size group, Keynote can't be beat. The Keynote app lets you create highly visual presentations that you can present on your iPad or through a larger monitor or projector. (You first have to connect your iPad to said monitor, of course.)

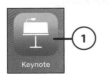

(**1**) From the iPad's Home screen, tap the Keynote icon to launch the Keynote app.

(**2**) You now see tiles for presentations you've previously created. Tap one of these tiles to reopen an existing presentation, or tap the Create Presentation tile (or the + at the top right) to create a new presentation.

(**3**) Tap to select the template you want to use for your new presentation.

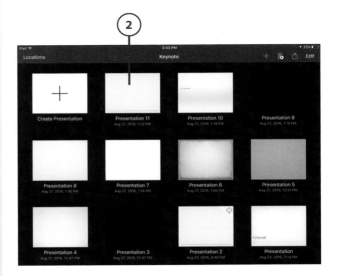

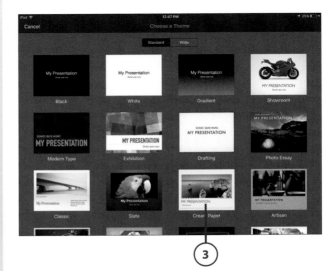

4. The new presentation includes a preselected visual theme, along with a single opening slide. The slides in your presentation are displayed in the slide sorter on the left side of the screen. Tap any slide to view it in the larger editing area.

5. Each new slide includes placeholder text and graphics. Double-tap any placeholder to replace its contents with your own.

6. Tap the paintbrush icon to format the slide's Style (background and text colors), format selected Text (font family and size, bold and italic formatting, and text alignment), and Arrange elements on the screen.

7. Tap the + icon to insert a table, chart, shape, or picture.

8. Tap the New Slide (+) icon to add a new slide to the presentation.

9 Tap to select the type of slide you want to add.

10 Repeat the preceding steps to add your own slide content and add additional slides to the presentation.

11 To add a transition between slides, tap a slide in the slide sorter and select Transition.

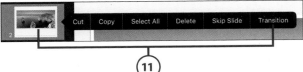

(12) Tap Effects to see available transitions.

(13) Tap to select the type of slide transition you want.

(14) Tap Options to set transition duration and how the transition is triggered.

(15) Tap the Play button in the tool-bar to play your presentation.

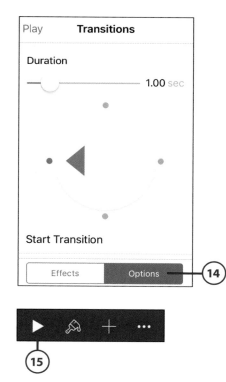

(16) Tap or swipe the screen to advance to the next slide.

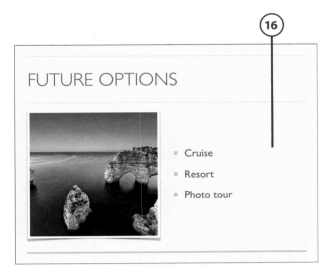

>>>*Go Further*

KEYNOTE REMOTE

The Keynote app lets you use your iPad as a remote control to present slideshows on other Apple devices, including Macs and iPhones. To use the Keynote Remote, open your presentation, tap More, and then tap Allow Remote Control. Follow the onscreen instructions to pair your iPad to another Apple device via Wi-Fi or Bluetooth.

Discovering More Productivity Apps

As good (and as free) as Apple's productivity apps are, they're not the only such apps available for your iPad. Google, Microsoft, and other software publishers offer similar productivity apps for iPad users, all available from Apple's App Store.

Evernote

Evernote is a popular app that lets you take and share notes, create to-do lists, and save content you find online, and then organize your notes in various ways. You can also sync your Evernote content across multiple devices, including iPhones, Macs, Windows PCs, and even Android phones and tablets. The Evernote app is free.

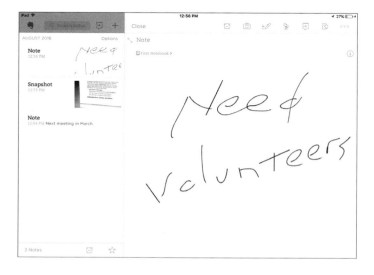

Other Note-Taking Apps

Other popular note-taking apps include GoodNotes 4 ($7.99), Notability ($7.99), and Notepad+ ($14.99—also available in a free version).

Google Docs, Sheets, and Slides

Taken together, Apple's Pages, Numbers, and Keynote apps comprise what some call an *office suite*—a collection of apps that let you perform most office productivity functions. Apple's apps are kind of an ad hoc or unofficial suite, compared to the more formal app suites from other companies.

Case in point is Google's office suite, dubbed Google Docs. The apps in the Google Docs suite include Docs (word processing), Sheets (spreadsheet), and Slides (presentations). These apps are a little more traditional in their operation than the iPad- (and Mac-) focused nature of Apple's productivity apps. But, unlike Apple's apps, they're cross-platform compatible; you can use the Google Docs apps on your iOS device, your Android device, your Windows computer, and your Google Chromebook, if you have one.

All three Google Docs apps are free, and work great on the iPad.

Microsoft Excel, PowerPoint, and Word

Speaking of office suites, the big daddy of all office suites is Microsoft Office. Long available only on Windows PCs, Microsoft now has Office apps available for all platforms, including Apple's iOS. The apps available—all free, by the way—include Word (word processing), Excel (spreadsheet), and PowerPoint (presentations).

Functionality of Microsoft's iOS apps isn't quite as robust as that of their PC counterparts, but files are fully compatible. If you're used to using Office apps in your office, then using those same apps on your iPad makes a lot of sense.

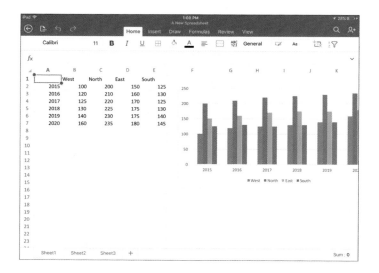

Paper

Paper is kind of a note-taking app with a twist. Use the Paper app to take hand-written notes and do any other type of writing and drawing. Paper makes it easy to not only create content, but to link that content to other content. You can connect text, photos, sketches, and more together, and thus better organize your ideas.

Paper is available for free from Apple's App Store. The original version of Paper won Apple's App of the Year award, and it's easy to see why.

| Settings | ‹ Storage & iCloud Usage | Storage |

| Notifications |
| Control Center |
| Do Not Disturb |

| Used | 34.8 GB |
| Available | 24.24 GB |

Videos	13.62 GB ›
Music	6.42 GB ›
Photos & Camera	2.15 GB ›
GarageBand	1.34 GB ›
iMovie	746.1 MB ›
C. Anatomy	685.2 MB ›
Keynote	572.2 MB ›
Excel	371 MB ›
FitStar Yoga	352.7 MB ›
Pages	348.4 MB ›
Numbers	337.1 MB ›
Farm Heroes Super Saga	245.4 MB ›

Settings list:
- Notifications
- Control Center
- Do Not Disturb
- General
- Display & Brightness
- Wallpaper
- Sounds
- Siri
- Touch ID & Passcode
- Battery
- Privacy
- iCloud
  millerwriter@icloud.com
- iTunes & App Store
- Wallet & Apple Pay

In this chapter, you learn how to manage the files stored on your iPad.

Managing Files on Your iPad and in the Cloud

How do you get your photos and other files from your iPad to your computer—or vice versa? How do you manage those files stored on your iPad? How can you share your files with others? This chapter shows you how to do all these things. (Hint: It's all about the "cloud.")

Managing Your iPad Storage

First off, let's find out how much storage you're using on your iPad. You have limited storage, after all; if you fill it, you won't have enough space to install new apps or shoot new pictures or videos.

Examine Available Storage

You can see how much storage space you've used—and have still available—from your iPad's Settings screen.

1. From your iPad's Home screen, tap the Settings icon to open the Settings screen.

2. Tap General in the left column.

3. Tap Storage & iCloud Usage.

4. The Used field displays the amount of storage space currently used.

5. The Available field displays how much storage space you have left to use.

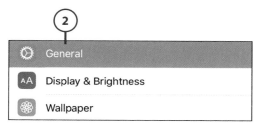

STORAGE	
Used	34.81 GB
Available	24.24 GB
Manage Storage	>

Manage Available Storage Space

Which apps are using the most storage space? If you're running short on space, which apps are the best to delete?

Fortunately, Apple makes it easy to look at storage on an app-by-app basis—and, just as easily, delete those apps and files that you're not using.

(**1**) From the Storage & iCloud Usage screen, in the Storage section, tap Manage Storage.

(**2**) You see a list of all the apps installed on your iPad, with the largest apps (those using the most storage space) first. Tap an app to view more details.

(**3**) The Music and Video apps both list the corresponding media files used by each app— individual songs (and songs by artist) for the Music app, and TV shows and movies for the Video app. Tap an item to view more details.

General	Storage & iCloud Usage	
STORAGE		
Used		34.81 GB
Available		24.24 GB
Manage Storage		>

(**1**)

(**2**)

Videos	13.62 GB >
Music	6.42 GB >
Photos & Camera	2.16 GB >
GarageBand	1.34 GB >
iMovie	746.1 MB >
C. Anatomy	685.2 MB >
Keynote	572.2 MB >

MUSIC	6.39 GB
All Songs	6.39 GB
ARTISTS	6.39 GB
Adele 19	87 MB >
Al Stewart A Beach Full of Shells and 14 more	1.4 GB >
Al Stewart; Dave Nachmanoff Uncorked: Al Stewart Live With Dave Nachmanoff	125.1 MB >
Big Star Radio City and 2 more	288.5 MB >
Billy Cobham The Best of Billy Cobham and Spectrum	175.1 MB >
Blood, Sweat & Tears Blood, Sweat & Tears and 7 more	703.4 MB >

(**3**)

(4) Delete a media item by tapping Edit in the top-right corner.

(5) Tap the red – icon.

(6) Tap Delete.

(7) Tap Done.

(8) Other apps display the amount of space used by that app and its data. Tap Delete App to delete the app and its corresponding data.

(9) Tap Delete App in the confirmation box.

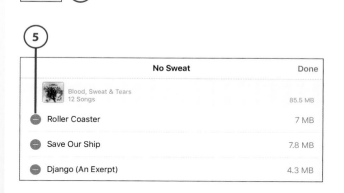

| Edit — (4) |

(5)		
No Sweat		Done
Blood, Sweat & Tears 12 Songs		85.5 MB
⊖ Roller Coaster		7 MB
⊖ Save Our Ship		7.8 MB
⊖ Django (An Exerpt)		4.3 MB

(6)(7)

No Sweat		Done
Blood, Sweat & Tears 12 Songs		85.5 MB
r Coaster	7 MB	Delete
⊖ Save Our Ship		7.8 MB

‹ Storage   Info

KEYNOTE
Version 2.6.2
App Size: 562.8 MB

Documents & Data   9.4 MB

Delete App

(8)

Delete App
Deleting "Keynote" will also delete all
of its documents & data.

Cancel   Delete App — (9)

>>>*Go Further*

WHAT TO DELETE

When you're looking to free up storage space on your iPad, it makes sense to look at the largest apps first—which is why Apple sorts them that way. You get the most bang for your buck by deleting a single large app than by deleting several smaller ones. So look at the apps in order of largest to smallest, and find those you no longer use or want. The first ones you come across are the ones you should delete.

Storing and Sharing Files on iCloud

It used to be that the only way to transfer media files to and from your iPad was by connecting your device to a computer. (And we'll talk about that method later in this chapter.) Today, however, most users rely on Apple's iCloud service to store and transfer media files on their iPads and iPhones.

iCloud is a cloud-based storage service, which means it stores your files on Apple's servers, over the Internet. All files are synced wirelessly when you're connected to a Wi-Fi network, so you don't have to physically connect your iPad to your computer.

>>>*Go Further*

UNDERSTANDING iCLOUD AND CLOUD STORAGE

When it comes to storing data, there are two types of storage: local and cloud. Local storage means that your data is stored locally, on your device. (In your case, your iPad.) Cloud storage stores your data on computer servers in the "cloud"—that is, on the Internet. The advantage of local storage is that you always have your data at hand, even if you don't have an Internet connection. The advantage of cloud storage is that you can access your data from any device connected to the Internet, from wherever you might happen to be. All you need is an Internet connection and the username and password for your cloud storage account.

Apple's cloud storage service is called iCloud, and it's integrated into iOS and your iPad. This is a good thing, as you have a lot more storage space available in the cloud than you do on your iPad itself. You can also access the photos and videos you shoot with your iPad from any other device—your iPhone, for example, or your desktop or laptop computer.

One nice thing about how iCloud works is that once you enable it, you really don't have to do much else. Any new photo or file you create on your iPad is automatically uploaded to iCloud; you don't have to manually transfer any files. This also syncs your data between multiple devices; if you have a shared calendar, when you add an event on your iPad's Calendar app that new event appears on all other devices linked to your iCloud account.

Access isn't limited to Apple devices, either. You can log onto iCloud.com from any computer or mobile device, using any web browser. It's all connected.

You were prompted to create an iCloud account when you first powered up your new iPad. You can also create a new account at a later date by going to iCloud.com and selecting the Don't Have an Apple ID? Option.

You get 5GB of free storage with your iCloud account. That's a lot, and it might be all you need. If it's not enough storage space, however, you can upgrade your account to get more storage. In the U.S., you pay $0.99/month for 50GB of storage (that's ten times the default storage space), $2.99/month for 200GB, or $9.99/month for a whopping 1TB (that's one terabyte, or 1,000 gigabytes!).

Configure iCloud on Your iPad

You probably set up iCloud when you first powered up your iPad. You can change any iCloud settings at any time from your iPad's Settings screen.

 From your iPad's Home screen, tap the Settings icon to open the Settings screen.

(**2**) Tap iCloud in the left column.

(**3**) Tap your username to change contact information, password, payment information, and other account info.

(**4**) Tap Set Up Family Sharing to share photos, music, movies, schedules, and more with other family members.

(**5**) The Storage section tells you how much iCloud storage space you have free. Tap Storage to manage your storage or buy more storage space.

(**6**) Tap iCloud Drive to enable/ disable storage for specific apps.

(**7**) Tap on the iCloud Drive switch to enable apps to store their documents and data in iCloud.

(**8**) Tap on the switch for each individual app for which you want to enable storage.

(**9**) Tap the back arrow to return to the previous screen.

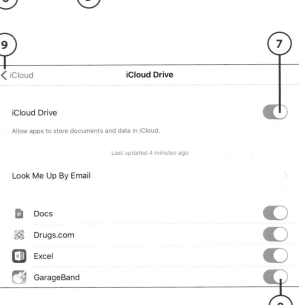

(10) Tap Photos to enable/disable photo sharing via iCloud.

(11) Tap on the iCloud Photo Library switch to automatically upload and store your photo library in iCloud.

(12) Tap Optimize iPad Storage to store all your photos online and automatically delete them from your iPad.

(13) Tap Download and Keep Originals to keep your original photos on your iPad (and copies in iCloud).

(14) Tap on Upload to My Photo Stream to automatically share your photos and videos with other iCloud-connected devices.

(15) Tap on iCloud Photo Sharing to create photo albums to share with other users.

(16) Tap the back arrow to return to the previous screen.

(17) Tap on the switch for any app or service that you want to sync via iCloud. (Probably all of them.)

☁ iCloud Drive	On >
❀ Photos	On >

(10)

(16) (12) (13) (14) (11)

‹ iCloud   P**hotos**

iCloud Photo Library

Automatically upload and store your entire library in iCloud to access photos and videos from all your devices.

Updated Just Now

Optimize iPad Storage

Download and Keep Originals   ✓

This iPad is currently storing original photos and videos. Turn on Optimize Storage to automatically manage storage on this device and keep originals in iCloud.

Upload to My Photo Stream

Automatically upload new photos and send them to all of your iCloud devices when connected to Wi-Fi.

iCloud Photo Sharing

Create albums to share with other people, or subscribe to other people's shared albums.

(15)

✉ Mail	⬤
👤 Contacts	⬤
📅 Calendars	⬤
Reminders	⬤
🧭 Safari	⬤
🏠 Home	◯
Notes	⬤
N News	⬤

(17)

(18) Tap Keychain to enable iCloud Keychain, which stores passwords and credit card information across other iCloud-connected devices.

(19) Tap Backup to enable iCloud Backup, which automatically backs up important data from your iPad to iCloud.

(20) Tap Find My iPad to enable the Find My iPad service, which helps you find or disable your iPad if it's lost.

🔑 Keychain		On >
🔄 Backup		On >
⚪ Find My iPad		On >

Find My iPad

Learn more about Find My iPad in Chapter 6, "Keeping Your iPad Safe and Secure."

Use the iCloud Drive App

You use the iCloud Drive app to view and manage those files you've stored in iCloud.

(1) From your iPad's Home screen, tap the iCloud Drive icon to open the iCloud Drive app.

(2) Files are stored in folders, by app. (Files not associated with a given app are stored separately on the main screen.) Tap a folder to view its contents.

(3) Tap an item to open that item.

(4) Tap Select to move or delete an item.

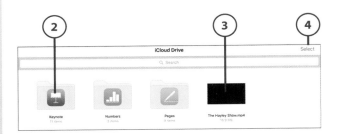

5 Tap to select one or more items. A blue check mark indicates selected items.

6 Tap Move to move this item to another folder.

7 Tap Delete to delete this item from iCloud.

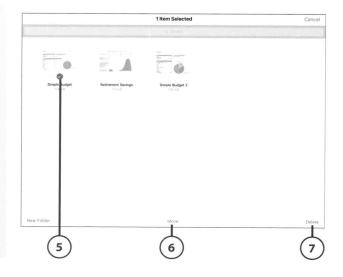

>>>Go Further

ACCESS iCLOUD FROM YOUR COMPUTER

You can view all items stored in your iCloud account from any connected device, including your desktop or laptop computer. Just open your web browser, go to iCloud.com, and then enter your Apple ID and password.

Once you've signed in, you see icons for all the iCloud-related services—Mail, Contacts, Calendar, Photos, and such. If you want to view your uploaded photos, click Photos. If you want to view other uploaded files, click iCloud Drive. From there you can navigate through the folders to view individual files.

Click to view iCloud photos

Click to view iCloud files

Syncing Files Between Your iPad and Your Computer

While your iPad is a freestanding device, you may want to connect it to your computer to synchronize ("sync") music, videos, eBooks, and other files between the two devices. You can also use your computer as a storage device to back up the files on your iPad.

Connect to Your Computer

You use the same cable to connect your iPad to your computer as you use to connect your iPad to the power adapter. You can connect to either Apple or Windows computers.

(1) Connect the Lightning connector on the cable to the Lightning port on the bottom of the iPad.

(2) Connect the USB connector on the cable to a USB port on your computer.

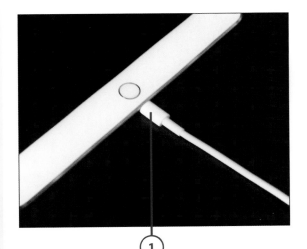

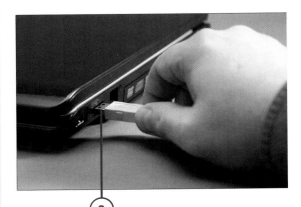

Sync with iTunes

When you connect your iPad to your computer, the iTunes software should launch automatically on your computer. If you don't yet have iTunes installed on your computer, go to www.apple.com/itunes/download; it's free.

You use the iTunes software to determine which files you sync (copy) between your computer and iPad. Select photos, music tracks, videos, eBooks, and other media files stored on your computer that you want to transfer to your iPad.

You can also use iTunes to update your iPad when there are updates to the operating system—although this can also be done wirelessly.

It's Not All Good

Launch iTunes Manually

If iTunes doesn't automatically launch on your computer when you connect your iPad, you might need to open it manually.

(1) Connect your iPad to your computer to launch the iTunes software on your computer.

(2) Within iTunes, click the iPad icon below the menu bar. This displays information about your connected iPad.

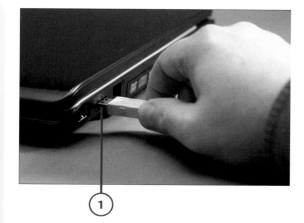

3 Click Summary in the left column to view key information about your iPad and to turn on automatic backups to either your computer or your iCloud account.

4 Click Apps to view and manage the apps and Home screen on your iPad.

5 Click Music to select which playlists, artists, albums, and genres on your computer to sync to your iPad.

6 Click Movies to select which movies on your computer you want to sync.

7 Click TV Shows to select which TV shows stored on your computer you want to sync.

8 Click Books to select which eBooks stored on your computer you want to sync.

9 Click Audiobooks to select which audiobooks stored on your computer you want to sync.

10 Click Photos to select which folders containing photos on your computer you want to sync.

11 Click any tab in the On My Device section to view the music, movies, TV shows, books, audiobooks, and ringtones that are stored on your iPad.

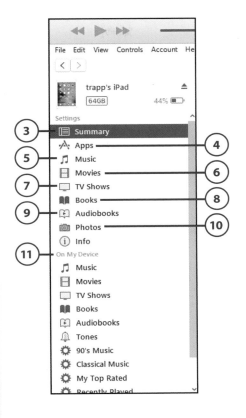

Using AirDrop and AirPlay to Share Content with Other Devices

One nice thing about committing to the Apple ecosystem (that is, using multiple Apple devices—iPads, iPhones, Mac computers, and the Apple TV set-top device) is that it's easy to share data and files between each device. This is particularly easy using Apple's AirDrop and AirPlay feature. AirDrop lets you easily sync files between devices, whereas AirPlay enables wireless streaming of music and videos to other devices.

Share Files with AirDrop

Use AirDrop to share photos, videos, locations, websites, and more with other compatible devices. AirDrop uses both Wi-Fi and Bluetooth to transfer data; if the other device isn't on the same Wi-Fi network as your iPad, you can connect them via Bluetooth, instead.

To use AirDrop, each device must be connected to the same network and signed into iCloud. All transfers are encrypted for security.

(1) Within an app, tap the Share icon.

(2) Nearby users are displayed in the top row of the share panel. Tap the name of a user to share this file with that user.

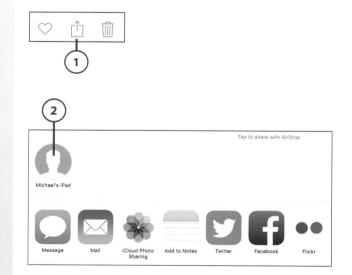

3 To receive files from another user, swipe up from the bottom of any screen on your iPad to display the Control Center.

4 Tap the AirDrop tile.

5 Tap Contacts Only to receive files from people in your contacts list only.

6 Tap Everyone to receive files from anyone nearby.

7 Tap Receiving Off to turn off AirDrop for receiving files.

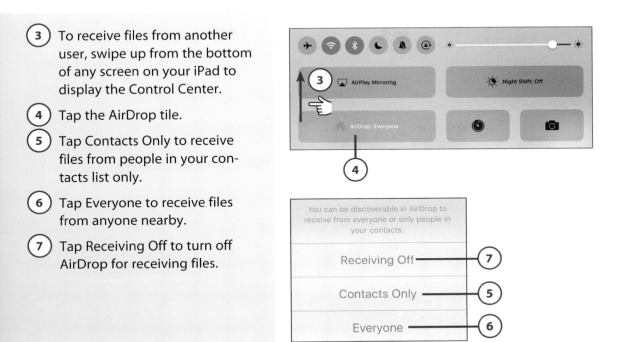

Stream Media with AirPlay

Use AirPlay to stream music and videos from your iPad to any compatible device in real time. You can share with Apple TV set-top boxes or other compatible set-top boxes, TVs, and audio/video receivers.

To stream media via AirPlay, both your iPad and the target device need to be connected to the same Wi-Fi network. You may also need to enable AirPlay on the other device.

1 Swipe up from the bottom of any screen to open the Control Center.

2 Swipe from right to left to display the music pane.

AirPlay Mirroring

You do *not* use the AirPlay Mirroring tile in the Control Center to stream music and videos to other devices. Tap AirPlay Mirroring if you want to "mirror" your iPad screen to an Apple TV set-top device.

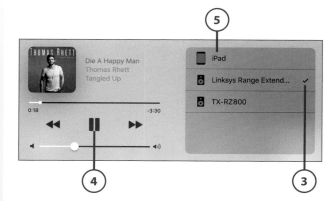

3 AirPlay looks for and displays nearby devices. Tap the device to which you want to stream.

4 Use the playback controls to start and pause playback. The current media is now streamed to the selected device—and *not* played on your iPad.

5 Tap iPad to return playback to your iPad.

Backing Up Your iPad

The data that you store on your iPad—pictures, videos, music, and more—is valuable to you. You don't want to lose these items if you happen to lose or damage your iPad, or if your iPad quits working.

Which is why you want to back up all your data—and settings and apps—in case something bad happens. When you have a backup of your important stuff, you can then restore those items to your iPad when it's found or fixed.

There are two ways to back up the data, settings, and apps on your iPad. You can back up online, to your iCloud storage account. Or you can back up to your computer, using the iTunes software.

Back Up to iCloud

The fastest and easiest way to back up your iPad is to iCloud. Backups happen automatically in the background whenever you're connected to the Internet via a Wi-Fi network.

1. From your iPad's Home screen, tap the Settings icon to open the Settings screen.

2. Tap iCloud in the left column.

3. Scroll down the list of apps and tap Backup.

4. Tap on the iCloud Backup switch.

5. If you want to back up your data now, tap Back Up Now.

Back Up to Your Computer via iTunes

If you'd rather not trust your data to the cloud, you can back up everything locally to your personal computer. All you have to do is connect your iPad to your computer, using the included USB cable, and then launch your computer's iTunes software.

1. On your computer, launch the iTunes software and make sure your iPad is selected.

2. In the Settings panel, click to select Summary.

3. In the Backups section, click to select This Computer.

4. Click the Back Up Now button to back up your iPad now.

5. Click Done when done.

In this chapter, you discover various accessories to personalize and power up your iPad.

→ Protecting Your iPad with Cases and Covers
→ Adding Functionality with Keyboards and Styli
→ Extending Your iPad with Bluetooth Devices

Accessorizing Your iPad

Numerous third-party companies make a variety of accessories you can add to your iPad. We're talking everything from covers to keyboards to wireless headphones. These accessories keep your iPad safer and make it more functional and more personalized.

Protecting Your iPad with Cases and Covers

The iPad is an exceptionally sleek and stylish bit of technological design. Unfortunately, this thin, light, mostly glass device is prone to break if you happen to drop it or give it a good twist.

This is why it's a good idea to encase your iPad inside some sort of protective cover. Of course, a rugged case tends to hide the sleek and stylish design, but that cool iPad design won't mean much if you crack the screen or just plain break the thing.

Smart Covers

There are all manner of covers and cases available for the iPad, whether you have a mini, Air, or Pro. One particularly useful type is the *smart cover*, which automatically puts your iPad to sleep when closed and wakes it up when opened. You can find smart covers from Apple and a variety of third parties, many of which feature foldable backs to function as stands for your device.

Apple's Smart Cover

Other Covers and Cases

Other companies make other types of covers and cases for your iPad. These range from soft silicone coverings to harder, more ruggedized protective cases. Some covers are optimized for use by children, making the device easier to hold and more impervious to unintentional destruction. There are even cases designed for presentation use, with hand straps or grips so you can hold the device in one hand when you give a presentation.

Ruggedized protective
iPad case from OtterBox

Desktop Stands

Some covers have folding backs that let you sit your iPad more vertically, but you might prefer a more single-purpose approach. Several companies offer desktop iPad stands that make it easier to read books and newspapers on your device, or to function as more of a desktop monitor—especially if you add a wireless keyboard.

Adding Functionality with Keyboards and Styli

If you want to use your iPad for office work, you need something other than the onscreen keyboard for typing. The good news here is that there are a variety of keyboards available that will turn your iPad into something more resembling a notebook computer—as well as "smart" styli to let you draw onscreen.

Apple's Smart Keyboard

If you're the proud owner of an iPad Pro, you need to seriously consider investing in Apple's Smart Keyboard. Functioning as a keyboard, cover, and folding stand, the Smart Keyboard connects to your iPad Pro via the device's Smart Connector. It's a wireless connection that transfers both data and power between the two devices.

Apple sells Smart Keyboards for both the 9.7-inch and 12.9-inch iPad Pros. The smaller model is priced at $149; the larger one goes for $169.

Apple's Smart Keyboard for the iPad Pro

Other Wireless Keyboards

You can use the Smart Keyboard only with the iPad Pro, but if you have an iPad Air or mini, there are lots of other wireless keyboard choices available—priced substantially lower, unsurprisingly. Some of these are freestanding keyboards; others come as part of a keyboard/cover/stand. Prices range from around $25 up to $100 or more.

VersaType keyboard case from Targus

Apple Pencil

The iPad Pro is a unique beast in the iPad jungle. It's designed for both heavy-duty office productivity and delicate onscreen drawing. If you plan to do drawing on your iPad, or even just take a lot of handwritten notes, the Apple Pencil is for you.

The Apple Pencil for the iPad Pro

The Apple Pencil is a wireless stylus that you can use to write or draw on the iPad Pro screen. It connects to your iPad Pro via the Smart Connector, and it's sensitive enough to let you vary line weight by increasing or decreasing pressure on the screen.

Like the Smart Keyboard, the Apple Pencil isn't cheap. We're talking $99, folks. But if you do a lot of onscreen drawing or note-taking, it's worth the price.

Other Styli

The Apple Pencil isn't the only stylus you can use with your iPad. Styli from other companies connect via Bluetooth, and can thus be used with any model iPad. You can find styli in all manner of shapes, sizes, and prices, so look for the model that fits best in your hand—and does what you need it to do.

The PenScript Active Stylus from IOGEAR

Active Versus Passive

Don't confuse active styli, such as the Apple Pencil, with passive styli. An active stylus connects to your iPad, typically via Bluetooth, to interact with the screen. A passive stylus is little more than a pointy stick that you tap the screen with instead of your finger.

Extending Your iPad with Bluetooth Devices

There are lots of other wireless devices you can connect to your iPad, all using Bluetooth technology. Setting up a Bluetooth connection is as easy as opening up the Settings page, tapping Bluetooth, tapping "on" the Bluetooth switch, and then selecting the desired device from the list displayed. (When Bluetooth is enabled, your iPad is discoverable by other devices—and discovers other devices, in return.)

Wireless Headphones and Earphones

Probably the most popular type of Bluetooth accessory for the iPad is the wireless headphone or earphone. When you want to use your iPad to listen to music or videos but don't want to disturb others nearby, just connect a Bluetooth listening device and you can crank it up as loud as you want.

Wireless Flexibility

Naturally, you can also connect wired headphones and earphones to your iPad, but Bluetooth models provide a degree of flexibility you just don't get when you're connected via a cable.

Beats Solo2
wireless headphones

Wireless Speakers

Speaking of sound, if you want to use your iPad to host the music for your entire living room, you don't have to settle for the two tinny little speakers built into the device. Connect one or more wireless speakers via Bluetooth and turn your iPad into the centerpiece of an honest-to-goodness home audio system.

— UE Roll Bluetooth wireless speaker from Ultimate Ears

>>>Go Further
SHOPPING FOR iPAD ACCESSORIES

Where can you find all the accessories mentioned in this chapter? iPad accessories are offered from a variety of different manufacturers and sold through Best Buy, Target, Walmart, and other traditional retailers, as well as Amazon.com and other online retailers. Prices do vary from store to store, of course, so make sure you shop around for the best price!

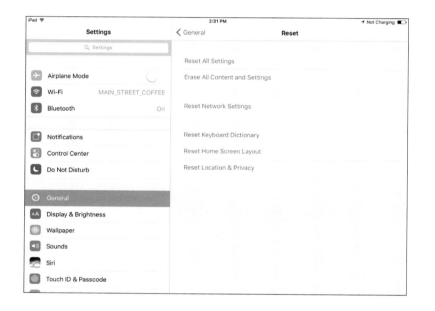

In this chapter, you learn how to troubleshoot and fix problems you may encounter with your iPad.

→ Troubleshooting iPad Problems
→ Updating and Resetting Your iPad

24

Fixing Common Problems

Something wrong with your new iPad? Maybe it's just running slow, or having trouble connecting to the Internet. Have no fear—most iPad problems are easy to fix, if you know what to do.

That's where this chapter comes in. Read on to learn how to trouble-shoot and fix the most common problems you might encounter with your iPad.

Troubleshooting iPad Problems

Your iPad is a technological marvel. The amount of computing power it packs into such a small device is nothing short of amazing. When I was growing up in the 1960s, before the dawn of personal computers, videogames, and even handheld calculators, we couldn't have con-ceived of such a device or the things it could do.

That said, with all technology comes some degree of complexity—and with complexity sometimes comes problems. You ever pick up your iPad and not been able to turn it on? Or have the screen freeze on you? Or have the darned thing drop an Internet connection? Then you know what I mean. The iPad is great, but it ain't always perfect.

So when your iPad is less than perfect, work through the troubleshooting tips in this section. Chances are, you'll have it up and running again in no time.

Your iPad Is Frozen

Okay. You're using your iPad, tapping along, when all of a sudden nothing you tap seems to work. You can do all the tapping in the world, but your screen is completely frozen. What do you do?

Well, the one thing you don't want to do is panic. That's because a frozen iPad, as scary as it may seem, typically isn't a major problem. There are a few simple things to try that will likely get your iPad working again.

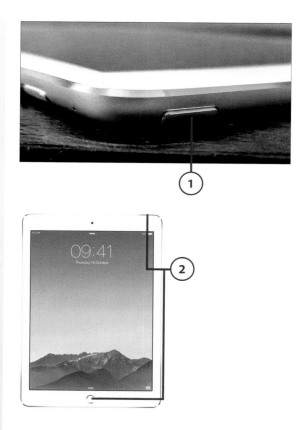

(1) Try restarting your iPad by pressing and holding the Sleep/ Wake button for a few seconds. When the slider appears, slide it to the right to power off. Then restart the iPad by pressing the Sleep/Wake button until the Apple logo appears.

(2) If your iPad won't restart then you need to do what Apple calls a *force restart*. (Don't worry; this won't delete any of your content.) Press and hold the Sleep/Wake and Home buttons at the same time, for at least 10 seconds, until you see the Apple logo onscreen. When you see the logo your device has restarted and should be unfrozen.

Your iPad Won't Turn On

What do you do if you can't even turn on your iPad? This situation may be caused by a few different problems.

(1) Your iPad may essentially be frozen in sleep mode. Try resetting the device by pressing and holding the Sleep/Wake and Home buttons at the same time, for at least 10 seconds. If you see the Apple logo onscreen, your iPad is good to go.

(2) It's also possible that your iPad is simply out of juice. Plug it in and let it charge up for 10 minutes or so, then try starting it up again. (If you see the charging screen with a low battery graphic a few minutes after you plug it in, this was your problem.)

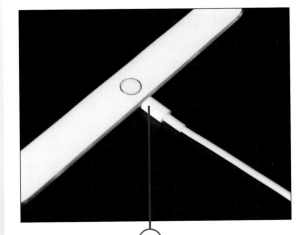

(3) If you don't see the charging screen when you plug it in, check the connecting cable, power adapter, and the connections between the cable, connector, and wall outlet. Make sure everything is firmly connected, and that the power outlet actually has power. (That is, turn on the wall switch!)

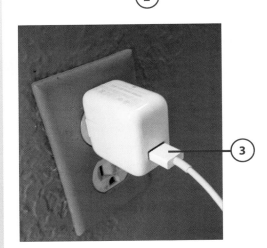

It's Not All Good

Freezing During Startup

If your iPad starts up but then freezes during the process (the Apple logo appears but doesn't go away), you can try connecting your device to your computer, launching iTunes, and then doing a force restart. When you get to the Apple logo screen, keep pressing the Sleep/Wake and Home buttons until you see the Recovery Mode screen. From here, choose the Update option, and iTunes will try to reinstall iOS without deleting any of the data stored on your iPad.

Your iPad Won't Turn Off

If you think it's a pain when your iPad won't turn on, imagine what it's like when your device won't turn off. If this happens to you, try the following:

(1) See if a given app is causing the problem. Press the Home button twice to display the App Switcher and then close each app individually. When all the apps are closed, try turning off your iPad.

(2) Do a force restart by holding the Sleep/Wake and Home buttons simultaneously for at least 10 seconds.

(3) If your iPad still won't shut off, just keep it running until the battery runs out and then recharge it.

An Individual App Freezes or Doesn't Work Right

If an individual app freezes on you, you have several options to try.

(**1**) Press the Home button twice to display the App Switcher. Drag the unresponsive app up and off the screen. You can then relaunch the app and see if it works properly.

(**2**) If the previous step didn't solve your problem, you might have to restart your iPad to close the frozen or misbehaving app. Press and hold the Sleep/Wake and Home buttons for about 10 seconds, until the Apple logo appears onscreen.

(**3**) If the app is still giving you trouble, uninstall and then reinstall the app. From the Home screen, press and hold the icon for the app until it starts to jiggle, and then tap the X to delete the app. You can then go to the App Store and reinstall a new version of the app.

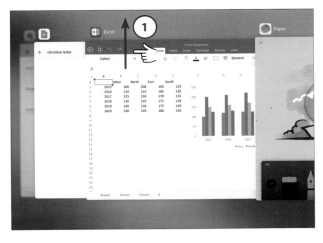

Your iPad Runs Slow

When your iPad seems slower than normal, it's probably because there's one or more apps running that are slowing things down. Here are a few things to try:

(1) Press the Home button twice to display the App Switcher and then close any app that you're not currently using. (If you have more than a half-dozen apps open, that's probably too many.)

(2) Do a force restart by holding down the Sleep/Wake and Home buttons simultaneously for at least 10 seconds.

Forced Restart

As you might have gathered, doing a force restart is an amazing cure-all. You'd be surprised all the problems that this solves!

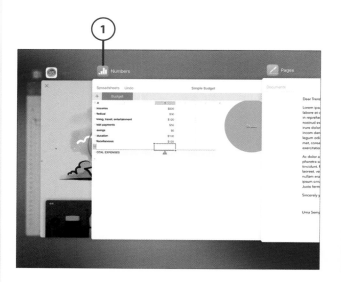

Your iPad's Wi-Fi Connection Doesn't Work

You're sitting in your living room or in a local coffeeshop, doing your daily Internet surfing, when all of a sudden you can't access any websites or send email. Something's happened to your Wi-Fi connection—but what?

1. Turn your Wi-Fi off then back on by opening the Settings screen, tapping Wi-Fi, and tapping off the Wi-Fi switch. Wait a few seconds, then tap the switch back on.

2. Make sure that you're connected to the right network. Open the Settings page, select Wi-Fi, and then look at the list of available Wi-Fi networks. If the wrong network is selected, tap the right one to connect.

3. If that doesn't work, try restarting your iPad. Hold down the Sleep/Wake button and then slide the slider to the right to power off. You can restart your iPad normally and see if the Wi-Fi is now working.

4. You can also reset your iPad's network settings. From the Settings screen, select General, tap Reset, and tap Reset Network Settings. This also restarts your iPad; you'll have to go in and choose the correct Wi-Fi network again.

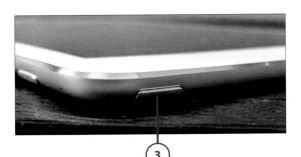

Wi-Fi	
Wi-Fi	⬤
✓ MAIN_STREET_COFFEE	🔒 📶 ⓘ

CHOOSE A NETWORK...	
A78A74_X2	🔒 📶 ⓘ
Esemble Creative	🔒 📶 ⓘ
Esemble Creative_5G	🔒 📶 ⓘ
Esemble Creative_5G-2	🔒 📶 ⓘ
Floraetc	🔒 📶 ⓘ
PinkDoor	🔒 📶 ⓘ
Other...	

‹ General	Reset
Reset All Settings	
Erase All Content and Settings	
Reset Network Settings	

Your iPad Charges Slowly or Not at All

If you find your iPad taking longer than usual to charge, not charging at all, or simply not holding a charge as long as it used to, there are several things to check.

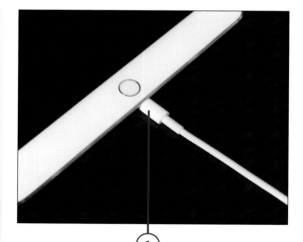

(1) Make sure the connecting cable is firmly plugged into your iPad, and to the power adapter. For that matter, make sure the power adapter is firmly plugged into a wall outlet—and that the wall outlet is turned on.

(2) Try changing charging cables. Cables do go bad, and when they do charging times suffer.

(3) If you have a spare power adapter around, try using that one instead of your old one. These gizmos go bad, too.

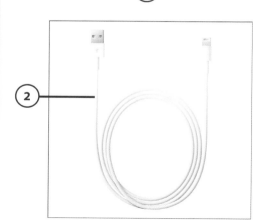

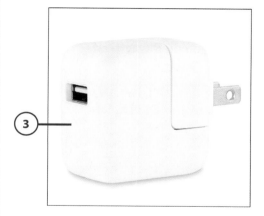

4 If you've been trying to charge your iPad by connecting to your computer (via USB), plug directly into the wall outlet (via the power adapter) instead. Charging via computer is much, much slower than charging via wall outlet. In fact, some computers simply don't send enough juice to their USB ports to charge your iPad at all!

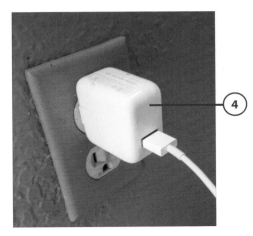

It's Not All Good

Old Batteries

If your iPad isn't holding a charge as long as it used to, it could be that your device's battery is getting old. iPad batteries become less efficient over time; if you've had your iPad for a year or more, it simply won't hold as much of a charge as it did when new. The only solution to this is to install a new battery, which you can't do yourself. (You'll have to go to an Apple Store or other service center for this.)

Your iPad Doesn't Rotate

One of the things I like about the iPad is how the screen rotates when you turn the device one direction or another. What do you do if your iPad *doesn't* automatically rotate?

1 First, know that not all iPad apps rotate. If you're using an app and turn your iPad and nothing happens, switch to another app or back to the Home screen and see if it rotated. If so, then the problem is a non-rotating app.

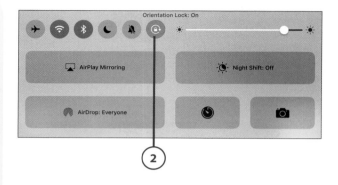

2. It's possible that you accidentally turned on something called *rotation lock*. With rotation lock enabled, your iPad screen simply won't rotate, no matter what you do. To switch this off, swipe up from the bottom of the screen to open the Control Center. If the rotation lock is enabled, the lock rotation button glows red. Tap this button to turn it off. (You need to close the Control Center for the auto-rotation to start working again.)

Your iPad Doesn't Appear in iTunes

It's happened to me. I connect my iPad to my computer to do some syncing of my music library, but iTunes doesn't launch automatically—and, when I launch it manually, my iPad doesn't appear on the list of connected devices. What's the problem?

1. Your iPad requires USB 2.0 or 3.0 to function properly. If you're connecting to an older computer, it may still have one or more USB 1.0 ports. Unplug your iPad from the current port and try another one, which hopefully will be USB 2.0.

2. Disconnect your iPad from your computer, then turn it off and back on again. Now reconnect your iPad to your computer and see what happens.

3. You could have a software problem on your computer. (This sometimes happens on Windows PCs.) Make sure you have the latest version of iTunes installed; if not, do the update. And if that doesn't work, try uninstalling iTunes from your computer and then reinstalling the latest version.

Your iPad Keeps Asking for Your iCloud Password

Here's another thing that's happened both to me and to my wife (on different devices). I start using my iPad, and sooner or later (mostly sooner) it nags me with a prompt to sign into my iCloud account. Even if I'm already signed into my iCloud account. It just keeps nagging me.

Is there any way to stop this constant nagging? Here's how.

(**1**) It may sound obvious, but try signing into your iCloud account. Sometimes doing what your device asks for is the proper approach.

(**2**) If the iPad keeps prompting you to sign into your iCloud account, something's stuck in the authorization process that makes your iPad think it needs the password when it really doesn't. Try restarting your iPad (by pressing and holding the Sleep/Wake button until you see the power-off slider) and see if this makes the annoying prompts go away.

(**3**) If this doesn't do it, try signing out of iCloud and then signing back into the service. You do this from the Settings screen; tap iCloud and then tap the Sign Out option. After this happens, return to the same Settings screen and sign back in again.

You Forgot Your iPad Passcode

Given how many passwords we're all required to keep in our heads for various devices, websites, and services, you're bound to forget one now and then. And if you can't remember the passcode you use to unlock your iPad, you're left with a locked device that is of no use to anybody.

That's because every iPad is programmed to lock out all users if the wrong passcode is entered six times in a row. It's a safety measure, to keep ne'er-do-wells from trying to force their way into a stolen device. Too many wrong passcodes and the iPad is disabled.

(This actually happened to my daughter-in-law, through no fault of her own. Her six-year-old son—my rambunctious little grandson—got hold of her iPad and tried to break into it by entering random numbers on the Lock screen. Six tries later, and her iPad was completely inaccessible.)

When this happens, the only way to get back into your iPad is to completely erase everything stored on your device, and revert to factory-fresh condition. You can then restore your data (if you've backed it up, that is) and create a new passcode.

The easiest way to erase your iPad is via iTunes. Follow these steps:

1. Connect your iPad to your computer and launch the iTunes software.

2. Wait for iTunes to sync your iPad to your computer and make a backup. Once the sync and backup are completed, click Restore.

3. Your iPad now is reset to factory-fresh condition and the setup process commences on your device. When you're prompted to restore your iPad, tap Restore from iTunes Backup.

4. Back in the iTunes software on your computer, select your device.

5. Select the most recent data backup and follow the onscreen instructions to restore the backed-up data.

>>>Go Further
APPLE SUPPORT

If you work through the tips in this chapter and still have problems with your iPad, it's time to turn to Apple's official technical support. You can get support at any Apple Store location, or online at https://support.apple.com/ipad. There are also many third-party repair companies who specialize in repairing iPads and other local devices; search Google to find one in your area.

Updating and Resetting Your iPad

It's important to keep your iPad up-to-date, which is what updating the operating system is all about. Operating system updates sometimes contain new features and almost always contain all manner of bug fixes. So if you've been having recurring issues with your iPad, chances are that they'll be fixed in the next version of the operating system.

Sometimes, however, things can get so gunked up that the only way to fix a recalcitrant iPad is to wipe it clean and reset it to the original factory condition. This should be the method of last resort, however, as it wipes out all the apps and data you've accumulated on your device.

Update to the Latest Version of iOS

Your iPad is controlled by an operating system that Apple calls iOS. This operating system is updated from time to time, and you want to make sure that your iPad is running the latest iOS version.

In most instances, your iPad tells you (via an onscreen notification) that a new version is available, and walks you through the update procedure. You can, however, manually check for and install iOS updates.

(1) From your iPad's Home screen, tap the Settings icon to open the Settings screen.

(2) Tap General in the left column.

(3) Tap Software Update. If a software update is available, follow the onscreen instructions to install.

Factory Reset Your Device to "Like New" Condition

If you've tried everything to get your iPad working again and nothing has worked, you might need to take the drastic step of resetting your iPad to "like new" condition. You should only attempt this device reset when all other steps have failed; it's a big thing.

What's big about it is that resetting your iPad erases all the data and apps stored on your device. You'll lose all your music, videos, pictures, you name it, and have to reinstall everything from scratch.

That said, the "reinstall from scratch" process isn't as dire as it sounds. If you've backed up your iPad in advance (via either iTunes or iCloud), you can reinstall all your backed-up data and settings.

Backing Up Your iPad

Learn more about backing up your iPad via either iCloud or iTunes in Chapter 22, "Managing Files on Your iPad and in the Cloud."

When the reset is done, your iPad is wiped and restarts with the original out-of-the-box setup process. You need to walk through the setup as if you just purchased the iPad, but then you can connect to iTunes or iCloud and reinstall your backed-up files.

It's Not All Good

Resetting Erases Everything

I will repeat this warning. *Resetting your iPad to factory-fresh condition erases all the data, apps, and settings stored on your device.* If you've previously backed up your iPad (to iCloud or iTunes), you can restore your data, apps, and settings. If you have not made a backup, your data and settings will be lost—*permanently*. (You can always restore apps you've previously downloaded from Apple's App Store.)

(1) From your iPad's Home screen, tap the Settings icon to open the Settings screen.

(2) Tap General in the left column.

(3) Scroll to the bottom of the page and tap Reset.

(4) Tap Erase All Content and Settings.

(5) Enter your passcode.

(6) When prompted, tap Erase. (Or tap Cancel to not proceed.) Your iPad—and all its data, settings, and apps—will be erased.

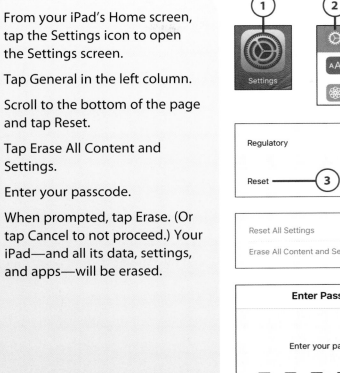

Settings

① General

AA Display & Brightness

🌐 Wallpaper

Regulatory

Reset ——— ③

Reset All Settings

Erase All Content and Settings ——— ④

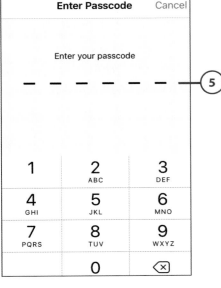

Enter Passcode   Cancel

Enter your passcode

— — — — — — ⑤

1	2 ABC	3 DEF
4 GHI	5 JKL	6 MNO
7 PQRS	8 TUV	9 WXYZ
	0	⊗

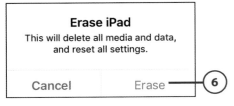

Erase iPad
This will delete all media and data, and reset all settings.

Cancel   Erase ——— ⑥

Restore from an iCloud Backup

When you reset your iPad, everything is wiped clean and your device is back to its factory-fresh condition. After the reset is complete, your iPad's initial setup process starts, and it's back to the "Hello" screen (discussed in Chapter 1, "Buying and Unboxing Your iPad").

You restore your iPad during this initial setup process—so look sharp at each screen you see and follow these instructions.

1. Proceed through the onscreen setup until you reach the Apps & Data screen and then tap Restore from iCloud Backup.

2. When prompted, sign into iCloud with your Apple ID.

3. On the next screen, choose a backup. You'll likely want to choose the most recent backup.

4. The backup starts. When prompted, you need to sign into the App Store with your Apple ID to restore your apps and purchases.

5. Make sure you stay connected to the Internet during the entire process, which might take up to an hour to complete. When the files are restored, you can finish the initial setup and start using your iPad as normal.

Restore from iTunes Backup

If you've previously backed up your iPad to your computer, via iTunes, you can restore your device from iTunes during the initial setup process.

1. Proceed through the onscreen setup until you reach the Apps & Data screen, then connect your iPad to your computer.

2. This should launch the iTunes software on your computer. Select your iPad from the available devices.

3. Back on your iPad, on the Apps & Data screen, tap to select Restore from iTunes Backup.

4. In iTunes, select Restore Backup.

5. Select the backup you want to restore from. (Probably the most recent one.)

6. Click Restore.

7. Keep your iPad connected to your computer until the restore process is complete. When it's done, you can finish your iPad's initial setup and start using it as normal.

A

Glossary

AirDrop   The feature that enables sharing of media files between an iPad and other Apple devices.

AirPlay   The feature that streams music and videos from an iPad to other Apple devices.

app   A software application running on the iPad or other mobile devices.

App Store   Apple's online store that offers apps and games for iPads and iPhones.

App Switcher   The screen mode that displays all running apps in a swipeable carousel.

Apple   The company that created the iPad and iPhone.

Apple Pay   Apple's mobile payment system.

Apple Pencil   The active stylus designed for use with the iPad Pro.

AssistiveTouch   A feature that overlays a group of large icons onscreen for common functions.

Bluetooth   Wireless technology designed to connect two devices together.

cloud storage   File storage on Internet-based servers.

Control Center   The panel that swipes up from the bottom of the iPad screen and enables control of many common system settings.

Do Not Disturb mode   An iPad operating mode that hides notifications, alerts, and system sound effects.

Dock   That area at the bottom of every iPad screen that displays the same four or five app icons.

eBook   An electronic book; a traditional book in electronic form.

email   Electronic mail; messages sent electronically from one computer or device to another.

FaceTime   Apple's video chat service.

FaceTime camera   The front-facing camera on the iPad, typically used for selfies and FaceTime conversations.

forced restart   The process of manually forcing the iPad to restart by pressing and holding the Sleep/Wake and Home buttons simultaneously.

front-facing camera   The camera above the iPad display, typically used for selfies and video chats.

HDR   High dynamic range, a process that combines the results of multiple photos to create a single high-contrast photo.

Home button   The small round button beneath the iPad screen.

Home screen   Those screens that host the icons for all the apps installed on an iPad.

hotspot   A location where you can get Internet access via Wi-Fi.

iCloud   Apple's cloud-based storage service.

identity theft   The fraudulent acquisition and use of an individual's personal information.

in-app purchase   The purchase of additional services from within an app or game.

iOS   The operating system used by iPad and Apple's other mobile devices.

iPad   Apple's popular tablet computer.

iPad Air   Apple's main iPad model, with a 9.7-inch screen.

iPad mini   Apple's smallest and most affordable iPad, with a 7.9-inch screen.

iPad Pro   The iPad designed for business productivity, with 9.7- and 12.9-inch models.

iPhone   Apple's smartphone.

iSight camera   The rear-facing camera on the Apple iPad.

iTunes   Apple's software that enables users to manage their iPads and iPhones on their Mac or Windows computers.

iTunes Store   Apple's online store that offers music and videos for purchase and rental.

Keynote   Apple's presentation app for the iPad and iPhone.

Lightning connector   The port on the bottom of the iPad that connects the iPad to the power adapter, computers, and other USB devices.

Lock screen   The screen that appears before you unlock your iPad.

malware   Short for malicious software—viruses, spyware, and other files that can damage a computer or mobile device.

multitasking   The capability of using more than one app at the same time.

Multi-Touch Display   Apple's touchscreen display.

newsreader   An app that consolidates news items from multiple sources.

Night Shift   The feature that enables you to adjust the color temperature of the iPad display for night-time viewing.

Notification Center   The iPad screen that displays system notifications and app alerts.

Numbers   Apple's spreadsheet app for the iPad and iPhone.

operating system   A core software program that controls a device's underlying hardware and operations.

Pages   Apple's word processing app for the iPad and iPhone.

passcode   On the iPad, a six-number code that must be entered to unlock the device.

Perspective Zoom   A type of parallax effect that displays a slight motion on the Home or Lock screens when you tilt your iPad.

pixel   A single dot or picture element that makes up a photo or video picture.

post   See *status update*.

predictive keyboard   A virtual keyboard that attempts to figure out what you're typing and enter that word for you.

rear-facing camera   The camera on the back of the iPad that faces away from you.

reset   Wiping your iPad of all data, settings, and apps and returning it to factory-new condition.

Retina display   The iPad display that offers 300 pixels or more resolution.

Safari   Apple's web browser app, included with iOS.

Safari Reader   A special reading mode, within the Safari browser, that makes some web pages easier to read by removing ads, images, videos, and other extraneous elements.

Search screen   That iPad screen that includes system notifications, widgets, and a search box.

selfie   A picture you take of yourself.

Siri   The voice-activated software that functions as a virtual personal assistant on your iPad and other Apple devices.

Sleep/Wake button   The physical button at the top-right corner of the iPad used to put the device to sleep and wake it up.

Slide Over   A feature that enables you to open a second app onscreen without closing the one you're currently in.

Smart Connector   The wireless connector unique to the iPad Pro, designed to connect the Smart Keyboard and Apple Pencil.

smart cover   An iPad cover that wakes the unit from sleep when open and puts it in sleep mode when closed.

Smart Keyboard   Apple's wireless keyboard designed for use with the iPad Pro.

social media   See *social network.*

social network   An Internet-based service that hosts a community of users and makes it easy for those users to communicate with one another.

spam   Also known as junk mail, any unsolicited email advertisement.

Split View   The mode that makes two apps active onscreen at the same time.

status update   A short message (with text and/or images and video) that updates friends on what a user is doing or thinking.

streaming media   Music and video that are transmitted in real time to a connected device.

tablet   See *tablet computer.*

tablet computer   A small computer in the shape of a handheld tablet. The iPad is a tablet computer.

text messaging   Short electronic messages sent from one device to another.

touch gestures   Taps and motions on the iPad screen that perform various common operations.

Touch ID   Apple's fingerprint sensing system.

touchscreen   A device display that can be operated by touch gestures.

URL   Uniform Resource Locator, the address of a web page.

USB   Universal Serial Port, a type of connection common to personal computers.

video chat   A face-to-face onscreen chat between two users.

VoiceOver   A feature that describes out loud any screen element or text on the iPad.

wallpaper   The background image on the iPad's Home and Lock screens.

Wi-Fi   Short for wireless fidelity, the wireless networking standard used by most computers and connected devices today.

YouTube   The Internet's largest video-sharing community.

Index

REGISTER THIS PRODUCT
SAVE 35%*
ON YOUR NEXT PURCHASE!

How to Register Your Product

- Go to quepublishing.com/register
- Sign in or create an account
- Enter the 10- or 13-digit ISBN that appears on the back cover of your book or on the copyright page of your eBook

Benefits of Registering

- Ability to download product updates
- Access to bonus chapters and workshop files
- A 35% coupon to be used on your next purchase – valid for 30 days
  > To obtain your coupon, click on "Manage Codes" in the right column of your Account page
- Receive special offers on new editions and related Que products

Please note that the benefits for registering may vary by product. Benefits will be listed on your Account page under Registered Products.

We value and respect your privacy. Your email address will not be sold to any third party company.

* 35% discount code presented after product registration is valid on most print books, eBooks, and full-course videos sold on QuePublishing.com. Discount may not be combined with any other offer and is not redeemable for cash. Discount code expires after 30 days from the time of product registration. Offer subject to change.

quepublishing.com